LOCAL COMMONS AND
GLOBAL INTERDEPENDENCE

LOCAL COMMONS AND GLOBAL INTERDEPENDENCE

Heterogeneity and Cooperation in Two Domains

edited by
Robert O. Keohane
and Elinor Ostrom

Published under the auspices of the
Center for International Affairs, Harvard University

SAGE Publications
London • Thousand Oaks • New Delhi

This edition first published 1995

Previously published as a Special Issue of the *Journal of Theoretical Politics*, Volume 6 (1994), no. 4.

SAGE Publications Ltd
6 Bonhill Street
London EC2A 4PU

SAGE Publications Inc
2455 Teller Road
Thousand Oaks, California 91320

SAGE Publications India Pvt Ltd
32, M-Block Market
Greater Kailash – I
New Delhi 110 048

British Library Cataloguing in Publication data

A catalogue record for this book is
available from the British Library.

ISBN 0 8039 7962 2
ISBN 0 8039 7963 0 pbk

Library of Congress catalog card number 94-68900

Typeset by Colset Pte Ltd, Singapore
Printed in Great Britain by The Cromwell Press Ltd,
Broughton Gifford, Melksham, Wiltshire

CONTENTS

Notes on Contributors   vii

1 Introduction
Robert O. Keohane and Elinor Ostrom   1

Part I: Theoretical Puzzles

2 The Problem of Scale in Human/Environment Relationships
Oran R. Young   27

3 The Politics of Scope: Endogenous Actors, Heterogeneity and
Institutions
Duncan Snidal   47

4 Heterogeneity, Linkage and Commons Problems
Lisa L. Martin   71

Part II: Evidence from the Laboratory

5 Heterogeneities, Information and Conflict Resolution:
Experimental Evidence on Sharing Contracts
Steven Hackett, Dean Dudley and James Walker   93

Part III: Evidence from the Field

6 Constituting Social Capital and Collective Action
Elinor Ostrom   125

7 The Conditions for Successful Collective Action
Gary D. Libecap   161

8 Self-interest and Environmental Management
Kenneth A. Oye and James H. Maxwell   191

9 Heterogeneities at Two Levels: States, Non-state Actors and
Intentional Oil Pollution
Ronald B. Mitchell   223

Index   253

NOTES ON CONTRIBUTORS

DEAN DUDLEY is Assistant Professor of Economics in the Department of Social Sciences at the United States Military Academy. Current working papers include 'Individual Choice in Common Pool Resource Environments: An Experimental Approach', 'Forecasting Behavior in Experimental Common Pool Resource Appropriation and Public Good Provision Environments' and 'Individual Provision Choice in Voluntary Contribution Public Good Environments: An Experimental Approach'. Current research focuses on strategies for downsizing large organizations. ADDRESS: Department of Social Sciences, United States Military Academy, West Point, NY 10996, USA; jd0099@usma8.usma.edu

STEVEN HACKETT is Assistant Professor, School of Business and Economics, Humboldt State University and Research Associate of the Workshop in Political Theory and Policy Analysis at Indiana University. His principal research focus is on contracting and the activities of firms, with recent attention to problems of ex-post contractual negotiations. Recent publications include 'A Comparative Analysis of Merchant and Broker Intermediation', *Journal of Economic Behavior and Organization*; 'Incomplete Contracting: A Laboratory Experimental Analysis', *Economic Inquiry*; and 'Bottlenecks and Governance Structures: Open Access and Long-Term Contracting in Natural Gas' (with T. Lyon), *Journal of Law, Economics, and Organization*. ADDRESS: School of Business and Economics, Humboldt State University, Arcata, CA 95521–8299, USA; hacketts@axe.humboldt.edu

ROBERT O. KEOHANE is Stanfield Professor of International Peace, Harvard University. He is the author of *After Hegemony: Cooperation and Discord in the World Political Economy*; co-author of *Designing Social Inquiry: Scientific Inference in Qualitative Research* and co-editor of *Institutions for the Earth: Sources of International Environmental Protection*. ADDRESS: Center for International Affairs, Harvard University, Cambridge, MA 02138, USA; keohane@husc.harvard.edu

GARY D. LIBECAP is Professor of Economics and Director of the Karl Eller Center at the University of Arizona, Tucson, and Research Associate with the National Bureau of Economic Research, Cambridge, MA. He received his PhD in economics from the University of Pennsylvania in 1976. His research areas involve investigations of property rights and regulatory arrangements, as well as bureaucratic behavior. ADDRESS: Karl Eller Center, University of Arizona, McClelland Hall, Tucson, AZ 85721, USA; glibecap@bpa.arizona.edu

LISA L. MARTIN is John L. Loeb Associate Professor of the Social Sciences in the Government Department at Harvard University. She received her PhD in Government from Harvard in 1989. She studies international cooperation and international institutions, and is the author of *Coercive Cooperation: Explaining Multilateral Economic Sanctions*. ADDRESS: Center for International Affairs, 1737 Cambridge Street, Harvard University, Cambridge, MA 02138, USA; lmartin.cfia@mhsgw.harvard.edu

JAMES H. MAXWELL is a visiting scholar at MIT's Center for International Studies and has served as Co-Director of MIT's Technology, Business, and Environment Program. He received his PhD in the field of Public Policy from MIT. He has written numerous articles on environmental policy, including recent articles on the political economy of the CFC phase-out, corporate environmental practices among the Japanese automobile transplants and on the policy issues surrounding recycling. ADDRESS: Center for International Studies, MIT, E38-648, 292 Main Street, Cambridge, MA 02139, USA.

RONALD B. MITCHELL holds a PhD in Public Policy from Harvard University and is currently an Assistant Professor of Political Science at the University of Oregon. His book, *Intentional Oil Pollution at Sea: Environmental Policy and Treaty Compliance*, will be published by MIT Press in 1994. ADDRESS: Department of Political Science, 1284 University of Oregon, Eugene, OR 97403-1284, USA; rmitchel@oregon.uoregon.edu

ELINOR OSTROM is Co-director of the Workshop in Political Theory and Policy Analysis and the Arthur F. Bentley Professor of Political Science at Indiana University, Bloomington. She is the author of *Governing the Commons* and *Crafting Institutions for Self-Governing Irrigation Systems*; co-author with Larry Schroeder and Susan Wynne of *Institutional Incentives and Sustainable Development* and co-author with Roy Gardner and James Walker of *Rules, Games, and Common-Pool Resources*. ADDRESS: Workshop in Political Theory and Policy Analysis, Indiana University, 513 North Park, Bloomington, IN 47408-3895, USA; ostrom@indiana.edu

KENNETH A. OYE is Director of the Center for International Studies and Associate Professor of Political Science at the Massachusetts Institute of Technology. He is author of *Economic Discrimination and Political Exchange: World Political Economy in the 1930s and 1980s*; co-editor of *Eagle in a New World: American Grand Strategy in the Post-Cold War Era*. ADDRESS: Center for International Studies, MIT, E38-648, 292 Main Street, Cambridge, MA 02139, USA; oye@mit.edu

DUNCAN SNIDAL is an Associate Professor in the Department of Political Science and the Harris Graduate School of Public Policy at the University of Chicago. His research focuses on issues of international cooperation and the role of international institutions. ADDRESS: Department of Political Science, University of Chicago, 5828 South University Avenue, Chicago, IL 60737, USA; snid@cicero.spc.uchicago.edu

JAMES WALKER is Professor of Economics and Associate Director of the Workshop in Political Theory and Policy Analysis at Indiana University. His principal research focus is the use of experimental methods in the investigation of behavior related to the voluntary provision of public goods and the use of common-pool resources. Recent publications include 'Covenants With and Without a Sword: Self-Governance is Possible' (with Elinor Ostrom and Roy Gardner), *American Political Science Review*, 'Probabilistic Destruction of Common-Pool Resources: Experimental Evidence' (with Roy Gardner), *Economic Journal*; and 'Group Size and the Voluntary Provision of Public Goods: Experimental Evidence Utilizing Large Groups' (with R. Mark Isaac and Arlington Williams), *Journal of Public Economics*. ADDRESS: Department of Economics, Indiana University, Bloomington, IN 47405, USA; walkerj@indiana.edu

ORAN R. YOUNG is Director of both the Institute of Arctic Studies and the Institute on International Environmental Governance at Dartmouth College. He is the author of *Resource Regimes: Natural Resources and Social Institutions; International Cooperation: Building Regimes for Natural Resources and the Environment;* and *International Governance: Protecting the Environment in a Stateless Society*. ADDRESS: Institute of Arctic Studies, Dartmouth College, 6193 Murdough Center, Hanover, NH 03755-3560, USA;oran.r.young@dartmouth. edu

1. INTRODUCTION

Robert O. Keohane and Elinor Ostrom

Neither modern states nor small farmers in remote areas of poor countries can appeal to authoritative hierarchies to enforce rules governing their relations with one another. In world politics, the lack of a world government means that states must find ways to cooperate with one another and to reach agreements that can be maintained through the use of reciprocity rather than through hierarchy. For small farmers in Asia, as well as many other people seeking to appropriate resources from a common pool, national governments are too remote or uncomprehending to be helpful in encouraging productive cooperation – whether such cooperation involves maintaining irrigation systems or other ways of sustaining common-pool resources (CPRs).

It is popularly believed that the actors involved in common-pool resource problems, whether individuals or governments, are trapped in an inexorable 'tragedy of the commons' from which they cannot extract themselves (G. Hardin, 1968). Empirical and theoretical work on multi-period CPR situations, however, has shown that the 'inexorable' nature of the problem results more from the assumptions used by theorists than from constraints that are universally present in all CPR situations. Indeed, research on local CPR problems has demonstrated that under some circumstances solutions worked out by those individuals directly affected prove more successful and enduring than resource regimes imposed by central political authorities.[1] Many successfully governed CPRs have survived for centuries relying on self-monitoring and self-enforcing patterns of human interaction. It is encouraging to realize that reliance on self-help schemes can be a positive advantage in small-scale CPR regimes.

Students of international politics have often made similar claims to those of observers who believe that the tragedy of the commons can only be over-

Support of the National Science Foundation in the form of grant number NSF SBR-9308633 is deeply appreciated. The authors wish to thank Nazli Choucri, Steve Hackett, Lisa Martin, Ron Mitchell, Duncan Snidal, Jimmy Walker and Oran Young for comments on an earlier draft and all participants in the October 1993 conference for their stimulating discussion leading to this introductory paper. We are particularly indebted to Patty Dalecki for her editing and production skills and to Stanra King and Brenda Bushouse for assisting us in putting this collection together.

1. See Berkes, 1989; Blomquist, 1992; Bromley et al., 1992; Feeny et al., 1990; Matthews, 1993; McCay and Acheson, 1987; McKean, 1992; Netting, 1981; E. Ostrom, 1990; V. Ostrom et al., 1993; Pinkerton, 1989; Tang, 1992.

come through hierarchical authority and coercion. 'Anarchy' is said to render infeasible sustained attempts at international cooperation (Waltz, 1959, 1979). However, critics of this pessimistic view have pointed out the existence of scores of 'international regimes' defined as 'implicit or explicit principles, norms, rules, and decision-making procedures around which actor expectations converge in a given area of international relations' (Krasner, 1983: 2). These regimes typically do not contain provisions for hierarchical enforcement of rules, but they do reduce transaction costs and provide information that facilitates cooperation (Axelrod, 1984; Keohane, 1984; Oye, 1986; Snidal, 1985; Young, 1989). They are functionally differentiated institutions, embodying rules that are often complex and detailed, existing in a world without clear hierarchies or centralized enforcement.

Thus, a remarkable convergence seems evident between two independent streams of literature in political science, economics, anthropology, sociology and related disciplines. At both local and global levels, researchers have found that when individuals or organizations (such as states) can make credible commitments, they are frequently able to devise new constraints (institutions, or sets of rules) that change the basic structure of incentives that they face. Such a conclusion is consistent with findings from other domains, such as principal–agent relationships in government or the theory of the firm (Moe, 1984; Williamson, 1985). Not surprisingly, many of the 'design principles' underlying successful self-organized solutions to CPR problems appear relevant to the design of institutions to resolve problems of international cooperation as well as those at a strictly local level. For example, both students of local CPRs and of international regimes have identified effective monitoring arrangements as crucial for promoting widespread compliance with rules: institutions typically provide for monitoring, increasing the likelihood that non-conformity with rules will be discovered (Haas et al., 1993; E. Ostrom, 1990; McKean, 1992). More generally, both literatures emphasize that institutions increase the availability of information and reduce transaction costs – the costs of devising, monitoring and enforcing rules. The significance of transaction costs in affecting actors' behavior and of institutions in affecting transaction costs is worth emphasizing. No analysis of institutions and cooperation can be persuasive without attention to the impact of transaction costs on the creation of institutions and, in turn, of institutions on transaction costs (cf. North, 1990; Eggertsson, 1990).

This convergence between the analytical orientations of work on local CPRs and international regimes is matched by the fact that in various domains people seek to create rules to enable them to cooperate. Locally, appropriators such as fishers or peasants often seek to devise rules to govern CPRs (Berkes, 1989; Bromley et al., 1992; Feeny et al., 1990; McCay and Acheson, 1987; Netting, 1981). Nationally, many political battles have been fought over the rules that should govern appropriation rights and about the allocation of costs for the provision of public goods (as well as private ones) by governments. At the regional level, governments have sought to cope with collective-action problems by building international regimes, such as those to protect regional seas or to reduce the incidence of acid rain in Europe (Haas, 1990; Levy, 1993; Young, 1982). At the global level, an international regime has been established to stop depletion of the stratospheric ozone layer (Benedick, 1991; Parson, 1993), conventions on global warming and biological diversity were signed at the United Nations Conference on Environment and Development (UNCED) held in Brazil in June 1992 and negotiations are in progress on desertification and migratory fish stocks (Haas et al., 1992).

Social scientists working on local and international issues often rely on models that assume a substantial degree of rationality on the part of the actors being studied, although these actors frequently lack complete information. The rationality assumption helps investigators create models that predict strategies and, where theoretically possible, outcomes, on the basis of actors' preferences given the constraints in a particular situation (including, for instance, the extent of information available to the actors). The rationality assumption also facilitates making inferences about preferences from observed behavior. The rationality assumption exacts a cost, by limiting the problems to be addressed. On the other hand, it confers the benefit of disciplining thought and permitting the use of relevant and insightful literatures from economics and fields affected by economic ways of thought.[2]

A further point of convergence between the CPR and IR (international relations) literatures derives from the emphasis in both on the underprovision of effective arrangements to enable participants to cooperate. Common-pool resources are frequently characterized by open access, which means that markets do not provide adequate incentives to preserve clean oceans, keep the ozone layer intact or more generally, to preserve the biosphere. As we explain at greater length below, they are not, strictly

---

2. Our recognition of the similarities between these two literatures began when we independently read one another's work. After some correspondence (we had never met), we organized, with the support of the National Science Foundation, two conferences. The first conference was held at the Center for International Affairs at Harvard University, 23–5 April 1992. Scholars from political science, economics, anthropology, natural resource management and international relations, most of whom had never previously met, spent two and half days vigorously reviewing a series of papers intended to begin the task of devising a common vocabulary and theoretical understanding that would help identify similarities and differences in both approaches. Revised papers from this first meeting were published in a Proceedings volume in January 1993 (Keohane et al., 1993). The first meeting was sufficiently promising for us to hold a second meeting, also supported by the National Science Foundation, at Indiana University, 15–17 October 1993, where drafts of the papers in this collection were presented.

speaking, public goods, since they are subject to problems of crowding: the fisher who catches too many cod or the herder who grazes too many sheep in a pasture deplete the resource for others. Yet like public goods, CPRs are subject to underprovision due to open access. At the international level, some rules and practices benefit all states, if they choose. For example, an international reserve currency with a stable value can be used as a standard of value and medium of exchange by financial markets worldwide, benefiting economies whose governments do not help to provide it as well as those that do (Kindleberger, 1973).[3] Few international institutions, however, are perfect public goods: for instance, states can be denied most-favored-nation (MFN) treatment and thus excluded from a liberal trade regime. International institutions also provide private benefit by helping to create gains from exchange, as Lisa Martin argues in article 4 in this collection.

The Impact of Number and Heterogeneity of Actors

Any theoretical approach to understanding cooperation and discord at local and global levels needs to recognize the multiplicity of variables that jointly affect outcomes. But for our scientific knowledge to increase, we need to focus at any one time on a limited set of explanatory variables. We have decided to focus on two such variables: the *number of actors* and the *degree of heterogeneity* among them.

In thinking about such explanatory variables, we began, in conversations with other participants in this project, by seeking to categorize potential variables according to whether research and thinking were likely to yield intellectual progress.[4] We identified some issues on which substantial agreement exists among researchers. For example, we have some understanding of the impact of different structures of preferences and of the impact of transaction costs, including monitoring costs, on the likelihood and extent of cooperation and of discord. With respect to the configuration of interests, it is hardly surprising that as the perceived ratio of benefits to costs of taking collective action rises, cooperation tends to become more likely. Furthermore, the implications of different patterns of transaction costs, including

3. Unlike CPRs, public goods are not subject to crowding or rivalry: one user's appropriation does not subtract from the amount available to others. We explore the implications of this difference below.

4. This collection has evolved through discussions and written interchanges among the authors; hence, this introduction should be read as part of that conversation, rather than as a prior template used by the writers of subsequent chapters.

costs of monitoring, have been extensively studied. More empirical and theoretical work is desirable on these issues, but the basic lines of analysis seem clear, at least in comparison to other significant questions.

A second body of work includes questions that are much more difficult to address. These questions are currently the subject of exploratory work, but they have not yet been sufficiently well defined to form the basis for a sustained research program, based on theories of collective action and choice. These include issues of identity, including the processes through which individuals (and collective actors) learn about and change their views of their own self-interest and how individual interests are affected by the type of community in which they are embedded. In our view, investigations of these issues need not contradict the assumption of rationality; but assuming ends–means rationality does not explain varying choices of ends. So far, at least, rationality-based theories have not accounted well for preferences, although some suggestive attempts have been made (Frank, 1988).

We focus in this collection on issues in a third category: those that are sufficiently well defined as to seem amenable to careful, well-specified research within the research program of rational collective action and choice: the *number of actors* and the degree of *heterogeneity* among them.

Number of Actors

In his contribution to this collection (paper 3), Duncan Snidal includes the question of the number of actors involved in a collective-action problem in the issue of *scope*. Originally, we thought of this issue as one for which fundamental analytic problems had been solved. From a variety of analytical perspectives and in a variety of domains it appeared that when centralized enforcement is ineffective, it is frequently more difficult to induce cooperative behavior in large groups than in small ones. A key reason given for this difficulty is that the costs of monitoring conditional strategies rise as group size increases (see Caporaso, 1992: 610–13; E. Ostrom, 1990: 202–3; Oye, 1986: 18–22; Taylor, 1987: 105). Snidal points out, however, the dangers of taking too simplistic a view toward the impact of the number of actors. Following Russell Hardin (1982), Snidal points out that changing the number of actors necessarily changes other elements of the problem: observed differences in behavior may be attributable as much to shifts along these dimensions as to changes in size per se (see also Bendor and Mookherjee, 1987; Isaac et al., 1993; Udéln, 1993). Frohlich et al. (1971) have also shown how effective leadership can counteract problems having to do with the number of actors involved.

Furthermore, the IR and CPR literatures have taken quite different perspectives on the impact of varying numbers of actors. Elinor Ostrom

(1990) points out that changes in numbers alone may not have strong effects by themselves and she regards small size as less important than other factors facilitating cooperation, such as common understandings of interests, low discount rates and low transaction costs.[5] Yet in international relations, it has almost become conventional wisdom that increasing the number of players magnifies the difficulty of cooperation.[6] As Snidal points out, drawing comparisons between the local CPR and international relations literatures could help international relations specialists at least to question this encrusted view.

Here the irony is that local CPRs frequently involve many more actors than the interstate system, which still remains below 200 units. Indeed, some of the local CPRs studied in recent years involve upwards of 15,000 to 20,000 actors and many involve communities that, while small in scale, contain more than 200 individuals. Of course, as Ronald Mitchell, Kenneth Oye and James Maxwell demonstrate, world politics involves other actors than states – chemical companies, tanker owners, insurance companies, non-profit organizations. Nevertheless, the key point is that although the scale of IR is much greater than of CPRs, the scope of CPRs, as indexed by the number of actors involved, is typically larger than in international relations.

Heterogeneity Among Actors

Our second theme focuses on heterogeneity among actors. Many of the analyses of problems of collective action at a local or global level have assumed homogeneous actors (see, for example, Gordon, 1954 and critique of this assumption in Johnson and Libecap, 1982). Formal analyses of such problems have typically assumed homogeneous actors, since this makes the analysis more tractable (Clark, 1980). While the assumption of homogeneity was made for theoretical simplicity, it has been regarded for too long as sufficiently close to reality to be able to be used as a basis for policy analysis,

---

5. In a recent overview of 21 case studies presented at a workshop that describe local cooperatives related to fisheries, forests, and water resources in India, Singh and Ballabh conclude that:

Size and composition of memebership of [Natural Resource Management Co-operative Societies] did not have any significant effect on the performance of the cooperatives. The literature is replete with studies which suggests that small and cohesive groups have higher chances of success in management of CPRs than large and heterogeneous groups. But the case-studies presented at the Workshop did not support that view, and it is not a necessary condition for a successful collective management of common pool resources (1993: 32).

6. It should be noted that in the balance of power literature before the 1960s, systems of five powers or more were seen as more stable than bipolar or tripolar systems. Hence, the view that cooperation is more feasible with smaller numbers of actors is rather new in international relations.

despite the fact that heterogeneity is a prominent aspect both of CPR and IR situations. Although heterogeneity has been obvious to empirical researchers, too little theoretical work has explored its consequences, hindering analysis at each level as well as comparison across these levels.[7]

We originally asked authors to examine two potential dimensions of heterogeneity: actors' capabilities and their preferences. We defined capabilities broadly to refer to actors' assets, whatever form these assets may take, that are used in attempting to achieve purposes. Preferences refer to evaluations of the individual benefits and costs of policies (in view of actors' expectations of likely resulting outcomes) and of the outcomes themselves: preferences over policies and outcomes, respectively. As a result of papers written for this collection and our discussions, we also focus on a third dimension of heterogeneity: information and beliefs. Although information could be considered a capability, because its impact on cooperation is sufficiently distinctive, it seems more illuminating to put it into its own separate category.[8]

We have also identified another dimension of heterogeneity, concerning internal authority and decision-making structures, which has been extensively discussed in international relations and in comparative politics (Waltz, 1959; Katzenstein, 1978; Doyle, 1983). Recently, students of national politics have begun to make creative use of theories of delegation to reinterpret power relationships between legislatures and bureaucracies (Moe, 1984; Ramsayer and Rosenbluth, 1993; Weingast and Moran, 1983). It is therefore plausible that a systematic investigation of the impact of heterogeneity of internal structures on cooperation would be rewarding. However, we do not pursue that line of analysis here.[9]

Insofar as the CPR literature has previously addressed the issue of heterogeneity, it has tended to argue that heterogeneity inhibits cooperation. Gary Libecap, for instance, shows in paper 7 of this collection that heterogeneity in endowments and information has made it remarkably difficult to implement oil field unitization, the known efficient solution to over-investment and waste in exploitation of common pools of oil. His findings

---

7. As this special issue was going to press, some related work on heterogeneity in mathematical sociology came to our attention, but its analysis has not been integrated into our work here (see Glance and Huberman, 1994).

8. There are, of course, as many different dimensions of heterogeneity as there are variables regarding which actors can be similar or different. The three dimensions on which we focus in this collection are all identified as important in subsequent articles. Other dimensions of heterogeneity, such as heterogeneity in internal authority and decision-making structures of actors (discussed in the text), may also be significant.

9. Lisa Martin has begun such a line of research, seeking to use theories of delegation to ·illuminate problems of international cooperation.

in case studies of fisheries and orange marketing reinforce this result: 'heterogeneities . . . among the parties, including differences in information, past production, costs and size, provide obstacles to reaching agreement on the allocation rules for sharing the net benefits that result' (Libecap, paper 7 in this collection).

In contrast, the international relations literature tends to argue, as Lisa Martin points out in her paper, that heterogeneity may facilitate cooperation. Different preferences or endowments are a condition for gains from trade. Furthermore, the international relations literature as well as some of the CPR literature – we do not wish to overdramatize the conflict – has emphasized that the concentration of capabilities in a few actors may increase the likelihood of successful collective action. As in Olson's insight into privileged groups, having actors of varying sizes can lead to cooperation. In international relations, work that emphasizes the impact of size differentiation on cooperation has been given the label of 'hegemonic stability theory' (Keohane, 1984; Snidal, 1985).

Heterogeneity of preferences has been less thoroughly explored; it seems likely that its impact will vary according to other conditions. For instance, controlling for the distribution of capabilities (which may itself affect preferences), heterogeneous preferences about the marginal desirability of goods may facilitate gains from trade in market situations but inhibit cooperation where public goods are involved. The contrast between the emphases of the local CPR and international relations literatures should help scholars join the issue: under what conditions does heterogeneity (of capabilities, preferences or information and beliefs) hinder or facilitate effective collective action?

Heterogeneity of Capabilities.   Since Aristotle's discussion of rule by one, few, or many, political scientists have been interested in the effects of differences in capability on political behavior. Even if individuals are essentially equal in their natural talents, as both Hobbes and Locke asserted, within societies they have different endowments of wealth, different degrees of influence over others and different degrees of access to force. Certainly, no one believes that states in world politics are equal! Where the exercise of influence over other players is feasible, as in most small-scale CPR situations and in world politics, players' power – that is, their ability to translate resources into influence over outcomes – will also vary (in part as a function of their payoffs at the no-agreement point). Industrial organization theory in economics has long studied the effects of heterogeneity of capabilities (for example, in the form of monopoly or oligopoly) on corporate strategy and similar analyses have been at the core of neorealist theories of international relations (Waltz, 1979). Ever since the publication of Mancur Olson's book, *The Logic of Collective Action* (1965), political scientists have paid much attention to the effects not only of concentration of capacity but also of the patterns of dispersion of benefits and costs among actors. The papers in Part II and Part III all seek in different ways to assess the impact of different players having different initial endowments, as such differences affect their behavior in a variety of situations, including those in which no agreement can be reached.

Heterogeneity of Preferences.   All political scientists are concerned with, in Harold Lasswell's words, 'who gets what, when, how?' (Lasswell, 1936). That is, we are concerned about distributive outcomes. How these outcomes are valued and therefore whether they are sought, depends on players' preferences. Actors are heterogeneous in preferences as well as in capabilities. Quite a few observations of CPRs have indicated that cooperation becomes more difficult when preferences are highly skewed; but, as Snidal and Martin both observe, in international relations heterogeneity of interests can facilitate cooperation. Scholars who have focused on frequency dependent behavior, such as Schelling (1978), Kuran (1987) and Granovetter (1978), have demonstrated that different distributions of preferences for taking cooperative actions dependent upon the actions of others have a strong impact on the level of cooperation achieved. Further, as all threshold models illustrate, a slight change in the initial distribution of preferences can lead to entirely different outcomes. Thus, if enough individuals initiate cooperation, others may follow in a domino cascade; with the initial cooperators absent, the same preference distribution may yield no cooperation at all.

In her paper, Martin extends the conception of preferences by examining the effects of heterogeneity of *intensities* of preferences: people may all value the same goods, but to different degrees. If we both value water from the local irrigation system, but I am lazier than you, we may be able to strike a mutually advantageous deal through which you receive more water in return for devoting more labor to maintain the system. Snidal introduces a similar concept in discussing heterogeneity among actors with respect to time horizons: if I need a lot of water in the early spring for my vegetable crop and you need more later in the year for your grain, we can make a mutually advantageous trade.

Heterogeneity of Information and Beliefs.   Francis Bacon said in the 16th century that 'knowledge is power'. Hence, it is hardly novel that individuals with different levels of information achieve more or less favorable outcomes. Modern analyses of bargaining and of organizational structure emphasize the significance of asymmetrical information and its effect on what Oliver Williamson calls 'opportunism', defined as 'self-interest seeking with guile' (Akerlof, 1970; Williamson, 1985: 30). Contemporary game theory increases our sensitivity to these issues, showing how even apparently small changes in the information at the disposal of actors can profoundly affect both the existence and the character of equilibria (Kreps, 1990; Kreps and Wilson, 1982). Experimental research has reinforced our awareness of the significance of communication among players (E. Ostrom et al., 1994). Recent discussions of 'social capital' (E. Ostrom, paper 6 in this collection; Putnam, 1993) have emphasized the importance not only of institutions and their associated rules, but of the networks of communication, norms of social practice and relationships of trust that facilitate cooperation within some communities – but whose absence can lead to violence-increasing and welfare-reducing cycles of conflict or deadlock. The notion of 'community' (Taylor, 1987) may extend beyond issues of homogeneity of beliefs and information and social capital; but surely it includes these components.

Institutions and Heterogeneity. To some extent heterogeneity in actor capabilities, preferences, internal structure and information is determined exogenously to the institutions designed to deal with specific collective-action problems. Inequality in property or status among individuals, or in power and wealth among nations, has its roots deep in history. It is important to recognize, however, that the nature of institutions affects heterogeneity as well as vice versa. Indeed, in carrying out their activities, institutions may decrease informational heterogeneity – by providing common, reliable information to a variety of participants – while (as Martin points out in her paper) increasing another aspect of heterogeneity, by delegating authority to specialized actors, thus increasing role differentiation. It will be particularly important for students of institutions not merely to look at the impact of heterogeneity on cooperation, but to examine how institutional arrangements affect various types of heterogeneity.

In this volume we seek to understand the impact on patterns of cooperation and conflict of the number of actors and the heterogeneity of those actors along three principal dimensions: capabilities, preferences and information and beliefs. Outside of the laboratory, this problem is very complex, since the type of problem, the ability to communicate, the ability to make credible commitments and the costs of monitoring also affect levels of cooperation and conflict. The papers in Parts I and III of this volume make a number of related specific arguments in an attempt to understand this complexity. Before these specific arguments are presented, however, we need to make a plausible case that problems of collective action at local and global levels are sufficiently similar to merit comparative analysis. Intuitively, they may seem too different to be comparable, either because they operate at very different scales or because of differences between CPRs and public goods.

Scale: How Much Does It Affect the Problem of Collective Action?

The principal assumption of this collection is that the structure of the situations that actors face, whether at a local or international level, creates strong similarities among problems, even at very different scales. That is, the similarities between local CPR problems and CPR problems involving international regimes are sufficiently great that we can learn a good deal from treating them within a comparable framework. Further, the similarities between the problems of providing local public goods and global public goods are such that much can be learned from both environments if looked at from a common framework. Yet the assumption of comparability is not self-evidently true. Indeed, the differences in scale between local regimes and international regimes may seem to make it implausible on its face. In local domains, the scale of the problem is much smaller than the jurisdiction of the relevant national government; in international domains, the scale of the problem exceeds any government's jurisdiction. Contrasted to work conducted at a global scale, Oran Young points out that work on local CPRs appears to be at a nano scale.

The difference in scale would have pronounced effects if governments necessarily dealt with problems within their jurisdictions by imposing authoritative rules on their subjects. Within states, effective hierarchy would be exercised, while in international relations no common government exists. However, governments' activities in local and national domains are not limited to the imposition of rules. The government of Nepal only provides very general laws to govern village life in rural areas of that country: as Ostrom indicates in paper 6, the villages manage most of their irrigation activities by themselves. Like relationships among states, their interactions are mostly governed through horizontal relationships involving reciprocity rather than the operation of effective hierarchical authority.

Indeed, exploration of what governments actually do about commons problems reveals a wide variety of actions. The successful management of California groundwater basins, discussed in *Governing the Commons* (E. Ostrom, 1990), suggests that governments may be able to provide rules and procedures that facilitate cooperation by appropriators: 'The design of a successful micro-constitution can create community where community did not previously exist' (E. Ostrom, 1992: 348). In paper 7, Libecap shows that the United States Government provided a legal system to enforce contracts with respect to oil field unitization, interfered with fishers' ability to self-regulate inshore fisheries by prohibiting local union restrictions on fishing harvests as violations of anti-trust laws and acted as a weak public entrepreneur with regard to orange-marketing agreements: proposing rules but not implementing them over the strong opposition of participants. The state of Kansas, as discussed by Oye and Maxwell in paper 8, responded to a request by a local water district to reinterpret an appropriation rule, which had major consequences on the allocation of drilling rights; with respect to air quality regulation, the American and Japanese governments behaved very differently during the 1970s and 1980s. Japan compensated those affected by regulations more fully and systematically than did the United States.

The fact that governments play varying roles in local or national problems – not just the classic role of sovereign rule-maker and rule-enforcer – resonates with the recent literature on international regimes previously referred to. Typically, regimes that govern aspects of international domains do not impose enforceable rules on states, nor do they provide a reliable system of law by which states can enforce commitments given to one another. However, they do provide a set of standards against which states can judge how closely their counterparts' behavior conforms to the rules that have been mutually agreed. For example, they may increase the 'audience costs' of reneging on commitments (Martin, 1993). As Martin suggests in paper 4, different international institutional arrangements involving delegation of authority imply varying roles of states and intergovernmental agencies on different sets of issues in world politics. Furthermore, international regimes may involve non-governmental organizations, such as the oil companies, tanker operators and insurance companies discussed by Mitchell in paper 9. Indeed, one mark of many successful international regimes is that they provide incentives for non-governmental actors to uphold the rules on which governments have agreed.

Obvious differences exist between the types of local and global problems discussed in this collection: furthermore, the geographic scale of a problem interacts with the number of actors and their heterogeneity to affect levels of cooperation and conflict. Nevertheless, we can learn from the similarities across different domains. In both domains, hierarchical authority plays a relatively minor role. At a local level, actors may need to take a considerable initiative in coping with collective-action problems without being able to rely heavily on external authorities. At an international level, actors cannot rely on an external authority and are forced back to self-help solutions. Furthermore, state action in both domains is often ineffective or even has perverse effects. Ostrom points out in paper 6 that state construction of large, modern irrigation works in Nepal has adversely affected productivity. Apparently, state intervention in this case has adversely affected farmers' incentives to maintain the works and to monitor the behavior of other appropriators. Mitchell points out that for decades, international regulation of tanker discharges was ineffective because tanker captains had no incentives to follow the rules.

In this collection, we compare two domains – local and international – and use 'scale' to signal the difference between them. Whether it turns out to be useful to compare these two domains remains for the reader to determine. Young addresses this issue directly in paper 2 and readers are urged to take his cautionary advice seriously.

CPRs and Public Goods

Some of the issues discussed in this volume are conventionally viewed as public goods. Potential beneficiaries cannot be excluded from jointly supplied public goods and use by one beneficiary does not affect another's appropriation of the good. Other problems, such as the governance and management of local fisheries and irrigation works, are seen as common-pool resources: depletable natural or human-made resources from which potential beneficiaries are difficult to exclude (Gardner et al., 1990: 335). Before we engage in comparisons between local and global situations, it is essential that we understand the relationships between CPRs and public goods.

It is costly to exclude potential beneficiaries of both CPRs and public goods from receiving value from their use; hence, it is difficult to induce individuals voluntarily to supply them.[10] In both types of situations, a key problem is how to induce contributions to provide benefits from as many beneficiaries as possible. The classic problem of public goods, which also afflicts CPRs, is underprovision. When there are many beneficiaries, each of whose contribution is small relative to the cost of provision, the good will not be supplied in optimal quantity, unless institutional arrangements exist that induce incentives to provide it, through such means as linking private with public goods or the activities of political entrepreneurs (Frohlich et al., 1971). However, as Mancur Olson argued almost 30 years ago, when one actor, or a small 'privileged group', can benefit from providing the good, public goods are likely to be provided even in the absence of such a political infrastructure.

Although the problem of underprovision is a possible outcome in any CPR, CPRs are afflicted by an additional problem that is not encountered in situations of public goods: use of the resource by one individual may have adverse consequences for others. When CPRs are open for anyone to use, individual beneficiaries may not take into account these adverse consequences. Participants acting independently have incentives to overuse the resource and thus reduce total returns. With respect to renewable resources, overappropriation can lead to the destruction of the resource itself. Thus,

---

10. As Snidal points out, the problem of exclusion is the result both of the intrinsic properties of a resource and of the boundary rules used to regulate the use of that resource. Thus, one strategy used in the governance of CPRs is to search for effective and easy-to-monitor boundary rules that keep non-contributors from benefitting from the contributions made by others.

renewable open access CPRs may be subject to overcrowding, inefficient use of resources, violence and potential destruction of the resource itself. CPRs, in short, are subject to rivalry, sometimes referred to as subtractability. The design issue in a CPR is therefore how to allocate subtractable benefits among appropriators.

Although this distinction is clear in the abstract, many physical resources can be viewed as public goods in regard to some aspects of their provision or use and as CPRs in regard to other aspects. Consider, for instance, the problem of managing a groundwater basin. In regard to appropriation or receiving benefits, the resource is clearly a common-pool resource – the water extracted by one user reduces the supply available to others. In regard to the regulation of the basin itself or its provision, protection of a groundwater basin from salt-water intrusion, soil compaction or pollution is a public good because protection of one user against destruction of the basin also increases the supply of protection available to others.

We can also think of the stratospheric ozone layer as a CPR for some purposes and as a public good for others. The incentives of those who produce chlorofluorocarbons (CFCs) are similar to those facing fishers or groundwater producers. The ozone layer is the 'sink' into which they can emit CFCs at little cost. They face incentives to overinvest in products that generate CFC emissions, because they do not bear the entire cost of the depletion of the ozone layer created by each additional ton of CFCs emitted. The more CFCs emitted, the less capable is the ozone layer of protecting people from skin cancer caused by exposure to the sun's radiation. On the other hand, one person's use of the protection provided by the ozone layer while sunbathing does not affect anyone else's ability to enjoy similar protection. Given an intact ozone layer, consumption of protection is not subtractable: there is no rivalry.

These examples suggest that the public goods–CPR distinction is more appropriately used to classify specific *aspects* of a physical resource rather than to characterize the physical resource as a whole. Some physical resources may involve rivalry in their provision and not in their consumption, while others may involve the opposite pattern. Few physical resources are pure public goods in all aspects of their provision and appropriation. The concept of a 'pure' public good with no aspects of subtractability, while important theoretically, has few real-world counterparts. John Dales (1968) has commented that the only physical example of a pure public good that he can specify is gravity – which is not something that humans can affect at all.

The ambiguity in these examples also suggests that the public goods–CPR distinction is not a classification that mimics divisions in the real world (such as that between male and female mammals) but rather one that reflects two ideal types in the Weberian sense. Public goods and CPRs are ideal types at either end of a continuum characterized by the degree of rivalry in consumption of the resource. Hence, the key to the public goods–CPR distinction seems to be the abundance of the resource relative to the function that it performs. Rivalry is not a problem for abundant resources, but it is for scarce ones. Hence, atmospheric oxygen is a public good because it is so abundant that one person's consumption does not affect that of another individual; but in much of the world, clean water is in short supply and therefore can be viewed as a common-pool resource.

Since the public goods–CPR continuum in part reflects relative abundance, a situation can move along that continuum over time. When human beings first begin to harvest from a previously unexploited fishing stock, the quantity of fish harvested by the first few fishers does not reduce the quantity available to others since the remaining fish have an increased opportunity to grow until maturity. Thus, in an early stage of development, a local fishery may seem more like a public good. As more and more harvesting occurs, however, rivalry increases and fisheries become CPRs. Before CFCs had been invented, the stratospheric ozone layer was a public good; and since it was provided by nature, there was no problem of underprovision. Now it is a common-pool resource, subject to human depletion.

In this collection of papers we hope to show that meaningful insights can be gained into the politics of collective action by explicitly comparing behavior with respect to public goods and CPRs within local and international domains. CPRs and public goods do not exhaust the problems faced in either a local or an international domain, but do include a wide variety of important problems faced at both ends of the geographic scale. Governments play a variety of roles in both local and international domains. The stark distinction between domestic hierarchy and international anarchy does not capture the rich set of ways in which political regimes can facilitate or hinder solutions of collective-action problems. Our information is incomplete and our findings are tentative; but we hope that this initial inquiry will stimulate more systematic work along these lines.

Scope and Heterogeneity: Insights from the Papers

Figures 1 and 2 depict the basic outlines of our analysis. Figure 1 asks how the factors that we have identified affect incentives to cooperate at a given time, with institutional arrangements regarded as fixed. In static analysis, existing institutional arrangements are treated as if they were exogenous. In the dynamic analysis depicted in Figure 2, however, changes in these institutions need to be explained and hence become endogenous.

As depicted in Figure 1, the variables on which this collection focuses are the number of actors and the heterogeneity of their abilities, preferences and information and beliefs. We treat these explanatory variables as

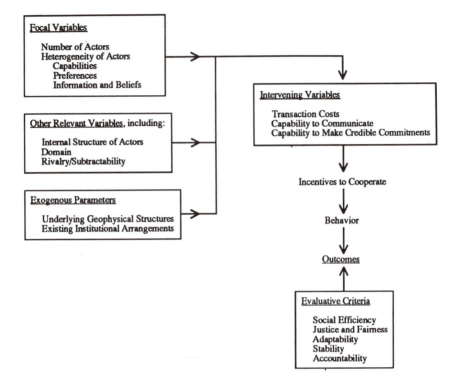

Figure 1. Relationships among variables at a given time.

exogenous; we do not explain them but take them as given. Many other potentially relevant exogenous variables, including internal decision-making structures, also affect behavior and outcomes in collective-action problems, but the papers in this collection refer primarily to domain (local to global) and whether problems have a CPR (subtractive) or public good (non-subtractive) structure. Factors such as the underlying geophysical structures also affect outcomes, but for a given problem and domain, they are fixed.

These exogenous factors affect three key aspects of the political processes that we study: the transaction costs that actors face, their ability to communicate and their ability to make credible commitments. Analyzing these costs and capabilities focuses attention on the key positive and negative incentives to cooperation involved in achieving collective action. We can then trace the behavior (with respect to the amount and type of cooperation or discord) that ensues, leading to outcomes. These outcomes then can be evaluated on a variety of grounds, including social efficiency, adaptability to exogenous shocks, stability over time, accountability of officials to those

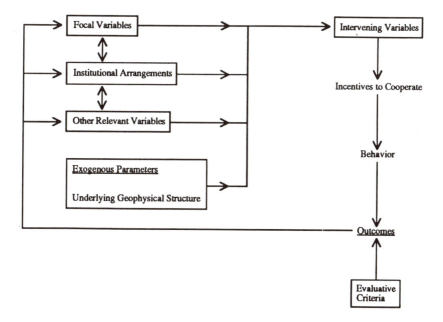

Figure 2. Relationships among variables over time.

who are affected by outcomes of their actions, and other normative criteria including justice and fairness.

Over time, institutional arrangements change as a result of patterns of cooperation and discord. As depicted in Figure 2, sustained cooperation to overcome collective-action problems requires changes in rules to adapt to new situations; enhanced cooperation typically entails changes in some rules; prolonged discord is likely to erode established institutions. Hence, to account fully for variations in cooperation over time one must also account for institutional change. Furthermore, once rules are changed, they may affect the number of actors and their heterogeneity. Thus, most of the left-hand variables are more or less subject to change over time as the outcomes of collective- and constitutional-choice processes affect them. Boundary rules, for example, that reduce the number of actors who are eligible to participate obviously change the size of the group. Allocational rules can operate over time so as to reduce or increase the differences in capabilities among participants and thus reduce or increase heterogeneity. Institutional changes thus tend to change the structure of a situation and the incentives and behavior of actors.

Using this more general framework, we can now discuss the papers that report analytical, empirical and experimental results. How do they contribute to an understanding of the effects on behavior and outcomes of

variations in the number of actors and of diverse dimensions of heterogeneity and number of players?

In paper 7, Libecap focuses on the effect of heterogeneity of capabilities
among appropriators from a CPR and how this is compounded by information asymmetries. Mining an oil pool, a non-renewable resource, at the
most efficient rate requires coordination among pumpers to extract oil
slowly rather than to race to pull it out before someone else does. The
capabilities of different oil producers vary dramatically depending on exogenous parameters such as the geological structure of the land under their
leasehold. It is very costly to obtain accurate information about these
exogenous parameters.

The effort to develop an agreement to allow one manager to organize
production from an entire pool as a unit – something that is clearly to
the long-term joint benefit of all producers – requires agreement to change
allocational rules. Whether this agreement is achieved early or late in the
development of an oil pool depends, according to Libecap, on the symmetric
or asymmetric information that actors possess. If enough development has
already occurred, each producer gains private information about its own
capabilities. Those who think their status quo position, if no agreement were
achieved, would yield them a high level of return are reluctant to agree to
a formula that does not adequately take their self-perceived earning capacity
into account. Since other participants cannot know whether a negotiator
has good information about capabilities or is bluffing, negotiations take a
long time once development of a pool has started. Where little individual
exploration has occurred before negotiations on unitization take place, by
contrast, producers lack information about their own capabilities. While
the producers have *less* information in the aggregate, the uncertain information they have is commonly shared. Without conflicting perceptions about
relative capabilities, actors are less likely to lose valuable time disagreeing
about the formulae used to allocate profits and losses.

Consequently, Libecap argues that the sequence of negotiations makes a
difference in whether and when agreements are reached to establish institutional arrangements that enhance joint returns. When negotiations are
undertaken before private information is obtained about individual differences in individual capabilities (what they could accomplish without an
agreement), the shared uncertainty of the future enhances the likelihood that
actors will agree to a new institutional arrangement. When negotiations are
undertaken after private information is obtained about diverse capabilities,
private information about the asymmetries in their capabilities leads to
highly conflictual negotiations and a much lower rate of agreement. Where
asymmetric information delays agreement, uncoordinated resource exploitation leads to reductions both in the common-pool resource itself and in
disparities among actors' capabilities. Hence, after many opportunities to

achieve higher joint returns have been foregone, agreements to cooperate become more likely.

Earlier studies by E. Ostrom (1990) and Blomquist (1992) concerning negotiations over renewable groundwater basins provide complementary findings. When groundwater producers used courts to make information commonly available about the underlying geologic structure of their ground-water basins as well as a reliable history of past extractions, they were able to agree to distribute future costs and benefits according to a sharing for-mula based on both aspects of this common knowledge. On the other hand, when the discovery process generated information that both capabilities and interests were highly disparate – as in the very large Mojave groundwater basin – efforts to bind producers with different interests into the same agree-ment failed (Blomquist, 1992).

Libecap's analysis of the interactive effects of heterogeneity of capabilities and information is supported by the experimental work of Steven Hackett, Dean Dudley and James Walker (paper 5). In both types of experiments, it was possible for participants to overcome the problems associated with dif-ferences in their capabilities (endowments) when they had common knowledge. In those CPR settings characterized by the stark institutions allowing no communication, actors with diverse capabilities overinvested their endowed assets. Allowing them to communicate enhanced their capacities to achieve a cooperative agreement. These outcomes approached full efficiency when information was generally available even though that revealed the extent of heterogeneities among the participants. Thus, it would appear that it is not simply heterogeneities of capabilities that deter agreements about changes in allocation rules but rather the particular com-bination of heterogeneities related to capabilities and information.

Martin's theoretical analysis of heterogeneity of capabilities and interests of international actors (bolstered by E. Ostrom's theoretical and empirical work on local actors) also examines the interaction among different aspects of heterogeneity rather than focusing on one dimension alone. As Martin states, 'Analysis of the impact of heterogeneity cannot rest on a straightfor-ward argument that conflicts of interest increase as heterogeneity does' (paper 4). She points to many instances in the creation and maintenance of international regimes where actors possessing substantially more capabilities than others – whose interests are also greater – adopt strategies that make agreement on cooperation easier to achieve, monitor and sustain. Even where actors are relatively homogeneous, their agreement frequently creates rules and enforcers of these rules whose powers are asymmetric with those of regular actors. Further, she points out that heterogeneities of interest intensity create possibilities for tradeoff among international actors that enhance the likelihood of stable, long-term agreements.

Ostrom's analysis in paper 6 of the asymmetry in capabilities between head-enders and tail-enders also illustrates how the interaction among diverse forms of heterogeneity may enhance or detract from possibilities of agreement. Tail-enders are in a weak bargaining situation when the labor or other material resources they could allocate to the maintenance of a CPR regime are of little value to head-enders. In such situations, the powerful may well act independently and no mutual gains are achieved from cooperation. In situations where head-enders could use the material resources of tail-enders, however, the cross-cutting interests can produce a stable, long-term and highly productive agreement. At the other extreme, if head-enders were also high-status individuals and owned large tracks of land, they could become completely intransigent in their unwillingness to enter into cooperative agreements. Thus, some combination of heterogeneities in capabilities and interests can create substantial benefits from trade and cooperation. Other combinations of heterogeneities exaggerate still further the bargaining power of some over others and become a major drag on the development of cooperative agreements.

From the contributions by Oye and Maxwell (paper 8) and Mitchell (paper 9), we learn that different patterns of incidence of costs and benefits may profoundly affect the provision of a public good or the maintenance of a CPR. In the typical local CPR, those who pay the costs tend also to be those who receive substantial benefits – although the distribution of costs and benefits may be asymmetrical. Likewise, insofar as a global public good can be achieved through regulation, everyone benefits, but the costs may be concentrated on a small number of actors – for example, firms producing CFCs or owners of tankers. For those actors, the salience of the costs they must bear is far greater than the small benefits that they also receive from improvement in the quality of the stratosphere or ocean. Hence, where costs of provision are concentrated and benefits diffuse, heterogeneity of interests makes the public good or CPR difficult to provide or maintain.

This conclusion is of course consistent with Mancur Olson's arguments about the provision of collective goods. However, Oye and Maxwell provide an interesting converse argument, drawn from work by George Stigler and others, on cartel theory and regulation. When the benefits of regulation to provide a public good are concentrated, regulation is much easier to supply than when they are diffuse; indeed, under these conditions regulation may be oversupplied, providing cartel-like protection to producers. Oye and Maxwell argue that leading producers of CFCs, such as DuPont, had incentives to support regulations phasing out such production in favor of new generations of chemicals on which they would enjoy competitive advantage. As Mitchell shows in paper 9, tanker owners and operators had fewer such incentives; hence, governments seeking to reduce the quantity of oil dumped in the oceans resorted to threats of denial of access to their ports. Yet even in this case the eventual regulatory solution took advantage of the heterogeneity of actors, such as the differences in interests between oil companies and private tanker operators and the professionalism and standard operating procedures of marine insurance companies. It is clear from the empirical studies in this volume that heterogeneity of actors can occur along a variety of dimensions, and that it can either hinder or facilitate cooperation.

Policy Implications

If the economists' typical policy advice is to 'get the prices right', ours is to 'get the institutional incentives right'. Government policies that have ignored the local knowledge of participants or underestimated their ability to solve collective-action problems have done great damage. In her article, Ostrom shows that government-managed irrigation systems have been, in general, notably unsuccessful in Nepal, compared with farmer-managed systems, despite much higher levels of capital inputs. Her argument is that government investment has often disrupted local institutions and practices, which constitute a form of social capital. In the absence of these institutions and practices, incentives for cooperation among farmers may disappear and productivity may suffer.

Likewise, focusing only on the polar extremes of a world state or uncooperative anarchy has stunted thinking about international cooperation. If we think about a range of institutions, from self-help to hierarchy, as Martin and Snidal do in their contributions, we can begin to ask how institutional variation affects efforts to cooperate. Furthermore, we can address issues of institutional design, which Young mentions in his article. An important aspect of institutional design, which both Ostrom and Snidal discuss, has to do with partitioning relatively large numbers of actors into smaller sub-sets, which may be able to meet frequently face to face (as with farmers in particular areas of large irrigation systems) or to negotiate on issues that particularly concern them, before returning to negotiate with the larger set of participants (as in GATT negotiations, with the United States, Europe and Japan often playing special roles). Institutions may create functional differentiation among actors, as Martin argues. Mitchell's article provides an example of such differentiation: the diverse complex of entities, from governments to insurance companies to international organizations, involved in implementing equipment standards for oil tankers.

This collection also illustrates how significant the flow of information is in enabling human beings to cooperate. A clear implication of several of these papers – hardly new, but reinforced by the work of Hackett and his colleagues and Libecap – is that extensive common knowledge and ease of information provision facilitate cooperation, while private information and barriers to communication make it much more difficult. From a policy standpoint, the implication is that the sequence of negotiations and the institutional arrangements that are devised should be crafted so as to increase the extent of common knowledge and to facilitate information exchange.

Another implication of research on local CPRs and public goods and on international regimes for international environmental institutions is the importance of achieving a match between the characteristics of a successful monitoring and sanctioning scheme and the characteristics of specific situations. In popular economic language, regulatory arrangements need to be 'incentive-compatible'. Furthermore, as evidence from the performance of local CPR institutions has repeatedly shown, arrangements worked out by participants, intimately knowledgeable about details of their activities, are likely to be more workable than blueprints developed by policy analysts and imposed by politicians and bureaucrats. Flexibility and a willingness to permit differently designed arrangements to develop on different issues will be required to deal with the continually expanding agenda of complex economic and ecological issues confronting the world today. Yet, these policy efforts are more likely to be successful if participants are guided in their creation by the results of rigorous theoretical studies of the design principles underlying successful cooperation in a wide variety of empirical contexts. We hope that the ideas and research directions outlined in these papers can make a significant contribution towards the design and execution of such studies.

Conclusion

We believe that this collection demonstrates the value of comparing collective-action problems at vastly different scales: local arrangements to maintain common-pool resources and international regimes both to provide public goods and to govern the distribution of privately appropriable resources. Under both sets of conditions, the actors involved are interdependent: their actions can impose costs or confer benefits on others. Typically, therefore, uncoordinated actions have welfare effects that are inferior to those of a variety of potential agreements. Hence, gains can be achieved through political exchange, involving the construction of institutions to make commitments credible, improve the flow of information and reduce the costs of enforcing agreements. But lack of effective hierarchical governance means that the participants themselves must provide such institutions: they cannot rely on outside authority but rather on self-enforcing agreements, maintained through strategies such as reciprocity.

Under these conditions, *scope* (the number of actors) and the *heterogeneity of actors* pose complicated issues for cooperation. Increasing scope may render cooperation more difficult; but the local CPR literature (as well as an older literature on the balance of power in international relations) should make one cautious about simplistic generalizations that increases in scope necessarily hinder cooperation. When scope changes, so do other features of the situation and it may be these changes that are causing observed effects. Furthermore, increases in the number of actors may, under some conditions, increase opportunities for constructing coalitions that facilitate cooperation.

Actors may be heterogeneous along a number of dimensions: we focus on capabilities, preferences and information and beliefs. The papers in this collection show clearly that heterogeneity can facilitate or hinder cooperation, depending on the type of heterogeneity and the context. The concentration of capabilities in a few actors may facilitate provision of public goods or CPRs, but only if these actors would benefit significantly from such provision. Heterogeneity of preferences can lead to gains from exchange, hence more cooperation. On the other hand, heterogeneous private information can be a great hindrance to negotiated agreements over CPRs.

This collection reports on an investigation of connections, previously unexplored, between issues involving local and global commons. Like most explorations, we have not thoroughly surveyed the terrain, only highlighted some of its more salient features. In particular, we have shown that issues involving both scope (the number of actors) and heterogeneity of actors are more complex than either the literature on international relations or that on CPRs has appreciated. We have not formulated rigorous propositions about the conditional effects of scope and heterogeneity on cooperation, much less tested such propositions. However, we hope to convince our readers that comparisons across scale can be illuminating, that scope and heterogeneity are important variables and that further work on these issues – empirical, experimental and theoretical – is likely to be rewarding. In surveying unexplored territory, even modest increases in knowledge are useful to those who follow.

REFERENCES

Akerlof, George (1970) 'The Market for Lemons', *Quarterly Journal of Economics* 55: 488–500.
Axelrod, Robert (1984) *The Evolution of Cooperation*. New York: Basic Books.
Bendor, Jonathan and Dilip Mookherjee (1987) 'Institutional Structure and the Logic of Ongoing Collective Action', *American Political Science Review* 81(1) (March): 129–54.
Benedick, Richard Elliot (1991) *Ozone Diplomacy: New Directions in Safeguarding the Planet*. Cambridge, MA: Harvard University Press.
Berkes, Fikret, ed. (1989) *Common Property Resources: Ecology and Community-based Sustainable Development*. London: Belhaven Press.
Blomquist, William (1992) *Dividing the Waters: Governing Groundwater in Southern California*. San Francisco, CA: Institute for Contemporary Studies Press.

Bromley, Daniel et al., eds (1992) *Making the Commons Work: Theory, Practice, and Policy.* San Francisco, CA: Institute for Contemporary Studies Press.

Caporaso, James A. (1992) 'International Relations Theory and Multilateralism: The Search for Foundations', *International Organization* 46(3) (Summer): 610–13.

Clark, Colin W. (1980) 'Restricted Access to Common-property Fishery Resources: A Game-theoretic Analysis', in Pan-Tai Liu (ed.) *Dynamic Optimization and Mathematical Economics*, pp. 117–32. New York: Plenum Press.

Dales, John H. (1968) *Pollution, Property, and Prices.* Toronto: University of Toronto Press.

Doyle, Michael W. (1983) 'Kant, Liberal Legacies, and Foreign Affairs', *Philosophy and Public Affairs* 12 (Summer and Fall): 205–35 and 323–53.

Eggertsson, Thráinn (1990) *Economic Behavior and Institutions.* New York: Cambridge University Press.

Feeny, David, Fikret Berkes, Bonnie J. McCay and James M. Acheson (1990) 'The Tragedy of the Commons: Twenty-two Years Later', *Human Ecology* 18(1): 1–19.

Frank, Robert (1988) *Passions Within Reason: The Strategic Role of the Emotions.* New York: Norton.

Frohlich, Norman, Joe A. Oppenheimer and Oran Young (1971) *Political Leadership and Collective Goods.* Princeton, NJ: Princeton University Press.

Gardner, Roy, Elinor Ostrom and James Walker (1990) 'The Nature of Common-pool Resource Problems', *Rationality and Society* 2(3) July: 335–58.

Glance, Natalie S. and Bernardo A. Huberman (1994) 'The Dynamics of Social Dilemmas', *Scientific American* (March): 76–81.

Gordon, H. Scott (1954) 'The Economic Theory of a Common Property Resource: The Fishery', *Journal of Political Economy* 62: 124–42.

Granovetter, Mark (1978) 'Threshold Models of Collective Behavior', *American Journal of Sociology* 83: 1420–43.

Haas, Peter M. (1990) *Saving the Mediterranean: The Politics of International Environmental Cooperation.* New York: Columbia University Press.

Haas, Peter M., Robert O. Keohane and Marc A. Levy, eds (1993) *Institutions for the Earth: Sources of Effective International Environmental Protection.* Cambridge, MA: MIT Press.

Haas, Peter M., Mark A. Levy and Edward A. Parson (1992) 'Appraising the Earth Summit: How Should We Judge UNCED's Success?', *Environment* 34(8) (Oct.): 6–11; 26–33.

Hardin, Garrett (1968) 'The Tragedy of the Commons', *Science* 162: 1243–8.

Hardin, Russell (1982) *Collective Action.* Baltimore, MD: Johns Hopkins University Press.

Isaac, R. Mark, James M. Walker and Arlington Williams (1994) 'Group Size and the Voluntary Provision of Public Goods: Experimental Evidence Utilizing Large Groups', *Journal of Public Economics*, forthcoming.

Johnson, Ronald N. and Gary D. Libecap (1982) 'Contracting Problems and Regulation: The Case of the Fishery', *American Economic Review* 72: 1005–22.

Katzenstein, Peter J., ed. (1978) *Between Power and Plenty: For Economic Policies of Advanced Industrial States.* Madison: University of Wisconsin Press.

Keohane, Robert O. (1984) *After Hegemony: Cooperation and Discord in the World Political Economy.* Princeton, NJ: Princeton University Press.

Keohane, Robert O., Michael McGinnis and Elinor Ostrom (1993) *Linking Local and Global Commons*, proceedings of a conference held at Harvard University, 23–5 April 1992. Bloomington: Indiana University, Workshop in Political Theory and Policy Analysis.

Kindleberger, Charles P. (1973) *The World in Depression.* Berkeley: University of California Press.

Krasner, Stephen D., ed. (1983) *International Regimes.* Ithaca, NY: Cornell University Press.

Kreps, David (1990) *A Course in Microeconomic Theory.* Princeton, NJ: Princeton University Press.

Kreps, David and Robert Wilson (1982) 'Reputation and Imperfect Information', *Journal of Economic Theory* 27: 253–79.

Kuran, Timur (1987) 'Preference Falsification, Policy Continuity and Collective Conservatism', *The Economic Journal* 97: 642–65.

Lasswell, Harold (1936) *Politics: Who Gets What, When, How*. New York: McGraw-Hill.

Levy, Marc (1993) 'European Acid Rain: The Power of Tote-board Diplomacy', in Peter M. Haas, Robert O. Keohane and Mark Levy (eds.) *Institutions for the Earth: Sources of Effective International Environmental Protection*, pp. 75–132. Cambridge, MA: MIT Press.

Martin, Lisa L. (1993) 'Credibility, Costs and Institutions: Cooperation on Economic Sanctions', *World Politics* 45(3) April: 406–32.

Matthews, David Ralph (1993) *Controlling Common Property: Regulating Canada's East Coast Fishery*. Toronto: University of Toronto Press.

McCay, Bonnie J. and James M. Acheson (1987) *The Question of the Commons: The Culture and Ecology of Communal Resources*. Tucson: University of Arizona Press.

McKean, Margaret A. (1992) 'Success on the Commons: A Comparative Examination of Institutions for Common Property Resource Management', *Journal of Theoretical Politics* 4: 247–81.

Moe, Terry M. (1984) 'The New Economics of Organization', *American Journal of Political Science* 28: 739–77.

Netting, Robert McC. (1981) *Balancing on an Alp: Ecological Change and Continuity in a Swiss Mountain Community*. Cambridge: Cambridge University Press.

North, Douglass C. (1990) *Institutions, Institutional Change and Economic Performance*. New York: Cambridge University Press.

Olson, Mancur (1965) *The Logic of Collective Action*. Cambridge, MA: Harvard University Press.

Ostrom, Elinor (1990) *Governing the Commons: The Evolution of Institutions for Collective Action*. New York: Cambridge University Press.

Ostrom, Elinor (1992) 'Community and the Endogenous Solution of Commons Problems', *Journal of Theoretical Politics* 4(3) July: 343–52.

Ostrom, Elinor, Roy Gardner and James Walker (1994) *Rules, Games, and Common-pool Resources*. Ann Arbor: University of Michigan Press.

Ostrom, Vincent, David Feeny and Hartmut Picht, eds (1993) *Rethinking Institutional Analysis and Development: Issues, Alternatives, and Choices*, 2nd edn. San Francisco, CA: Institute for Contemporary Studies Press.

Oye, Kenneth A., ed. (1986) *Cooperation Under Anarchy*. Princeton, NJ: Princeton University Press.

Parson, Edward A. (1993) 'Protecting the Ozone Layer', in Peter M. Haas, Robert O. Keohane and Marc A. Levy (eds) *Institutions for the Earth: Sources of Effective International Environmental Protection*, pp. 27–74. Cambridge, MA: MIT Press.

Pinkerton, Evelyn, ed. (1989) *Co-operative Management of Local Fisheries: New Directions for Improved Management and Community Development*. Vancouver: University of British Columbia Press.

Putnam, Robert D. (with Robert Leonardi and Raffaella Y. Nanetti) (1993) *Making Democracy Work: Civic Traditions in Modern Italy*. Princeton, NJ: Princeton University Press.

Ramsayer, Mark and Frances McCall Rosenbluth (1993) *Japan's Political Marketplace*. Cambridge, MA: Harvard University Press.

Schelling, Thomas C. (1978) *Micromotives and Macrobehavior*. New York: Norton.

Singh, Katar and Vishwa Ballabh (1993) 'Cooperatives in Natural Resource Management', Workshop Report no. 10. Anand, India: Institute of Rural Management.

Snidal, Duncan (1985) 'The Limits of Hegemonic Stability Theory', *International Organization* 39(4) Autumn: 579–615.

Tang, Shui Yan (1992) *Institutions and Collective Action: Self-governance in Irrigation*. San Francisco, CA: Institute for Contemporary Studies Press.

Taylor, Michael (1987) *The Possibility of Cooperation*. Cambridge: Cambridge University Press.

Udéln, Lars (1993) 'Twenty Five Years with *The Logic of Collective Action*', *Acta Sociologica* 36: 239–61.

Waltz, Kenneth N. (1959) *Man, the State and War*. New York: Columbia University Press.

Waltz, Kenneth N. (1979) *Theory of International Politics*. Reading, MA: Addison-Wesley.

Weingast, Barry and M. Moran (1983) 'Bureaucratic Discretion of Congressional Control? Regulatory Policymaking by the FTC', *Journal of Political Economy* 91: 765–800.

Williamson, Oliver (1985) *The Economic Institutions of Capitalism*. New York: Free Press.

Young, Oran R. (1982) *Resource Regimes: Natural Resources and Social Institutions*. Berkeley: University of California Press.

Young, Oran R. (1989) *International Cooperation: Building Regimes for Natural Resources and the Environment*. Ithaca, NY: Cornell University Press.

Part I

Theoretical Puzzles

2. THE PROBLEM OF SCALE IN HUMAN/ENVIRONMENT RELATIONSHIPS

Oran R. Young

Long familiar to natural scientists, the problem of scale does not figure prominently in the discourse of the social sciences. Yet, in principle, matters of scale are just as pertinent to the growth of knowledge about social systems as they are to the development of understanding of physical and biological systems. In this essay, I endeavor to bring the problem of scale to the attention of students of social phenomena. My strategy for doing so is to consider in some depth similarities and differences between analyses of institutions that arise to govern human/environment relationships at the micro level of small-scale, local societies and the macro level of international society. In the process, I hope to initiate a more wide-ranging dialogue regarding the problem of scale among social scientists concerned with a broad array of subjects.

The problem of scale revolves around the transferability of propositions and models from one level to another in the dimensions of space and time. Scaling up, then, refers to the application of propositions or models about micro-scale systems to meso-scale and macro-scale phenomena. Scaling down involves the opposite tack, the application of propositions or models about macro-scale systems to meso-scale or micro-scale phenomena. A few examples from the natural sciences will lend substance to these conceptual points. Those working on the development of general circulation models (GCMs) as a means of understanding changes in the global climate system are regularly asked about the prospects for scaling down from the global to the regional level. That is, many of those concerned about climate change want to know whether models of the global climate system can shed light on the prospects for climate variability at the regional or even the subregional level. Conversely, ecologists working on self-contained, local ecosystems are often asked whether their knowledge of ecosystem dynamics applies at the landscape level or even at the planetary level. Much of the thinking underlying the Gaia hypothesis, for instance, is based on the premise that the Earth as a whole is an ecosystem that ought to behave in accordance with principles derived from the study of smaller scale ecosystems.

Similar examples are easy to come by with regard to the dimension of time. There is great interest today, for example, in the feasibility of scaling up from propositions about interannual climate variability, caused by such forces as the El Nino phenomenon or volcanic eruptions, to propositions about variability at the decadal level, as in the case of cycles associated with variations in the amount of solar energy reaching the earth. At the same time, those who work on macro-scale phenomena, like glacial cycles or the controversial Milankovich cycle, are concerned with the prospects for scaling down or, in other words, investigating the applicability of their findings about long cycles to interannual or decadal cycles. Although space and time are distinct dimensions, the problem of scale is the same in both instances. Ultimately, it concerns the extent to which the underlying mechanisms at work at the various levels are similar enough to allow us to make use of ideas and insights developed at one level in our efforts to understand phenomena occurring at other levels.

Human/Environment Relationships

The last decade has witnessed a striking growth of interest in the study of human/environment relationships on two distinct scales. One of the resultant bodies of literature, centered on the idea of governing the commons (Ostrom, 1990), focuses on common-pool resources (CPRs) and explores the role of social institutions as determinants of collective outcomes in small-scale, stateless societies. Inspired by the observation that the so-called 'tragedy of the commons' (G. Hardin, 1968) frequently does not occur in practice, analyses of CPRs have done much to illuminate the conditions under which self-interested actors are able to use natural resources sustainably in the absence of an overarching or hierarchical public authority capable of making and enforcing rules governing the use of the resources at stake (McCay and Acheson, 1987; Bromley et al., 1992).

The other body of literature, closely tied to the 'new institutionalism' in international relations, seeks to delineate the conditions under which cooperative arrangements can emerge and operate effectively in international society (Hughes, 1992; Milner, 1992). Energized by the realization that many international interactions do not conform to the non-cooperative logic of the prisoner's dilemma (Axelrod, 1984), studies of resource regimes at the international level have gone some way toward pinpointing the conditions that account for the variance in outcomes flowing from conscious efforts to devise governance systems dealing with human/environment relationships (Young, 1989a).

The problem of scale posed by the emergence of these two bodies of literature is straightforward. Can we scale up from the study of CPR arrangements in local societies to the level of international society? To what extent, for example, do propositions concerning the conditions governing success in avoiding the 'tragedy of the commons' in small-scale systems hold at the international level? Conversely, can we scale down from the level of international society to small-scale systems? Is the process of establishing social practices to guide the use of CPRs in small-scale, stateless societies, for instance, governed by the same forces as the formation of international resource regimes? In the following discussion, I explore this subject in some detail. To make the analysis easy to follow, I organize the argument around seven themes: (1) analytic puzzles, (2) social settings, (3) the nature of institutions, (4) the formation of institutions, (5) the consequences of institutions, (6) the performance of institutions and (7) design principles.

1. Analytic Puzzles

Each of the literatures under consideration rests squarely on the premises that interactive decision making is the norm in human affairs and that collective-action problems are endemic in a world of interactive decision making (R. Hardin, 1982). They both assume as well that a sizable fraction of the variance in human/environment relationships can be explained in terms of the effects of social institutions operating in the absence of a centralized government or hierarchical structure of public authority (Elster, 1989; Furubotn and Richter, 1991). These are major points of tangency. Despite these striking similarities, however, studies of CPR arrangements and of resource regimes exhibit pronounced differences. This is attributable, in the first instance, to the way in which each stream of analysis frames its central analytic puzzle.

At the heart of the literature on CPRs lies the concept of a common pool or, in other words, a resource used by a group of appropriators that is both non-excludable and depletable (Feeny et al., 1990). Resources of this type that do not give rise to access rules raise the specter of the 'tragedy of the commons', a vicious circle involving overuse and eventual exhaustion of the

resources caused by the unwillingness or inability of individual appropriators to internalize the social costs of their own actions (Gordon, 1954;
Scott, 1955). Conventional wisdom has long held that the way to avoid these
problems in human/environment relationships is to introduce systems of
private property or, on some accounts, public property (G. Hardin and
Baden, 1977). In a sense, the study of CPR arrangements can be seen as an
effort to refute this conventional wisdom and to put in its place a set of propositions recognizing the important role that structures of restricted common property play in many small-scale societies. The key move in this
analytic project is the observation that the basic elements of common property are regularly coupled with more or less extensive codes of conduct or
social practices capable of guiding the behavior of users of CPRs. Once
made, this move leads to a search for conditions governing the establishment
of such codes of conduct as well as to an effort to compare and contrast the
performance of the resultant restricted common-property arrangements with
structures of private or public property in terms of criteria like sustainability,
efficiency, and equity (McKean, 1992).

The literature on resource regimes in international society, by contrast,
starts from a concern with the nature of collective-action problems more
generally. Rather than focusing on the behavior of users of CPRs, it seeks
to identify analytically differentiable types of collective-action problems (for
example, coordination, battle of the sexes, chicken, prisoner's dilemma) and
to investigate the prospects for avoiding suboptimal outcomes arising from
interactive decision making in situations exhibiting these characteristics
(Rittberger, 1990; Snidal, 1985a, 1991). One response, now receiving concentrated attention on the part of students of international relations, is that
the answer lies in the capacity of states to create appropriate institutions or,
in other words, socially defined systems of roles, rules and relationships
(Krasner, 1983). The result is a generic analysis of the factors at play in the
formation of regimes or governance systems and of the conditions that determine the effectiveness of these institutional arrangements or their capacity
to solve the problems motivating their establishment once they are in place.
In bringing this type of analysis to bear on human/environment relationships at the international level, those interested in resource regimes have
sought to differentiate a number of classes of problems that arise repeatedly
in this realm (for instance, international commons, shared natural resources,
transboundary externalities) and to evaluate the institutional mechanisms
needed to solve each type of problem (Haas et al., 1993; Young, 1994).

Whereas the literature on small-scale systems starts with the specific problem of avoiding the 'tragedy of the commons' in the use of common pools
and seeks to extend the analysis step by step to other (closely related)
problems, therefore, the literature on international society begins with the
more abstract problem of understanding the bases for sustained cooperation

in connection with a range of analytically distinct situations and endeavors to apply its conclusions to an array of substantive matters, including the collective-action problems associated with common-pool resources. The virtue of the first approach is its focus on a well-defined puzzle that is widely understood to be important. Its weakness is that it sometimes proves difficult or awkward to frame more complex concerns (for example, issues relating to the mixed systems of property rights characteristic of common-field agriculture or subsistence hunting and gathering) within this conceptual framework (Berkes, 1987; Campbell and Godoy, 1992). The picture emerging from the study of international resource regimes is just the opposite. This literature offers a more comprehensive taxonomy of problems associated with human/environment relationships. But it lacks the sharp focus afforded by the intense concern for escaping the 'tragedy of the commons' that provides the motivating puzzle of the literature on CPRs.

2. Social Settings

Underlying this difference in analytic strategies and partially obscured by the framing of the central puzzles energizing the two lines of enquiry are some important differences in the nature of the social settings under consideration. Whereas structures of property rights, in the sense of sets of rights and rules organized around the entitlements of ownership, loom large in small-scale societies, they have no direct or immediate counterparts in a society of sovereign states. As members of international society, states do not own the territories they occupy in the ordinary sense of the term (though it is perfectly true that some governments hold title to large quantities of public property). Rather, they possess jurisdiction over human activities taking place throughout their territories and exercise authority over the activities of users of resources lying within their jurisdictional boundaries (Schachter, 1991).

This is the point of the classic distinction in international law between *imperium*, which is a matter of jurisdiction and authority, and *dominium*, which is a matter of ownership and rights. From this vantage point, *res communis* (in contrast to what international law knows as *res nullius*) differs significantly from structures of common property in domestic or municipal systems. The category of *res communis*, containing such diverse phenomena as the high seas, the stratospheric ozone layer, the global climate system, the electromagnetic spectrum and outer space, encompasses resources with respect to which groups of states (which may but need not include all the members of international society) share jurisdiction rather than the entitlements of ownership. Under this arrangement, actual use rights regarding such resources typically run with individuals or organizations (such as fishers, shipping companies or airlines), subject to codes of conduct adopted and implemented by groups of states sharing jurisdiction over the resources in question.

This leads directly to the observation that resource regimes in international society involve an added dimension that does not arise in small-scale societies. Although the members of international regimes are ordinarily states, the actors whose behavior is at stake are often private individuals or corporations who are nationals of member states or who are subject to the jurisdiction of one or more of the member states for other reasons. In effect, states work out the relevant codes of conduct among themselves and assume responsibility for implementing the provisions of the agreements they reach within their own jurisdictions (Jacobson and Weiss, 1990). This requires a second level of rule making – often in the form of implementing legislation – coupled with an effort on the part of national authorities to elicit compliance from the users of the resources in question; sometimes it raises questions about the capacity of public agencies to deal effectively with obligations relating to implementation and compliance they have assumed under the terms of international regimes. It is hardly surprising, under the circumstances, that rules making perfectly good sense in connection with the activities of individual users of CPRs do not always prove effective in the two-stage process of institution building characteristic of international society.

To this we must add that the states which form the membership of international regimes are collective entities whose interactive behavior is the product of domestic processes that are often both complex and unpredictable. This is the central insight of those who speak of the logic of two-level games (Putnam, 1988; Evans et al., 1993) and who advocate bringing the second image back in (Zurn, 1993) to understand both the processes of regime formation and the effectiveness of institutional arrangements once they are in place. Of course, it is possible to argue that the individuals who constitute the principal subjects of common-property arrangements in small-scale societies sometimes experience cognitive dissonance or inner conflict regarding their participation in such arrangements. Where clans, siidas, moieties and so forth are the real decision-making units, moreover, the distinction is even less sharp. Still, it is hard to avoid the conclusion that the complexities arising from the fact that states are collective entities add a whole new dimension to the study of the collective-action problems associated with interactive decision making among goal-directed actors.

Among other things, this raises important questions about the role of community in solving collective-action problems. If by community we mean a social group possessing shared beliefs, a stable membership, the expectation of continuing interaction and a pattern of relations that are direct and multiplex (Singleton and Taylor, 1992), it is apparent that there are sharp differences between international society and many small-scale societies on this dimension. Of course, it is easy to allow sentimentality to lead us to exaggerate the role of community in local societies. Many of these societies have been characterized by deep social fissures, not to mention rapid change at a variety of levels. Similarly, there is a case to be made that shared beliefs do exert real influence on the behavior of policymakers at the international level and through them on the behavior of states themselves. Even so, we should be wary about casual assertions regarding the existence of an international community and, as a result, about the transferability of arguments pertaining to the role of community in solving collective-action problems from the level of small-scale societies (Ostrom, 1992) to the level of international society.

3. The Nature of Institutions

Both streams of analysis reflect the influence of the 'new institutionalism', an intellectual movement now making its mark throughout the social sciences (Eggertsson, 1990; Furubotn and Richter, 1991; Powell and DiMaggio, 1991). They are unified in their commitment to the proposition that social institutions, in contrast to material conditions and ideas (Cox, 1986), account for a large proportion of the variance in the collective outcomes flowing from interactive behavior. They agree, as well, on a conception of institutions as rules of the game or codes of conduct that define social practices, assign roles to the participants in those practices and guide interactions among the occupants of these roles. Among other things, this conception accents the distinction between institutions, on the one hand, and organizations, treated as material entities possessing offices, personnel and budgets, on the other. This has led to a newly emerging interest in the idea of governance without government at both levels (Young, 1989a).

These are strong bonds. Even so, there are notable differences between the two lines of enquiry regarding the domain of institutions or, in other words, the boundaries of the class of phenomena to be included under the rubric of institutions. Focusing on institutions that are often construed as spontaneous or self-generating arrangements, the literature on CPRs includes informal or de facto codes of conduct passed from generation to generation through a process of socialization. This implies, among other things, that individuals may have little choice regarding participation in the social practices they inherit. Their identity may be determined, at least in part, by the nature of the institutions in which they participate. By contrast, students of resource regimes have moved toward a conception of institutions centering on roles and rules articulated explicitly in the provisions of treaties, conventions or other (not necessarily legally binding) international agreements (Regimes Summit, 1991). Given the prevailing understanding of sovereignty, individual members of international society are regarded as free from any obligation to comply with the terms of regimes unless and until they make an explicit decision to participate in them.

It is easy to overdo this distinction. A growing body of case studies suggests that participants in CPR arrangements often articulate the rules of the game in an explicit manner, whether or not they choose to formalize them in constitutive documents. Regardless of the force of social pressure, moreover, individual users of CPRs are not wholly programmed by processes of socialization. It is now apparent, for instance, that many – perhaps most – ecosystems change too rapidly and unpredictably as a consequence of natural forces to allow static institutional arrangements to succeed in producing sustainable human/environment relationships. Nor are international resource regimes confined to the formal provisions laid out in constitutive documents. In some cases, the provisions of treaties and conventions (for example, many articles in the 1982 Convention on the Law of the Sea) simply ratify arrangements that have emerged informally over a period of time. What is more, international practices regularly evolve with the passage of time to meet changing circumstances, whether or not they are amended or altered in any formal sense. Equally important is the fact that individual states commonly experience social pressure to participate in resource regimes, regardless of their sovereign rights. The result, more often than not, is a complex combination of behavior that actually conforms to the requirements of regimes coupled with declaratory policies asserting sovereign rights.

Nonetheless, the two lines of enquiry pose contrasting dilemmas for those engaged in the analysis of social institutions and concerned with the transferability of propositions between micro-scale and macro-scale phenomena. Stressing informal arrangements, the literature on CPRs faces problems in pinning down the rules of the game precisely and, therefore, in separating institutions clearly from the encompassing social settings in which they operate. There is the danger here that ensuing ambiguities regarding the boundaries of the universe of cases will not only make it difficult to generalize about institutional matters with confidence, but also raise the specter of analysts falling prey to the temptation to save hypotheses through ex post facto adjustments in the boundaries of the universe of cases under consideration. Focusing on codes of conduct articulated explicitly in constitutive documents, by contrast, the literature on international resource regimes avoids these problems of operationalization. Instead, it runs the risk of excessive formalism in the sense of assuming that rules in practice conform to the rules articulated in constitutive documents; it tends as well to ignore institutional arrangements that are important determinants of behavior though they are informal in nature. Each of these dilemmas is significant in its own right. But in terms of the present discussion of scale, their significance is that they raise serious questions concerning the comparability of the universes of cases considered by the two streams of analysis.

4. The Formation of Institutions

Why do institutions form to deal with some collective-action problems but not others? What is the nature of the process through which institutions (re)form in specific social settings? To what extent are lessons regarding institutional dynamics transferable from small-scale, local societies to international society and vice versa? Given what I have said already, it will come as no surprise that the two literatures start from divergent vantage points regarding both the problem and the process of regime formation.

The literature on CPRs features a relatively uniform conception of the problem to be solved in creating resource regimes. The focus, in almost every case, is on depletable but non-excludable resources that are used or appropriated by a number (sometimes a large number) of actors who are assumed to form a relatively homogeneous group in terms of both their preferences and their capabilities. The problem, then, is to devise rules or codes of conduct that restrict the behavior of individual appropriators in such a way as to avoid overuse or exhaustion of the relevant resources. For its part, as might be expected from the framing of its analytic puzzle, the international regimes literature proceeds to differentiate among types of problems and to investigate the implications of these differences for the prospects of success in efforts to create institutional arrangements. This yields the suggestion, for instance, that coordination problems in which there are stable and optimal equilibria will be easier to solve than collaboration problems where equilibria are either suboptimal or absent (Martin, 1992). Similarly, this line of analysis treats the number of actors as an important variable, suggesting that problems involving small numbers will be easier to solve than large-number problems. Differences among the individual actors involved may also play a role; the presence of a single dominant actor, for example, may help to produce success when institutions are treated as public goods and the actions of the dominant actor give rise to what is known as a privileged group (Olson, 1965; Snidal, 1985b).

Equally important are the vantage points of the two literatures on the process of regime formation. Approaching institutions as self-generating arrangements (von Hayek, 1973), the mainstream literature on CPRs seeks to explain the development of codes of conduct in terms of the diffusion of ideas and the convergence of expectations in the absence of formal negotiation. The evolution of de facto rules governing exchange relationships – including the barter arrangements characteristic of subsistence systems as well as natural markets – constitutes a prominent case in point.

Students of international regimes, on the other hand, have concentrated on explicit negotiations leading through a process of institutional bargaining to agreement on the terms of treaties or conventions (Young and Osherenko, 1993). The central debate in this intellectual community concerns the relative importance of structural power in contrast to other driving forces as determinants of the content of the agreements reached (Keohane, 1984; Haggard and Simmons, 1987; Young, 1989b).

How can we reconcile these analytic disparities? Several responses to this question are worthy of consideration. From the perspective of those who belong to the relevant social groups, institutions exhibit the attributes of public goods (that is, non-excludability and jointness of supply or non-rivalness), whether they are designed to prevent the 'tragedy of the commons' among appropriators of local common pools or to regulate human activities in international commons like Antarctica or transboundary flows of pollutants like acid rain in Europe. What is more, information regarding problem structures available to those involved in regime formation is ordinarily highly imperfect. In the typical case, the parties are apt to be well aware that they have a problem to solve. But they seldom devote much time to thinking about or seeking to determine such things as the extent to which their problem is one in which an optimal equilibrium exists. This means, among other things, that regime formation at both levels is a kind of problem-solving exercise in which groups of actors seek to devise sets of rules that seem likely to cure the specific problem at hand in a way that everyone can accept (Young, 1989b).

Additionally, it seems helpful at this juncture to introduce a distinction between the negotiation stage and the prenegotiation or agenda setting stage of institutional development (Stein, 1989). Prenegotiation encompasses those processes through which issues emerge on the public agenda, are framed or defined for consideration on the part of those concerned with collective action and rise to a sufficiently prominent place on the agenda to merit concentrated attention. The negotiation stage, on this account, refers to efforts to arrive at mutually agreeable arrangements once a problem is well-defined and ripe for action. The point of introducing this distinction is to suggest both that the formation of resource regimes in international society includes a prenegotiation stage that is heavily influenced by the diffusion of ideas and the convergence of expectations and that the emergence of structures of property rights in small-scale societies often encompasses a stage that can be properly construed as negotiation, even when the results are not formalized in constitutive documents. In effect, both stages occur at the micro or local level as well as the macro or international level, though the prominence of each may vary from case to case and analysts working at the different levels have chosen to highlight one or the other stage in their thinking about the development of social practices.

It now seems apparent as well that equifinality figures prominently in processes of institutional development at all levels of social organization (Young and Osherenko, 1993). What this means is that we can identify several distinct tracks or paths leading to success in the (re)formation of institutional arrangements in small-scale societies and in international society alike. Just as the participation of a dominant actor may be critical in the establishment of international regimes, the leadership of a particularly influential individual may be an essential feature of institution building in small-scale settings. Similar observations are in order about paths characterized by explicit or overt negotiation among a group of actors more or less evenly matched in terms of their bargaining strength and by tacit interactions driven by the convergence of expectations around salient solutions in contrast to the convergence of offers through some reciprocal concession mechanism. All these processes – producing what may be described as imposed arrangements, negotiated arrangements and self-generating arrangements (Young, 1989a) – are clearly in evidence in the case studies produced by students of international regimes and students of arrangements arising to deal with CPRs in small-scale societies. There may, of course, be differences from one society to another in the prominence of these paths. But the point I want to emphasize is that some of the apparent disparity between the two streams of analysis regarding institutional development is a matter of emphasis on the part of analysts rather than actual differences in the phenomena under consideration.

5. The Consequences of Institutions

Do institutions matter (P. Haas, 1989)? Put another way, what proportion of the variance in collective outcomes in the realm of human/environment relationships can we explain in terms of the operation of systems of property rights or resource regimes (Young, 1992)? The initial responses of the two streams of analysis to these questions are strikingly different. The mainstream literature on CPR arrangements – like the mainstream literature on most micro-scale and meso-scale social systems – simply takes it for granted that institutions are major determinants of collective outcomes and concentrates on assessing these consequences in terms of a variety of criteria of evaluation. Students of international regimes, by contrast, must confront the deep-seated skepticism of most realists and many neo-realists who see institutions largely as epiphenomena at the international level. The argument here is that institutional arrangements are fundamentally reflections of the underlying configuration of power in international society and that they can be expected to change whenever the underlying configuration of power shifts (Strange, 1983; Grieco, 1990).

Whatever the merits of these disparate perspectives in their own terms, the clash between them suggests the importance of addressing the issue of demonstrating the existence and strength of causal connections between institutions and collective outcomes at all levels of social organization. The mere fact that changes in collective outcomes follow the establishment of new institutions or the restructuring of existing institutions is not sufficient to prove a causal link; the danger of spurious correlation is far too great for that. What is more, the usual statistical procedures for weeding out spurious correlations cannot offer much help in assessing the role of institutions at either the micro level or the macro level. Not only is it hard to operationalize the key variables for purposes of quantitative analysis but we are also seldom in a position to draw the representative samples from larger universes of cases that are central to the application of most relevant statistical procedures.

Two lines of attack seem helpful in this connection (Levy and Young, 1993). In the first instance, it is possible to probe the strength of inferred links between social practices and collective outcomes through a combination of natural experiments, thought experiments and even laboratory experiments. It makes sense, for example, to look for situations that resemble each other closely, except in terms of the character of prevailing institutions, and then to ask about differences in the collective outcomes that ensue. There is much to be said, as well, for making use of the method of counterfactuals to ask what would have occurred in the absence of the relevant institutions (Fearon, 1991; Biersteker, 1993) and for engaging in a sustained effort to account for apparent links between institutions and outcomes in terms of rival hypotheses.

In the final analysis, however, it seems essential in addressing this problem to take another step and to work toward exposing the behavioral mechanisms through which institutions operate to affect behavior (Levy et al., 1991). Because social scientists do not agree on the adequacy of a single model of behavior – especially where collective entities are concerned – this endeavor inevitably requires the specification of a set of behavioral models together with an effort to show step by step the causal chains leading from the existence of institutions to the interactive behavior of the relevant set of actors (Levy, 1993). This is not an easy task; it is unlikely to produce a simple litmus test to be used in demonstrating the effectiveness of institutions. But in the long run, the construction and testing of behavioral models will surely produce sizable rewards for those who currently take it for granted that institutions matter as well as for those who now face extreme skepticism from colleagues who believe that material conditions in general and structural power in particular determine the content of collective outcomes, regardless of the character of prevailing institutional arrangements.

6. The Performance of Institutions

Among those who are satisfied that institutions do account for a sizable proportion of the variance in collective outcomes, it is natural to move on to a study of the performance of social practices. In the first instance, this is a matter of problem solving or, in other words, the capacity of institutional arrangements to meet the challenges that motivate their establishment. Here, too, the initial biases of those who think about small-scale societies and those who focus on international society diverge quite sharply. Among students of CPR arrangements, there is a distinct optimism regarding the capacity of institutions to circumvent the 'tragedy of the commons', producing sustainable human/environment relationships in the process. Most students of international affairs, by contrast, are inclined to see institutions as weak instruments that face an uphill battle in solving collective-action problems, except in those all too uncommon cases of assurance or coordination where no major conflicts of interest or incentives to cheat are involved.

What should we make of this disparity? On their own terms, these biases are difficult to justify. It is easy enough to find failures as well as successes in the efforts of the members of local societies to solve collective-action problems. Equally important, there are striking differences among international resource regimes in their performance as problem-solving devices. This suggests that those who are now endeavoring to pin down conditions governing the success of institutional arrangements – on whatever level they operate – are on the right track (McKean, 1992). It also affords striking opportunities for mutually beneficial interactions between those focusing on micro-scale systems and those who work at the macro scale. Recent studies dealing with matters like the importance of institutional flexibility as a means of dealing with changing ecosystems and of the role of transparency as a determinant of compliance with regulative rules (Chayes and Chayes, 1993) offer strong evidence of the value of efforts to scale up and scale down in this area of enquiry.

Beyond this, any consideration of the performance of social institutions must come to terms with issues pertaining to efficiency and equity, as well as with the issue of problem solving per se. A frequent criticism of common-property arrangements, for example, is that they harbor strong biases toward the status quo because they do not provide adequate incentives for innovation or growth, whatever their merits in avoiding the 'tragedy of the commons' (Field, 1990). International regimes, by contrast, are sometimes criticized as devices created by the privileged members of international society for the purpose of perpetuating the current highly asymmetrical distribution of wealth between the rich and the poor. My point in introducing these examples is not to debate their validity at either the micro scale or the macro scale. Rather, I want to suggest, to begin with, that once the causal role of institutions is acknowledged, it is natural to begin asking pointed questions about their performance in terms of criteria like efficiency and equity and, beyond this, that this is another area where students of small-scale societies and students of international society have much to contribute to each others' thinking. In effect, it is time to set aside the preoccupation with the 'tragedy of the commons' at the micro scale and the battle over the consequentiality of institutions at the macro scale and move toward a more sophisticated analysis of the performance of institutions fueled by an ongoing dialogue between those concerned with the two scales.

7. Design Principles

It is natural for those who study institutional arrangements governing human/environment relationships to take a strong interest in the development of design principles (Ostrom, 1990). Partly, this is a matter of joining theory and practice in the interests of deepening our knowledge of social institutions. There are obvious advantages from an analytic point of view in linking basic and applied research in such a way as to test and refine theoretical arguments in the light of actual experience and to organize thinking about current problems in terms of theoretically significant categories. In considerable part, however, it is the prospect of extracting design principles from the study of institutions that makes research in this field relevant to the concerns of policymakers and that provides the rationale for continuing to provide the resources needed to underwrite ongoing research programs in this promising field enquiry.

This said, it is worth noting that students of small-scale systems and international society alike face serious questions concerning the feasibility of formulating design principles that will prove helpful to those responsible for working out the terms of institutions in specific cases. For their part, those interested in CPRs have emphasized the spontaneous or self-generating nature of common-property systems, a position likely to appeal to conservatives who maintain that deliberate intervention in the processes through which institutions develop is either unnecessary or infeasible or both (Ellickson, 1991). Additionally, this stream of analysis does better in dealing with self-contained traditional societies than with contemporary situations featuring complex mixes of traditional common-property arrangements and recent interventions stemming from the policy initiatives of modern states (Jodha, 1993). There is a real danger, under the circumstances, that the design principles emanating from this stream of analysis will be most relevant to a universe of cases encompassing a shrinking set of members.

Turning to international society, the questions concern the causal role of institutions and the extent to which it is feasible to generalize from one case to another. To the extent that the realists are right in treating international institutions as epiphenomena, any effort to formulate design principles will be fundamentally an exercise in futility. It is this observation that has led some to cite the fact that policymakers regularly work hard to devise international institutions together with the supposition that it is improbable that they are all deluded as evidence that institutions really do matter in international society (Chayes and Chayes, 1993). It is undeniable, as well, that this stream of analysis includes a good deal of facile thinking regarding the generalizability of findings about resource regimes from one case to another. Many recent efforts to apply ideas drawn from the case of ozone depletion to other current concerns, like climate change and the loss of biological diversity, illustrate this danger (Sebenius, 1991).

What is more, the process of forming institutions is itself a matter of collective action at all levels of social organization (Young, 1982). Put another way, the terms of social practices are products of interactions among self-interested parties, whether the process is one featuring the convergence of expectations as envisioned by those who focus on spontaneous arrangements or institutional bargaining as suggested by those who think in terms of negotiated arrangements. In either case, it follows that institutions are not created by unitary actors able and willing to apply design principles in a rational or goal-directed manner (Young, 1989b). Certainly, this does not make the search for design principles irrelevant. But it does politicize and, therefore, greatly complicate the view of institutional design implicit in many accounts of the role of knowledge in the creation of social institutions (P. Haas, 1992).

None of this is likely to deter analysts from seeking to extract design principles from their studies of social institutions suitable for use by policymakers struggling to deal with specific cases. What is to be gained, then, from revisiting the problem of scale with a concern for the formulation of design principles? The answer, I now believe, depends on how problems to be solved through the creation of institutions are framed. To the extent that students of international regimes focus on the implementation of the provisions of treaties within the domestic legal and political systems of the member states, for example, there is little prospect that propositions derived from the study of small-scale systems will prove helpful. Yet it seems distinctly interesting to compare the findings of the two streams of analysis regarding the role of transparency, monitoring and implementation review procedures as determinants of compliance on the part of those subject to the rules of social institutions. Similarly, many of the arguments about the role of culture articulated by students of small-scale societies (McCay, 1993) seem to me to have limited applicability to the world of international regimes. But there is mounting evidence to suggest that social learning, in contrast to the deployment of bargaining strength, plays an important role in the evolution of institutional arrangements at both the micro scale and the macro scale (E. Haas, 1990). The conclusion I draw from these observations is that the solution to the problem of scale is by no means clear-cut in connection with the streams of analysis under consideration. Transferability is hardly an all-or-nothing affair; the feasibility of applying propositions across levels will often be affected by the way in which the issues to be addressed are framed.

Conclusion

What can we conclude from this brief account of scaling up and scaling down in connection with social institutions governing human/enviromnent relationships that will be of interest to social scientists contemplating the problem of scale more generally? First and foremost is a warning about the dangers of simplistic reasoning. Macro-scale systems are not merely small-scale systems writ large. Nor are micro-scale systems mere microcosms of large-scale systems. It follows that we cannot simply assume that the mechanisms at work at the two levels are the same and that any effort to transfer propositions from one level to another or, in other words, to scale up and scale down, should be treated with a healthy sense of skepticism. This may be unwelcome news for social scientists who adhere to doctrines like methodological individualism. But it seems difficult to justify any other conclusion on the basis of this case study.

This said, however, the case I have discussed does suggest that there is considerable scope for cross-fertilization among studies of social phenomena conducted at different scales. The literatures under consideration here have in common a focus on interactive decision making, a concern with collective-action problems and an interest in the role of institutions as devices for solving or avoiding these problems. These are major points of tangency. Under the circumstances, there is much to be said for thinking carefully about both common themes that unite the two literatures and analytic disparities that divide them. The observation that transparency is an important determinant of compliant behavior on both scales, for example, is a striking finding. By contrast, the realization that two streams of analysis that share so much can frame their central analytic puzzles so differently is a sobering thought. But in either case, we all stand to benefit from an effort to sort out what is transferable across scales and what is peculiar to micro-scale or macro-scale systems in the realm of human/environment relations.

REFERENCES

Axelrod, Robert (1984) *The Evolution of Cooperation*. New York: Basic Books.

Biersteker, Thomas (1993) 'Constructing Historical Counterfactuals to Assess the Consequences of International Regimes: The Global Debt Regime and the Course of the Debt Crisis of the 1980s', in Volker Rittberger (ed.) *Regime Theory and International Relations*, pp. 315–38. Oxford: Oxford University Press.

Berkes, Fikret (1987) 'Common-property Resource Management and Cree Indian Fisheries in Subarctic Canada', in Bonnie J. McCay and James M. Acheson (eds) *The Question of the Commons: The Culture and Ecology of Communal Resources*, pp. 66–91. Tucson: University of Arizona Press.

Bromley, Daniel W. et al., eds (1992) *Making the Commons Work: Theory, Practice, and Policy*. San Francisco: Institute for Contemporary Studies Press.

Campbell, Bruce M. S. and Ricardo A. Godoy (1992) 'Commonfield Agriculture: The Andes and Medieval England Compared', in Daniel Bromley et al. (eds) *Making the Commons Work: Theory, Practice, and Policy*, pp. 99–127. San Francisco: Institute for Contemporary Studies Press.

Chayes, Abram and Antonia Handler Chayes (1993) 'On Compliance', *International Organization* 47 (Spring): 175–205.

Cox, Robert (1986) 'Social Forces, States and World Orders: Beyond International Relations Theory', in Robert O. Keohane (ed.) *Neorealism and Its Critics*, pp. 204–54. New York: Columbia University Press.

Eggertsson, Thráinn (1990) *Economic Behavior and Institutions*. Cambridge: Cambridge University Press.

Ellickson, Robert (1991) *Order Without Law: How Neighbors Settle Disputes*. Cambridge, MA: Harvard University Press.

Elster, Jon (1989) *The Cement of Society: A Study of Social Order*. Cambridge: Cambridge University Press.

Evans, Peter B., Harold K. Jacobson and Robert D. Putnam, eds (1993) *Double-edged Diplomacy: International Bargaining and Domestic Politics*. Berkeley: University of California Press.

Fearon, James (1991) 'Counterfactuals and Hypothesis Testing in Political Science', *World Politics* 43 (January): 169–75.

Field, Barry C. (1990) 'The Economics of Common Property', *Natural Resources Journal* 30 (Winter): 239–52.

Feeny, David, Fikret Berkes, Bonnie J. McCay and James M. Acheson (1990) 'The Tragedy of the Commons: Twenty-Two Years Later', *Human Ecology* 18(1): 1–19.

Furubotn, Eirik G. and Rudolf Richter, eds (1991) *The New Institutional Economics*. College Station: Texas A&M University Press.

Gordon, H. Scott (1954) 'The Economic Theory of a Common-property Resource: The Fishery', *Journal of Political Economy* 62 (April): 124–42.

Grieco, Joseph M. (1990) *Cooperation among Nations: Europe, America, and Non-tariff Barriers to Trade*. Ithaca, NY: Cornell University Press.

Haas, Ernst B. (1990) *When Knowledge is Power: Three Models of Change in International Organizations*. Berkeley: University of California Press.

Haas, Peter M. (1989) 'Do Regimes Matter? Epistemic Communities and Mediterranean Pollution Control', *International Organization* 43 (Summer): 377–403.

Haas, Peter M., ed. (1992) 'Knowledge, Power, and International Policy Coordination', *International Organization* 46 (Winter, special issue).

Haas, Peter M., Robert O. Keohane and Marc A. Levy, eds (1993) *Institutions for the Earth: Sources of Effective International Environmental Protection*. Cambridge, MA: MIT Press.

Haggard, Stephan and Beth A. Simmons (1987) 'Theories of International Regimes', *International Organization* 41 (Summer): 491–517.

Hardin, Garrett (1968) 'The Tragedy of the Commons', *Science* 162 (13 December): 1243–8.

Hardin, Garrett and John Baden, eds (1977) *Managing the Commons*. San Francisco: W. H. Freeman.

Hardin, Russell (1982) *Collective Action*. Baltimore, MD: Johns Hopkins University Press for Resources for the Future.

Hughes, Barry B. (1992) 'On Global Cooperation: A Literature Review and Partial Integration', paper prepared for the annual meeting of the International Studies Association, Atlanta, Georgia.

Jacobson, Harold K. and Edith Brown Weiss (1990) 'Implementing and Complying with International Environmental Accords: A Framework for Research', paper prepared for the annual meeting of the American Political Science Association, San Francisco, California.

Jodha, Narpat S. (1993) 'Property Rights and Development', paper prepared for the Beijer Institute, Stockholm, Sweden, September.

Keohane, Robert O. (1984) *After Hegemony: Cooperation and Discord in the World Political Economy*. Princeton, NJ: Princeton University Press.

Krasner, Stephen D., ed. (1983) *International Regimes*. Ithaca, NY: Cornell University Press.

Levy, Marc A. (1993) 'European Acid Rain: The Power of Tote-board Diplomacy', in Peter M. Haas, Robert O. Keohane, and Marc A. Levy (eds) *Institutions for the Earth: Sources of Effective International Environmental Protection*, pp. 75–132. Cambridge, MA: MIT Press.

Levy, Marc A., Gail Osherenko and Oran R. Young (1991) 'The Effectiveness of International Regimes: A Design for Large-scale Collaborative Research' (mimeo) Hanover, NH: Dartmouth College, Institute of Arctic Studies.

Levy, Marc A. and Oran R. Young (1993) 'Results of the November 1992 Workshop on Regime Effectiveness' (mimeo) Hanover, NH: Dartmouth College, Institute of Arctic Studies.

McCay, Bonnie J. (1993) 'Management Regimes', paper prepared for the Beijer Institute, Stockholm, Sweden, September.

McCay, Bonnie J. and James M. Acheson, eds (1987) *The Question of the Commons: The Culture and Ecology of Communal Resources*. Tucson: University of Arizona Press.

McKean, Margaret A. (1992) 'Success on the Commons: A Comparative Examination of Institutions for Common Property Resource Management', *Journal of Theoretical Politics* 4 (July): 247–81.

Martin, Lisa L. (1992) 'Interests, Power, and Multilateralism', *International Organization* 46 (Autumn): 765–92.

Milner, Helen (1992) 'International Theories of Cooperation among Nations: Strengths and Weaknesses', *World Politics* 44 (April): 466–96.

Olson, Mancur (1965) *The Logic of Collective Action*. Cambridge, MA: Harvard University Press.

Ostrom, Elinor (1990) *Governing the Commons: The Evolution of Institutions for Collective Action*. New York: Cambridge University Press.

Ostrom, Elinor (1992) 'Community and the Endogenous Solution of Commons Problems', *Journal of Theoretical Politics* 4(3) (July): 343–51.

Powell, Walter W. and Paul J. DiMaggio, eds (1991) *The New Institutionalism in Organizational Analysis*. Chicago: University of Chicago Press.

Putnam, Robert D. (1988) 'Diplomacy and Domestic Politics: The Logic of Two-level Games', *International Organization* 42 (Summer): 427–60.

Regimes Summit (1991) 'Workshop Report: 22–4 November' (mimeo) Hanover, NH: Dartmouth College, Institute of Arctic Studies.

Rittberger, Volker, ed. (1990) *International Regimes in East–West Politics*. London: Pinter Publishers.

Schachter, Oscar (1991) 'The Emergence of International Environmental Law', *Journal of International Affairs* 44 (Winter): 457–93.

Scott, Anthony C. (1955) 'The Fishery: The Objective of Sole Ownership', *Journal of Political Economy* 63: 116–24.

Sebenius, James K. (1991) 'Designing Negotiations Toward a New Regime: The Case of Global Warming', *International Security* 15 (Spring): 110–48.

Singleton, Sara and Michael Taylor (1992) 'Common Property, Collective Action and Community', *Journal of Theoretical Politics* 4(3) (July): 309–24.

Snidal, Duncan (1985a) 'Coordination Versus Prisoners' Dilemma: Implications for International Cooperation and Regimes', *American Political Science Review* 79 (September): 923–42.

Snidal, Duncan (1985b) 'The Limits of Hegemonic Stability Theory', *International Organization* 39 (Autumn): 579–615.

Snidal, Duncan (1991) 'Relative Gains and the Pattern of International Cooperation', *American Political Science Review* 85 (September): 701–26.

Stein, Janice G., ed. (1989) *Getting to the Table: The Processes of International Prenegotiation.* Baltimore, MD: Johns Hopkins University Press.

Strange, Susan (1983) '*Cave! hic dragones*: A Critique of Regime Analysis', in Stephen D. Krasner (ed.) *International Regimes*, pp. 337–54. Ithaca, NY: Cornell University Press.

von Hayek, Friedrich (1973) *The Political Order of a Free People, Vol. 3 of Law, Legislation and Liberty.* Chicago: University of Chicago Press.

Young, Oran R. (1982) *Resource Regimes: Natural Resources and Social Institutions.* Berkeley: University of California Press.

Young, Oran R. (1989a) *International Cooperation: Building Regimes for Natural Resources and the Environment.* Ithaca, NY: Cornell University Press.

Young, Oran R. (1989b) 'The Politics of International Regime Formation: Managing Natural Resources and the Environment', *International Organization* 43 (Summer): 349–75.

Young, Oran R. (1992) 'The Effectiveness of International Institutions: Hard Cases and Critical Variables', in James N. Rosenau and Ernst-Otto Czempiel (eds) *Governance without Government: Order and Change in World Politics*, pp. 160–94. Cambridge: Cambridge University Press.

Young, Oran R. (1994) *International Governance: Protecting the Environment in a Stateless Society.* Ithaca, NY: Cornell University Press.

Young, Oran R. and Gail Osherenko, eds (1993) *Polar Politics: Creating International Environmental Regimes.* Ithaca, NY: Cornell University Press.

Zurn, Michael (1993) 'Bringing the Second Image (Back) In: About the Domestic Sources of Regime Formation', in Volker Rittberger (ed.) *Regime Theory and International Relations*, pp. 282–311. Oxford: Oxford University Press.

3. THE POLITICS OF SCOPE: ENDOGENOUS ACTORS, HETEROGENEITY AND INSTITUTIONS

Duncan Snidal

Do large numbers of heterogeneous actors inhibit cooperation? This question is central both to local common-pool resource (CPR) problems and to international relations (IR). Yet no consistent answer emerges across the two settings. The IR conventional wisdom is that large numbers strongly inhibit cooperation, but CPR analysts find no strong independent effect. IR analysts argue that heterogeneity promotes cooperation, but CPR analysts find homogeneity more conducive to cooperation. These puzzles are only partly resolved by recognizing the different forms and thus impact of heterogeneity. The deeper resolution lies in the fact that different institutional settings not only mediate key actor characteristics but determine them. Thus, this paper argues that the number and heterogeneity of actors are not purely exogenous determinants of cooperation but rather are codetermined along with other aspects of institutional scope.

The development of NATO illustrates the codetermination of heterogeneity and scope. The end of World War II did not simply present a few Western states with a well-defined problem that determined the nature of

---

I thank Harvey Starr, Elinor Ostrom, Robert Keohane, John Freeman, Robert Meyer and Amit Sevak for useful comments on earlier drafts of this paper.

NATO. Instead, considerations of different alternatives led to decisions over membership, issues to include and relations to other international institutions. Choices were made to exclude the former Soviet ally but include Germany and to include some non-European members (US and Canada) but not others (Japan). The issue focus was to be security in Europe and not Asia and economic issues were left to other venues. Indeed, NATO arguably helped create – or at least define – the very collective-action problem of containing the Soviets that it then set out to overcome. Finally, NATO reflected a US decision to pursue security through specialized regional alliances rather than through the UN framework. Once made, these choices provided a relatively fixed framework within which common policies were coordinated for over 40 years.

The post-Cold War era presents a crisis and an opportunity for NATO. Its original mission has greatly diminished in importance while new issues of instability in Eastern Europe and around the globe have gained greater prominence. In considering a recasting of NATO's mission and membership, key issues of institutional design are tightly intertwined with all aspects of the problem. The *scope* of this 'new' institution in terms of membership, issues covered and its new institutional setting will not be strictly determined by the nature of the problem or the participants.[1] Instead, key decisions in the institutional design process will include what states to admit, what issues to handle and how NATO should connect with its broader institutional setting.

This paper examines the impact of the membership dimension of scope (number and nature of actors) on collective action in IR and CPRs. But I argue that scope is itself sometimes endogenous so that membership cannot be taken as a fixed parameter of the problem. Instead, the determination of membership, other institutional rules and the outcome are tightly interrelated. This 'simultaneity' is increased within the institutional design approach of this collection precisely because good design is forward-looking and seeks both to establish effective institutions and to create environments that make institutions more effective.

The paper borrows from lessons on achieving collective action in local

---

1. Institutional scope refers to the range of inclusion and extent of effective coverage of institutions and rules. In this paper I focus on membership while only implicitly and briefly discussing other aspects of scope, including issues covered, temporal scope and nested relations among various institutions and rules systems. Ostrom's (1990: 90) institutional design principles of 'clearly defined boundaries' and 'nested enterprises' are directly related to scope. Note that scope differs from scale as discussed in papers 1 and 2 in this collection by Young and by Keohane and Ostrom.

CPR problems[2] and examines their applicability to IR. Comparisons across these different contexts raise questions about the impact of the number and heterogeneity of actors that clarify the more general use of those concepts. The first section of the paper addresses the analytic similarities and possible contextual differences that affect transference from CPR experiences to the IR realm. Even emphasizing the differences between the settings, it is clear that some instructive lessons are available across them.

The second section expands on the methodological point introduced above that institutional scope cannot be considered simply as a fixed environmental factor. The reason is that the choice of scope rules helps determine other key variables including the heterogeneity of actors, which is the key independent variable of this volume. Because our CPR observations are primarily institutional equilibria resulting from protracted but largely unobserved processes, sorting out issues of exogeneity and endogeneity is more difficult than usual. Even where we can observe the sequence of institutional development more closely, the forward-looking nature of institutional design complicates ordinary causal analysis. Thus, extra care is required in specifying the interrelations among the key variables.

The following two sections compare the impact of the number and heterogeneity of participants in the CPR and IR settings. Some of the observed differences across IR and CPR are due to inherent differences in the problems faced, while others are due to different types of heterogeneity. But the greatest difference is due to political–social factors that make membership rules endogenous and alter the incentives and therefore the behavior of actors. The different degrees of success in achieving cooperation between CPRs and IR, or between examples within each area, are then better explained by features of the political setting than by the numbers or heterogeneity of actors. The concluding section summarizes some general implications from this comparison with CPRs for understanding the role of institutions in promoting collective action in IR.

Comparing CPRs and IR

Local CPRs and IR have exploitable similarities because both involve collective-action problems, broadly defined, where independent behavior leads to collectively suboptimal outcomes. However, the two research agendas emphasize different variants within this general category. Local

---

2. I use Ostrom (1990; see also Ostrom et al., 1994) as an icon for the larger body of local CPR research in several disciplines. Ostrom's work is of special importance because of its theoretical thrust and its ambitious attempts to generalize across cases.

CPR analysis focuses on the provision and appropriation of goods that are not joint in consumption (like private goods) but where exclusion is difficult (like public goods). Standard cases are natural resources, like forests or water, where the quantity available is less than the desired consumption of potential appropriators. This particular problem occurs at the international level as well (e.g. global commons issues) but is not nearly as central in the literature. Much greater attention (probably too much) has been paid to the provision of international public goods that are both joint and non-exclusive.[3] More recently, there is an increasing awareness among IR scholars that no single model of collective action deserves pride of place and that different models are appropriate for different problems (Stein, 1982; Snidal, 1985a; Krasner, 1991; Martin, 1992). The obvious corollary is that great care needs to be taken in transferring design principles discovered through analyzing CPRs to any IR problems better characterized as public goods or by other models.[4]

Several other possible differences between local CPRs and IR should be noted. First, local CPRs often *appear* more clearly bounded by physical and technological parameters than do typically messy IR problems. The Law of the Sea negotiations, for example, included not only global fishing matters but issues of navigation and mineral exploitation as well as general consideration of economic development and global equity. For other international issues such as money, nuclear proliferation or migration, the nature and even existence of a collective-action problem remains open to definition. By contrast, while collective action is difficult in the stereotypical CPR problem, it is greatly simplified insofar as the technology of the resource defines the issue, the actors affected by it and their possibilities for action. However, Ostrom (1990) shows that many real CPRs are not so clear-cut and finds the absence of such 'boundary conditions' a prime contributing factor to their failure. Her fishery examples are plagued by outsiders who move into a CPR and frustrate local attempts to manage the resource. Similarly, complex interconnections of underground water sources mean physical boundaries of water basins are not understood and this impedes collective action. On closer analysis, local CPR problems are not inherently more clearly bounded than

---

3. Public goods is the category of analysis against which Ostrom (1990: 32) is reacting as *partially* inappropriate for CPR problems because they differ on the property of jointness.

4. The other two categories defined by the jointness–exclusion typology are also of interest in international relations. One is that of *private goods* (i.e. exclusive but not joint), which is relevant to many problems such as international trade. Note that the IR literature often transforms this to a public goods problem of providing appropriate trade institutions, a move that sometimes obscures as much as it reveals. The fourth case of *club goods* (joint and exclusive) has been surprisingly underexploited as a way to understand international organizations that provide benefits only to their members.

IR problems and, when they have clearer boundaries, the explanation often lies with political or social factors rather than simply technological ones. Thus, clear boundary definitions are often as much a result as a cause of successful cooperation.

A second substantive difference is that the IR sociopolitical environment *appears* very different from various CPR settings. The convention among IR scholars is to presume an anarchy where security concerns impede cooperation and lawlessness is a major problem. One consequence is a strong emphasis on regimes as providers of the public good of 'order' otherwise absent from international affairs. This difference should not be overstated, however, since CPRs often involve the very livelihoods of the participants. Their security is very much at stake and violence is a very possible outcome.[5] A more important point is that, even where formally anarchic in the sense of the absence of a strong central government, local CPRs are often embedded in well-articulated societies ranging from peasant villages to highly institutionalized modern democracies. Successful solutions are usually nested in broader social–political relations that support local agreements. But comparison to CPR arrangements contains an instructive lesson that external support need not entail the strong central enforcement implicit in the standard IR anarchy–hierarchy dichotomy (Waltz, 1979).

A third difference is between successful CPR institutions that have evolved and prospective IR institutions that need to be designed. Although many local CPRs developed over extended periods, we have no good record of their evolution, but only a snapshot of the final institutional equilibrium. The final design principles may tell us little about how they were achieved; successful CPR arrangements might even be unintended consequences unattainable by rational design.[6] Moreover, evolutionary design principles

---

5. See the description of violence among Valença fishers (Cordell, 1972 in Schlager, 1994), which might reassure the most hard-core realists, although they might find its gradual elimination (not through power-balancing) troublesome. See also Ostrom's examples of violence among Mawelle fishers (1990: 152) and on the Spanish huertas (1990: 77) where participants were orderly in terms of their collective CPR rules, even though their larger society was marked by significant potential for violence. I thank Elinor Ostrom for correcting my tendency in an earlier draft to exaggerate the extent to which the IR setting was distinguished by greater insecurity and violence.

6. Bardhan (1989) cites a compelling example from Langlois (1985). A regulatory institution created by populists to limit monopoly power may then be captured by the capitalist interests it was intended to regulate. The resulting agency is maintained because it serves the interests of large industry even though the principles behind its operation are exactly contrary to the principles embodied in its design. Ironically, such a system of captured agencies probably could never have been established through rational design. This illustrates the possibility of rather sharp divergence between evolutionary and rational design principles. I thank Michael McGinnis and Robert Keohane for a stimulating conversation regarding this issue.

may be inappropriate for other settings. A crude but sufficient example is found with early aspirants to flight who looked towards the evolutionary principles embodied in birds. Wings were a good idea, but flapping them was not a good idea. Alternative design principles for flight, embodied in helicopters and rockets, require no wings and have no direct counterpart in the animal world. This does not mean, of course, that evolutionary examples are not useful – only that they must be used with caution. A design principle that occurs in a successful CPR setting cannot be taken as necessary or sufficient for other problems.

Thus, differences between CPRs and IR are great enough to provoke skepticism in transferring conclusions from one realm to the other, but not so great as to make that infeasible. Indeed, variation within each category on these key factors is probably as great as the variation across categories. The greatest difference is not the technological nature of the underlying issues, or even the political–social environment that surrounds them. Instead, it lies in their combination whereby politics redefines problems to facilitate their solutions. Here lies the strongest parallel between the local CPR literature and the 'regime' literature in IR. Each explores how self-interested actors regulate their behavior in mutually beneficial ways through rules and institutions that sit between the unregulated 'self-help' behavior of anarchy on the one hand and the strong central regulation of the state or world government on the other. The conceit of the institutional design approach is that principles that work in one arena will work well in the other with appropriate tailoring to particular circumstances. Because our observations are final institutional equilibria and given the forward-looking nature of institutional design, however, it is difficult to sort out issues of cause and effect. This requires us to pay special attention to issues of endogeneity addressed in the next section.

Endogeneity, Exogeneity and Institutional Design

Specifying what is exogenous versus what is endogenous, or independent versus dependent variables, is a difficult first step in theoretically informed empirical analysis. Normal issues of whether our theoretical knowledge is sufficient for this task are further complicated by key properties of institutional analysis. One is that we often observe only the end result of institutional change (e.g. the evolved resolution of a CPR problem) rather than the sequence of steps through which the final institutions developed. This makes it hard to sort out causal patterns among variables that we observe only in the final institutional equilibrium.[7] Second, because actors are forward-looking in considering institutional design, current choices will anticipate future conditions that themselves are in part a product of current choices. This further complicates the attempt to sort out cause and effect. In the extreme situation, 'everything is endogenous', which is a recipe for intellectual chaos since it is impossible to find firm ground on which to draw meaningful conclusions about causal processes.[8]

Proper specification of an empirical argument also requires clear distinctions among variables and parameters. Variables are factors whose values fluctuate either for reasons outside the model (exogenous) or for reasons specified inside the model (endogenous). Questions of exogeneity or endogeneity are typically fought out over variables since their status is seen as open to debate. By contrast, parameter values are usually fixed in the model and therefore exogenous. This specification is a claim that the fundamental processes governing behavior are constant over the time frame covered by the model. Note that the fourth category in this fourfold categorization – endogenous parameters – is not typically used.[9] Below, I argue that this missing category is useful for thinking about the relations among institutions, performance in collective problems and change.

Institutions are usually treated as exogenous parameters that provide the

---

7. For related discussions on institutions as equilibria see Schotter (1981) and two terrific papers by Calvert (1992a, b). Calvert builds on Schotter to argue that institutional analysis should focus on equilibria as providing simultaneous accounts both of the institution and of behavior within the institution. The current discussion accepts that basic point, but parts with Calvert (1992b: 13, 61; 1992a: 29) insofar as he suggests that the equilibrium analysis 'draws a sharp line between givens ... and the results' or implicitly defines institutions only endogenously in terms of the equilibrium to the neglect of other aspects of the institution defined exogenously in the rules of the underlying game. Calvert (1992a: nn. 4, 6, 17) recognizes the practical advantages of treating some institutional features as fixed.

8. The econometrics literature is instructive for these issues. On the first point see the controversy surrounding Wold (1960) on the seeming simultaneity in data induced when units of time (i.e. the distance between institutional equilibria that constitute our observation points) are lengthy even if the causal relationships among variables are clear (recursive) on a finer time line. More generally, the identification problem (Fisher, 1966) concerns the impossibility of making sound inferences without a clear set of exogenous variables, supplemented by other theoretical knowledge (e.g. other linear restrictions) about their interrelations. The difficulty increases whenever forward-looking 'rational expectations' make model specification in terms of exogenous and endogenous variables treacherous at best or even impossible (Sims, 1980).

9. In the econometrics literature this corresponds to the case of time-varying coefficients (Jackson, 1992; Judge et al., 1985: chs 13, 19) although there are further complications of simultaneity here.

fixed environment in which social and political processes take place. This is true both in the behavioral tradition and in game-theoretic specification of institutions through the rules of the game.[10] Such a conception accords with the standard normative presumption that the value of institutions lies in providing a stable background against which actors can make intelligent choices. Thus, significant invariance over time is an essential aspect of what we mean by an institution. In the longer term, of course, institutions are affected by the behavior that goes on within them. But this effect is typically slow and cumulative, whether in the development of legal precedent or the gradual evolution of a social custom. Under these circumstances, it is analytically appropriate to treat the institution as parametric and exogenous to the situation.

Institutional change and especially institutional design require us to consider the (partial) endogeneity of institutions. The very notion of institutional design is one of reshaping boundaries between what is endogenous and what is exogenous. Formal institutions create rules to govern the behavior of actors and thereby limit or expand the scope of their endogenous choices. The emergence of informal institutions, such as norms, affects individual behavior by altering the collective belief system that constitutes an important part of each individual's fixed external choice environment.[11] In either case, some institutional factor changes, becomes parametric and then constrains or channels future individual behavior.

The normal distinction between exogenous and endogenous variables is thus awkward for institutional analysis. Institutions cannot be considered strictly exogenous since we are interested in how they are created and changed by actors seeking to improve their circumstances. Nor are institutions purely endogenous in the same sense as other choice variables (including how actors behave *given* an institutional setting): institutions matter because they circumscribe and constrain actor behavior, are at least sticky and are sometimes much more rigid than that. For these reasons, institutions are usefully thought of as *endogenous parameters* where the former term indicates that they are susceptible to change and the latter term that they provide a relatively fixed setting for other endogenous choices or

---

10. Beliefs are the area where game theory has moved closest to endogenizing institutions in the form of updating through the model. However, the beliefs studied tend to concern specific facts of the situation (e.g. is my opponent tough or not?) rather than more general facts about expected behaviors within a multilateral setting. Thus, there has been less progress in building 'focal points' or 'conventions' into the models.

11. 'Fixed', like exogenous, is relative to the time frame. For example, beliefs may be frequently updated and modified and so evolve continuously rather than in discrete jumps. In a sufficiently short time frame, however, beliefs may be sufficiently stable as to be usefully treated as fixed.

variables.[12] The tension between the terms reflects the fact that while institutions are a consequence of human agency and history, they are valuable precisely because they lie outside the domain of short-term choice and thereby constrain it. The important exceptions are those momentous occasions that correspond to constitutional choices and crises. Otherwise, institutions change either slowly through gradual accretion of experience and precedent whose effect is not contemporaneous or else in the guise of small institutional changes that adapt the institution better to immediate circumstances, but do not themselves reflect a fundamental change in the institution.

The status of institutions as usually exogenous, but sometimes endogenous, has been recognized in both the CPR and the IR literatures. Ostrom's distinction between operational, collective-choice and constitutional-choice rules provides an ordering of rules that are progressively more difficult to change and therefore increasingly likely to be exogenous.[13] Stephen Krasner's (1982) discussion of the difference between changes within regimes and changes of regimes has similar implications for different levels of exogeneity. In any institutional design problem, some rules will be seen as possible targets for change – hence endogenous parameters – and others will be seen as strictly exogenous parameters. Even when we speak of fairly grand 'changes of regimes', however, there must be some defining environment or else, in Ostrom's words, 'the structure of the problem would unravel'. Thus, even changes of regime are almost certainly changes within some larger regime.

A further and significant complication is that forward-looking institutional design implies a cascading endogeneity that can affect other seemingly exogenous variables. Because institutions define environments for future choice and since the choice of design principles depends on their anticipated consequences, good institutional design should select future exogenous variables in salutary ways. Rather than explaining the success of

---

12. I thank Andrew Dunne for suggesting the term 'endogenous parameters' to describe institutional stability and change. To complete the fourfold typology, other institutions and institutional rules will constitute constant and 'exogenous parameters' in which endogenous institutional change is nested. There also will be 'exogenous variables' whose changes will affect behavior within both evolving and constant institutions. Finally, the key 'endogenous variables' of interest in these analyses will be the behavior of actors under the constraints and opportunities provided them.

13. See Kiser and Ostrom (1982) and Ostrom (1990: 50–5). The distinction here is implicit in the general problem of categorizing variables as exogenous or endogenous. In any dynamic framework, the determination depends on the time period chosen. In the short run, most factors are exogenous, whereas in the very long run almost everything is endogenous. Institutional analysis is complicated because many of its important questions lie in the intermediate territory where there is no easy delimitation of endogeneity and exogeneity.

the institution, these 'exogenous' variables are a consequence of its design. In terms of the focus of the papers in this collection, the number and heterogeneity of actors may themselves be a product of prior institutional choice rather than independent factors. Thus the possibility of institutional design not only makes institutions endogenous: it raises general questions about whether other variables are exogenous or have been affected by the institutional design process.[14]

The implications for institutional analysis are twofold. First, it may be difficult to sort out exogeneity, endogeneity and hence causality – especially where design as opposed to evolution is the underlying process. We should look instead for combinations of design principles, circumstances and (favorable) outcomes that are compatible with one another in constituting an equilibrium. Determination of causality among these requires more detailed knowledge of the underlying process, whether it is one of design or of evolution, than may be available. Without that knowledge, we cannot be sure whether an institutional principle is a necessary consequence of a particular environment or if the environment is a consequence of the rule. Second, and for this reason, in discussing long-term institutional change it is important to reconsider the exogeneity of the environment of the institution. For example, the level or cost of exclusion is typically taken as a defining characteristic of CPR or public good problems. But since exclusion itself is a function not only of technical properties of the good but also of legal–political ones, it may be partially endogenous over the longer term. Thus, in understanding the determinants of institutional scope we must also consider the extent to which those determinants are themselves a product of institutional scope.

---

14. Exogenous parameters other than institutions also can be made endogenous in some circumstances. Even physical constraints are endogenous under conditions of technological change. As Ostrom et al. (1994) point out, for example, we cannot repeal the law of gravity but we can make water run uphill. Similar possibilities of change apply to other exogenous parameters (perhaps including the nature of humans and states), especially if the time frame is sufficiently long. Of course, our research goal is not to make everything endogenous but to identify the endogenous factors we wish to explain and the exogenous factors that help explain them. Our policy goal is to find factors that can be manipulated to change the outcomes. On an operational basis this means exogenous variables, but on a constitutional basis it means institutional parameters. The difference, of course, is that operational variables (e.g. monetary policy) may be effective even when changed fairly frequently (though this is debated) whereas institutional variables are valuable precisely because they change slowly.

The Number of Actors (n)

The determination of regime membership illustrates the tension between the exogenous and endogenous aspects of institutional scope. The point that scope both determines and is determined by its environment is fully apparent since actors and their characteristics appear here both as an independent and dependent variable.

The standard view is that collective action becomes more difficult as the number of actors (n) increases, but that this may be offset by increasing asymmetries among group members (Olson, 1965: 15; Oye, 1986).[15] However, except for a few special cases such as the privileged public good group, there has been remarkably little detailed analysis of either the impact of changing numbers of actors or variations among their important characteristics. In addition, available evidence does not give as clear a conclusion as the Olsonian hypothesis would suggest. After briefly reviewing the differing conclusions from the CPR and IR literatures, this section examines the determinants of n and how institutions might affect those in desirable directions. The basic argument is that institutions play an important role in determining the number and character of participants in an issue and thereby mitigate the independent effect of n and actor heterogeneity (discussed in the next section) on institutional performance and cooperation.

Local CPR and IR literatures differ in their assessments of the importance of n. Ostrom (1990: 188–9, 212) concludes that n is overrated as a determinant of success or failure in collective action, so none of her design principles explicitly address it.[16] She observes successful cooperation in very large groups, collective action failures in fairly small groups and no obviously strong correlation between group size and success. Yet Ostrom's diagnosis recognizes that cooperation is easier among small groups. She argues for the importance of 'nested enterprises' whereby individuals are organized through smaller groups that are then organized into larger groupings. Such hierarchical federation allows large group cooperation to be built upon the advantages of small group cooperation so that n is secondary to other considerations, especially organizational or institutional structure.

By contrast, the IR literature emphasizes n as a central factor for understanding international affairs. Adding or subtracting even a single state fundamentally changes an international interaction. Balance of power is the classic example. Despite wide disagreement over the precise relationship

---

15. Hardin (1982: 42–9) points out that n cannot change without some change in other elements of the problem, so this claim needs elaboration and modification according to the specific contextual circumstances. See also Bendor and Mookherjee (1987).

16. Two design principles, 'clear boundaries' and 'nested enterprises,' implicitly affect n as discussed below.

between numbers of major powers and the stability of the international system, there is broad consensus that even one great power more or less can make a decisive difference.[17] A second example is that the zero-sum setting precludes cooperation among two actors but is fundamentally transformed once a third actor is included.[18] The multilateral setting cannot be uniformly zero-sum and room for joint gain must exist at least among some of the possible coalitions. This has important substantive implications for international politics, including the circumscription of relative gains arguments as a basis for realist pessimism regarding cooperation among states (Grieco, 1990; Snidal, 1991). A final example is the contrast between games of collaboration and games of coordination which shows that the impact of increasing n is not uniform across cases. Increasing numbers impede cooperation in Prisoners' Dilemma games but not necessarily in coordination problems where increased n may increase the stability of cooperative outcomes (Martin, 1994; Snidal, 1985a). Thus while the direction of impact depends on additional factors, group size is important for collective action in IR.

In some local CPRs, the physical problem and available technology determine the number and nature of the actors. For historical or whatever reasons, a group of farmers who have fields along an irrigation canal (or fishers who live near a coastal fishing area) face a problem of joint provision or allocation of the common pool resource. The participants may be in a symmetric position and depend equally on the common pool or they may have asymmetric positions because some are located near the head of the irrigation system (or have historic priority to a particular fishing location). Regardless of the specifics, Ostrom (1990: 91) finds that clear 'boundaries' defining both the participants and the CPR are a key condition for successful resolution of CPR problems. Often these are set historically, sometimes independently of the CPR itself, and provide an exogenous basis for subsequent institutional development.

The historical evolution of local CPRs shows that boundaries are not always fixed and both the number and characteristics of participants fluctuate through time. Such change can destroy a successful CPR institution.

---

17. Gulick (1955) and Kaplan (1957) see the five-power system of 19th-century Europe as the paradigmatic situation for international stability, whereas Waltz (1979) believes bipolarity provides a magical recipe for stability. Recent more analytic treatments explore possibilities involving different numbers of powers (Niou et al., 1989; Wagner, 1986; see also Wagner, 1993).

18. Non-IR readers may feel I am stretching even the broad definition of collective action by including zero-sum settings where there are no collective gains to be made. However, the relative gains argument has gained prominence as a critique of the possibility of international cooperation because states maximize differences in payoffs (i.e. 'relative' gains, power). Moreover, important examples of collective action in international polities, such as alliances, clearly concern cooperation of one group at the expense of another.

An example is the Mawelle fishery in Sri Lanka where demographic and market pressures, combined with the inability of the local community to control its rules, resulted in the breakdown of a viable set of collective rules. Of chief importance was a rapid rise in the number of fishers combined with a shift from owner-producer to wage-labor production and a corresponding dilution of kinship groups. The success of the Törbel alpine pasture, by contrast, depended on a stable population maintained by late marriages, spaced births and emigration. The failure or success in each case depended on clear rules delimiting which actors had rights to the common pool. The Törbel case is particularly interesting because n was endogenous insofar as marriage and family plans were influenced by anticipated access to the CPR, while emigration provided the ultimate relief valve for commons access.[19] In such situations, successful governance institutions limit the number of participants to what can be sustained within the productive capacity of the CPR.[20]

The IR cases share these properties of both physical–technological and political determination of n. Geographic factors largely determine the necessary actors in some international environmental CPRs such as the Mediterranean basin. But in other CPRs, the participant states are fundamentally a product of international politics. Antarctica has been partitioned among a set of states with more or less arbitrary claims, just as the third world was a CPR (from a very ethnocentric Western view) partitioned among imperial rivals in the 19th century. Fishing grounds, navigation rights and seabed minerals all depend heavily on political agreements regarding property rights of individual states. The same is true for IR problems not analytically equivalent to CPRs. NATO mixes geographic imperatives with political considerations to define its problem as well as its membership. The GATT trading regime is not constructed around 'technological' considerations of comparative advantage that cut across North–South lines but, like the European Union (EU), has been primarily a club of industrialized countries. Technological considerations may even follow politics here in

---

19. The parallel in the Mawelle case was that CPR breakdown came at a time of changing connections to the external environment in terms of increased market pressures and improved transportation. This suggests that the self-regulating equilibrium of the Mawelle CPR was upset by outside intrusion on boundary rules.

20. Other examples in Ostrom et al. (1994) are also suggestive: Tang (1994: 322) notes that participation in a wide range of irrigation CPRs depends on landownership, irrigation-shares, membership in an organization or payment; Schlager (1994: 358, 368) notes that participation in a fisheries CPR depends on residency, use of certain technology, membership or a few other criteria; and Agrawal (1994: 375–6) notes that participation in Indian forest CPRs depends on residency, sometimes modified by contributions to maintaining the CPR. None of the cases offers a rich description of the origin or change of rules that could provide an interesting window into how endogenous institutions affect membership.

that, after an extended period of trading together, a set of countries may become inherently better suited to trading with each other (e.g. compatible standards, types and quality of goods produced) than with other countries. Thus, in both CPR and IR settings, n is defined by a combination of technological and political–institutional factors.

The most important way that political arrangements affect n is through mechanisms that exclude non-contributors or threaten punishment to induce contributions. Although pure CPR and public goods models assume exclusion is very difficult, significant exclusion occurs in many real settings. This is the result of conscious efforts (or of evolutionary good fortune) to overcome difficult collective problems by redefining them through political institutions. The CPR cases are instructive because they display how exclusion (or contributions) can be attained through a multiplicity of mechanisms even in situations where we should expect it to be most difficult.

The least relevant possibility from an IR perspective is exclusion or enforcement based on *external* political institutions. Ostrom's (1990) clearest examples are Los Angeles water basin problems where state courts determine the status and rights of various appropriators and thereby the basis for local bargaining towards an agreement. The failure of the Mawelle CPR previously mentioned rests in large part on the failure of external authorities to enforce boundary rules by preventing new entrants to the fishery. Finally, weekly water courts composed of representatives of adjacent Spanish irrigation districts (*huertas*) provide sanctioning power to each local CPR for the management of its irrigation agreements. Note that these CPR problems are not 'solved' externally, since local participants design the governing rules, but external enforcement of locally designed rules is what makes the solutions stick. Insofar as international anarchy is defined by the lack of such strong external institutions, however, international agreements must be enforced in different ways.[21]

At the other extreme, exclusion/enforcement can be *local and decentralized*. The best example is the 'Port Lameron', Nova Scotia fishers who defend their CPR territory through warnings and threats of destroying the equipment of intruders (Ostrom, 1990: 175). The assignment of fishing locations in the Turkish Alanya fishery is also enforced by the fishers themselves

---

21. Note that some forms of external enforcement operate at the international level. One is hegemonic enforcement where a dominant state enforces an agreement between two subordinate states, as the United States has in the Camp David accord. A more controversial example is whether the European Union is becoming sufficiently strong to represent a de facto external authority for some agreements between its members. Finally, an insufficiently understood case is where external authority is effective through the 'legitimation' of local rules rather than any direct enforcement apparatus. Ostrom (1990: 177-8) provides several examples where the opposite occurs and lack of external support undermines local rules.

since those assigned more desirable sites are prepared to defend them. Although such decentralized enforcement would seem to be a natural model for IR, the CPR examples indicate several drawbacks. An obvious one is the reliance on threats of violence by individual actors. Given the scale, potential and history of decentralized international violence, this is an unacceptably dangerous way to organize cooperation even if the evidence is that *use* of violence at the local level is infrequent.[22] A second reason is that these solutions of CPRs are much more fragile than those rooted in external authority.[23] A final (and, in my mind, decisive) reason is that at least the Alanya enforcement regime is not completely decentralized, since enforcement of the rules receives support from other fishers who are not directly involved, but who value the maintenance of a rule system that improves their situation. The local coffeehouse emerges as a significant institution that provides a forum for conflicts to be resolved as well as a nexus for other social relations that support the fishing arrangement. Thus, even small-scale CPRs require more than strictly decentralized enforcement.

This leads us to the third mixed case where exclusion/enforcement of the CPR is managed locally but in a *locally centralized* way. The Alpine and Japanese mountain CPRs are essentially coextensive with the preexisting social and political fabric of their respective villages. The village assembly determines land rights, as well as membership and participation rights, both in the political community and in the commons. It provides a framework within which the CPR rules are decided, plays a direct or indirect role in the monitoring of those rules and provides the muscle behind the imposition of sanctions. This central connection is important even when Japanese detectives fine violators and take the proceeds for their personal use because it enables and legitimizes their seemingly decentralized practice. In addition, the informal networks and interconnections of small societies play an important role in supporting cooperative behavior since social ostracism is perhaps the greatest penalty. Thus, the commons are managed by a combination of formal and informal mechanisms that mimic some functions of the state at the local level. While there is no state in a strong sense, the setting for the resolution of these problems is not anarchic either.

IR resolutions of collective-action problems fall somewhere between these last two cases. Enforcement relies fundamentally on individual states but is facilitated and even orchestrated through more centralized efforts. As with the Japanese detectives, the rules of the international community justify

22. See note 5 above.
23. Port Lameron and Alanya are two of the three cases that Ostrom (1990: 180, Table 5.2) describes as fragile. The third is Gal Oya, Sri Lanka, which cannot be categorized in terms of this exclusion/enforcement trichotomy due to missing information on sanctions.

retaliatory behavior and distinguish such behavior from arbitrary violations of international norms. Moreover, even if they do not face direct retaliation, states worry about ostracism from international society just as villagers do from their society. It matters because their standing in the community facilitates their ability to achieve their other goals as, for that matter, does the maintenance of rules that promote collective ends.

The technology of many IR problems makes it easier for individual states and international institutions to determine n than in typical CPR cases. In particular, CPRs (and public goods) assume that exclusion is impossible for technical reasons whereas in many important international problems exclusion is a matter of choice. States decide with whom to trade and with whom to ally. When collective action is not tightly defined by physical imperatives, international communities may play a stronger role in defining their boundaries. In organizations like alliances and trading groups, benefits may accrue primarily to members or, even if there are spillovers to non-members, the additional benefits of membership may still exceed its costs. Moreover, there are often alternative ways to organize collective action (e.g. specific rules for a trading regime) with different distributional consequences for individual states. Now membership that provides a voice in shaping the content of collective action may be preferable to free riding.

Finally, local CPR cases raise interesting questions regarding the common presumption that the number of states involved in many international issues is a major impediment to cooperation. It is not uncommon for IR scholars to presume that small groups with fairly similar interests (e.g. the five states of G-5) will have difficulty cooperating and that cooperation among large numbers of states (e.g. G-77) must fail. A comparison to local commons problems suggests that IR theorists have overemphasized this problem. For example, the irrigation problems in the Spanish huertas involve upwards of 13,000 participants who are able to successfully resolve their collective action problem. Here the institutional arrangement of nesting (Ostrom, 1990: 184) mitigates the impact of large n. Even more telling is that 100 fishers – a number that would be large in IR – are able to cooperate in managing the Alanya fishery in a setting that is weakly institutionalized. Thus, international relations analysts must look beyond simple head counts to explain the failure of international collective-action problems since n and its impact are contingent on the institutional setting.

Heterogeneity Among Actors

Heterogeneity describes variation across actors on some significant attribute. Olson's (1965) famous privileged group argument is that an actor with a preponderant interest in a public good will unilaterally provide it to the benefit of all. This has been imported into IR as the 'theory of hegemonic stability' (Kindleberger, 1973; Keohane, 1984) that the presence of a single dominant actor benefits the international system through its willingness to provide international public goods. Thus, the standard IR argument is that extreme asymmetry or heterogeneity promotes cooperation. By contrast, the CPR literature (Ostrom, 1990: 89, 210–13; Libecap, paper 7 in this collection) generally concludes that homogeneity promotes collective action. The striking difference in these claims arises because of their concern with different aspects of heterogeneity.

This section analyzes different types of heterogeneity and their impact on collective action in the two areas. The variety of forms and consequences of heterogeneity leads to a less than satisfying conclusion: the impact of heterogeneity is heterogeneous. Nevertheless, this is a useful advance over tendencies to conflate different types of heterogeneity and directs our attention to the differential impact of variations in actor characteristics. It thereby highlights key ways in which the design of institutions affects heterogeneity and thereby collective action.

Consider first the differences between CPR and IR arguments in terms of heterogeneity defined over capability. Hegemonic stability theory sees capability–heterogeneity as promoting cooperation because larger actors produce a public good whose benefits are joint across all states. Here benefits accrue to all, but costs fall on producers. By contrast, in CPRs the benefits of appropriation are not joint and accrue only to appropriators, while the costs of CPR depletion fall on all. These technological differences explain why capability–heterogeneity has a different impact across the two settings, since in the former case more powerful actors work in the common interest whereas in the latter case they work against it.[24]

Arguments based on capability are typically inattentive to equally important variations in interests. In the hegemonic stability model, for example, interest and capacity are collapsed into willingness/ability to contribute to the collective effort.[25] This overlooks possible variations among states' interests by stipulating strong common interest in a public good. Now asymmetry (heterogeneity) is beneficial in the pure public goods model because

24. Moreover, homogeneity eases the tough bargaining problem in achieving cooperation on CPRs insofar as symmetry makes equal payoffs more compelling (Libecap, paper 7 in this collection). The same effect is likely with respect to a potential cooperating k-group in non-privileged public goods situations (Snidal, 1985b) – suggesting that the impact of heterogeneity is not monotonic for small groups.

25. The IR security literature distinguishes more clearly between interest and capability through concepts like resolve. In economics, by contrast, capability and interest are typically collapsed into the single concept of demand.

actors have different amounts of the *same* interest.[26] But when distributional issues are important because states have different interests – for example, if they have differences over *which* public good should be provided (e.g. debates over the purpose of NATO) – then heterogeneous preferences inhibit cooperation. In other situations, the impact of interest–heterogeneity can be completely reversed again. In market and issue linkage situations, for example, heterogeneous interests provide an essential basis for cooperative exchange whereas homogeneous actors have no incentives to cooperate (Martin, paper 4 in this collection). Thus, arguments about heterogeneity require careful specification since its different aspects need not have uniform impact.

Ostrom suggests that actors' time horizons and therefore discount rates are an important aspect of interest–heterogeneity and therefore determinant of collective action. The longer the horizon over which actors are concerned and the longer the CPR can be expected to operate, the more interest they will have in maintaining it. This reinforces the importance of institutions in lengthening participants' time horizons by creating boundaries that prevent non-contributors from appropriating from the CPR and, more generally, by increasing the stability of the CPR. However, heterogeneous discount rates, as well as heterogeneous preferences across goods at different points in time, can complicate collective-action problems. For example, industrialized and less-developed countries will find cooperation on the international environment difficult insofar as the latter are (quite reasonably) less willing to trade off current growth for longer-term environmental benefits. Thus, time horizons provide another aspect of heterogeneity that affects cooperation.

At least two additional types of heterogeneity are important for both IR and CPRs. One is that an issue may be populated by two or more fundamentally different types of actors. In this collection, Ronald Mitchell's discussion of maritime oil pollution (paper 9), for example, treats not only states but oil companies and independent shipping lines as significant actors while Kenneth Oye and James Maxwell (paper 8) focus on the pivotal role of individual private firms in the Montreal Protocol. Local CPRs also may be populated by differentiated actors, such as families or firms, or by fishers whose different technologies make their uses of the CPR fundamentally antagonistic. Many (but not all) of these differences can be captured by differences among capabilities or interests while others require a more serious consideration of subgroups as illustrated in the cited analyses. One of the interesting (but unexplored) institutional design questions at the international level is when, and in what way, states should allow non-state actors to participate in international rule-making.

---

26. Of course, public goods settings still produce mixed motives since even if actors all want more of the same public good, they still want others to pay for it.

A second important type of *non*-heterogeneity, or homogeneity, occurs when actors share vital characteristics that define them as a community. In discussing the virtues of homogeneity in resolving CPRs, Ostrom implicitly argues the advantage of common factors that tie the relevant community together and facilitate cooperation. The connections here may include common interest, but also go well beyond it. They are easiest to see in their absence (as in the Sri Lankan irrigation schemes that involve Sinhalese and Tamils from very different backgrounds) or when subgroups are in opposition to one another (as inshore fishers often are against offshore trawlers). Common language surely lowers the transaction costs of inter-Sinhalese (versus Tamil–Sinhalese) cooperation, but a common sense of identity and history also facilitates collective action within any homogeneous group. Similarly, inshore fishers have common interests, but it is probably more significant that they live together in small and fairly isolated villages and share no similar connections with the offshore trawlers. The same is true at the international level among states that share common cultural, geographic or historical experiences, whether in the Atlantic Community or the Islamic one.[27] Some of this effect is explained by the incentives offered by their multifarious interactions, but some of the effect goes beyond that to a shared sense of identity. The resulting community is supportive of collective action for the reasons discussed under 'local and decentralized' enforcement in the previous section. In any event, 'community' is a plausible candidate as a factor that reduces group heterogeneity in a way that promotes collective action.[28]

This dimension of homogeneity raises the advantages and possible dangers of addressing international problems in terms of community subgroups. Subgroups can take advantage of their homogeneity, as well as their smaller size, to organize collective action. An optimistic view would see subsequent cooperation among these groupings paving the way to wider international

---

27. The danger of exaggerating this point is about as great as that of ignoring it. Japan has joined the 'Western' community because of its shared interests even though its historical–cultural legacy is very separate. The Islamic community too is clearly in the process of construction rather than being purely a predetermined affiliation. Oran Young (1994) provides a skeptical view of transferring arguments about the role of community in small-scale societies to the international level.

28. The partial success of the Gal Oya irrigation project in Sri Lanka, even though cultural heterogeneity was reinforced by the asymmetric locations of the respective ethnic communities in the irrigation system (with Sinhalese as 'head-enders' and Tamils as 'tail-enders'), shows that lack of community is not fatal to collective action. Moreover, successful collective action provides a partial basis for developing community as suggested by the solidarity among the Gal Oya farmers during a subsequent period of ethnic violence (Ostrom, 1990: 170–1).

cooperation, as in Ostrom's conception of nested enterprises.[29] But several drawbacks to this form of solution are apparent. Obviously if exclusion is too expensive, then restricting participation to the subgroup is infeasible. Another problem is that subgroups may achieve only a fraction of the possible cooperative potential posed by the problem (Oye, 1986); ironically, the opposite danger is that they will achieve enough of the benefit to inhibit further extension of cooperation.[30] Current arguments about the dangers of regional trade hinge partly on this concern. Finally, increased subgroup *homogeneity* may increase the impact of heterogeneity in the larger group. The history of blocs in IR suggests the danger that subgroups can become antagonistic and create new problems much worse than the one being solved.

These several categories of heterogeneity can each be affected by political and social institutions. Boundary rules that affect *n* can also determine the composition of the membership. Criteria such as family and community membership in local CPRs, or sovereignty and liberal democracy in international politics, may create homogeneity that promotes collective action. In other cases, group boundaries might be chosen to increase heterogeneity because that increases joint benefits. Regardless, a key point is that heterogeneity is not strictly exogenous but rather is a consequence of the institutional arrangements through which collective action is organized.

Finally, are the actors in IR problems more or less heterogeneous than those in local CPR settings? The two settings seem similar insofar as the predominant actors, states and individuals respectively, are formally homogeneous in each sphere. But a brief look beneath this veneer reveals substantial differences among the actors in each setting. Individuals in local CPRs often vary in their interest in and capacity to affect collective action. Some will be located near the head of the irrigation system, others at the tail; some fishers have several nets, others only a share in one. Similar disparities exist in international politics. They are perhaps greater when comparing the very biggest and very smallest actors, or the richest and the poorest. But for many other groupings of states that confront collective-action problems, the intragroup disparities may be similar to those found in local CPRs. The one area where international politics is much less homogeneous than *certain* local CPRs is with respect to the 'community' conception of homogeneity. The isolated mountain and fishing communities almost certainly have deeper

---

29. This differs from the conception of 'minilateralism' (Kahler, 1992) where leadership by a few great powers produces multilateral collective action.

30. Technically, if subgroups are too effective there is no core and the collectively efficient outcome is not stable. This means a successful subgroup cannot expand its membership without either decreasing benefits of current members or treating new members less well. The resulting bargaining problems could prevent full collective action.

interconnections and stronger common identities than are found in international politics. But other local CPRs seem comparable to IR in the extent of 'community' and the overall importance of this form of homogeneity remains an open question.[31]

Conclusion: Lessons for IR from CPR

Institutional analysis concerns the three-way interaction between institutions, their environment and behavior. Although providing a relatively fixed *parametric* setting in which political behavior occurs, over the longer run institutions *endogenously* change in response to their environment and the choice of actors. The relationship is further complicated because the construction of institutions proceeds in part through the selection of the very environmental factors that are central determinants of the institutional form. Finally, these processes can occur in ways better described as 'evolutionary' and not directly the product of rational design, or in ways better described as 'rational' and thus primarily the result of conscious decisions, or most often as a complicated combination of the two.

CPR–IR comparisons focus research on the variety of cooperation problems and expose the dangers of over-reliance on particular models as paradigmatic in either area. There is important diversity not only across the two categories but also within each. Some differences are physical or technological as illustrated by the different levels of jointness or the technical difficulty of enforcing property rights. But political and social factors that determine the possibilities for achieving collective action are equally important sources of diversity. More importantly, the diversity is not always given but is subject to determination within an issue area. Thus, variables that have been taken as central exogenous determinants of international outcomes – such as the number of actors and their characteristics – themselves need to be explained. Other factors, such as the nature of anarchy, are seen not to be single-valued but rather to take on a range of different specific forms in particular circumstances. Finally, if international problems are messier and more difficult to resolve than local CPR problems, those differences demand explanation in terms of the politics and society of the two settings.

Comparisons across categories demonstrate the variety of solutions to collective-action problems and the accompanying variety of institutional roles. First, local CPRs show the importance of boundaries in defining cooperation problems and their possible solutions. International decision makers have long understood this (for better and worse) as reflected in

---

31. See Buzan (1993) for a recent discussion of international society.

decisions to exclude communist states from many postwar institutions, in the struggles by newly independent states to increase their influence in international organizations and in the multitude of G-groups constituted to address various international issues.

Second, the anarchy–hierarchy distinction that is often presented as the fundamental defining difference between domestic and international politics is grossly insufficient and misleading for both if taken too seriously. Broader forms of social relations among individuals that we characterize in terms of society or community provide alternative ways to organize cooperation that in certain respects are much more effective than coercive centralized institutions. While international society is less developed in some areas, in other areas the development of society compares favorably with that found in local CPR problems that have been successfully resolved.

Third, there is a wide range of institutional possibilities between anarchy and hierarchy and these intermediate forms may remedy the deficiencies of purely decentralized cooperation in ways that are more effective than is possible even through hypothetically strong centralized institutions. The expansive definition of international regimes including everything from norms to laws to expectations (Krasner, 1982) has been useful in identifying this range. But the IR field has been retarded in developing deeper understanding of the differential operation of these institutional forms and their relationship to specific functions of cooperation. Greater attention to informational considerations has been the best example of IR scholarship probing more deeply into the specific operations of international institutions that fall neither at the extreme of pure anarchy nor central government.

Finally, the local CPR literature provides a corrective to naive or overly optimistic views regarding the possibility of institutional design, as well as to unduly pessimistic ones. Successful CPR principles are not simply selected and then imposed on a situation. Ostrom's work is full of examples where well-intended central policymakers impose 'solutions' from above only to find their intentions frustrated by their lack of information regarding the underlying problem, by variations in the problem from one locale to another and, especially, by the unanticipated reactions of involved parties. Successful institutional design implicitly involves experimentation and learning as solutions are implemented and then modified in the face of results. The international politics corollary is that the absence of strong central authority is only a part of the problem. Even if we could establish world government – or a pocket of strong centralized authority over some aspect of international affairs – we could not solve such complex problems simply by writing rules and laws. Instead, we would need a process of learning and adapting rules to the problems and the states involved. Conversely, if we combine these 'evolutionary' lessons with what we can learn about rational design principles from local CPRs and other settings, then solving international collective-action problems need not rest heavily on strong central authority.

REFERENCES

Agrawal, Arun (1994) 'Rules, Rule Making, and Rule Breaking: Examining the Fit between Rule Systems and Resource Use', in Elinor Ostrom, Roy Gardner, and James Walker (eds) *Rules, Games, and Common-pool Resources*, pp. 267–82. Ann Arbor: University of Michigan Press.

Bardhan, Pranab (ed.) (1989) *The Economic Theory of Agrarian Institutions*. New York: Oxford University Press.

Bendor, Jonathan and Dilip Mookherjee (1987) 'Institutional Structure and the Logic of On-going Collective Action', *American Political Science Review* 81(1): 129–54.

Buzan, Barry (1993) 'The English School Meets American Theories', *International Organization* 47(3) (Summer): 327–52.

Calvert, Randall (1992a) 'Rational Actors, Equilibrium, and Social Institutions', mimeo. Rochester NY: University of Rochester.

Calvert, Randall (1992b) 'The Rational Choice Theory of Institutions: Cooperation, Coordination, and Communication', mimeo. Rochester NY: University of Rochester.

Cordell, John C. (1972) 'The Developmental Ecology of an Estuarine Canoe Fishing System in Northeast Brazil', PhD dissertation, Stanford University.

Fisher, F. M. (1966) *The Identification Problem in Econometrics*. New York: McGraw Hill.

Grieco, Joseph M. (1990) *Cooperation among Nations: Europe, America, and Non-tariff Barriers to Trade*. Ithaca, NY: Cornell University Press.

Gulick, Edward Vase (1955) *Europe's Classical Balance of Power*. Ithaca, NY: Cornell University Press for the American Historical Society.

Hardin, Russell (1982) *Collective Action*. Baltimore, MD: Johns Hopkins University Press.

Jackson, John (1992) 'Estimating Models with Variable Coefficients', *Political Analysis* 3: 27–51.

Judge, George, W. E. Griffiths, R. Carter Hill and Tsoung-Chao Lee (1985) *The Theory and Practice of Econometrics*. New York: Wiley.

Kahler, Miles (1992) 'Multilateralism with Small and Large Numbers', *International Organization* 46(3) (Summer): 681–708.

Kaplan, Morton (1957) *System and Process in International Relations*. New York: Wiley.

Keohane, Robert O. (1984) *After Hegemony*. Princeton, NJ: Princeton University Press.

Kindleberger, Charles P. (1973) *The World in Depression*. Berkeley: University of California Press.

Kiser, Larry L. and Elinor Ostrom (1982) 'The Three Worlds of Action: A Metatheoretical Synthesis of Institutional Approaches', in Elinor Ostrom (ed.) *Strategies of Political Inquiry*, pp. 179–222. Beverly Hills, CA: Sage.

Krasner, Stephen (1982) 'Structural Causes and Regime Consequences: Regimes as Intervening Variables', *International Organization* 36(2): 1–21.

Krasner, Stephen D. (1991) 'Global Communications and National Power: Life on the Pareto Frontier', *World Politics* 43: 336–66.

Langlois, Richard N. (1985) *Economics as a Process*. Cambridge: Cambridge University Press.

Martin, Lisa L. (1992) *Coercive Cooperation: Explaining Multilateral Economic Sanctions*. Princeton, NJ: Princeton University Press.

Niou, Emerson, Peter Ordeshook, and Gregory Rose (1989) *The Balance of Power*. Cambridge: Cambridge University Press.

Olson, Mancur (1965) *The Logic of Collective Action*. Cambridge, MA: Harvard University Press.

Ostrom, Elinor (1990) *Governing the Commons: The Evolution of Institutions for Collective Action*. New York: Cambridge University Press.

Ostrom, Elinor, Roy Gardner and James Walker (1994) *Rules, Games, and Common-pool Resources*. Ann Arbor: University of Michigan Press.

Oye, Kenneth A. (ed.) (1986) *Cooperation Under Anarchy*. Princeton, NJ: Princeton University Press.

Schlager, Edella (1994) 'Fishers' Institutional Responses to Common-pool Resource Dilemmas', in Elinor Ostrom, Roy Gardner and James Walker (eds) *Rules, Games, and Common-pool Resources*, pp. 247–65. Ann Arbor: University of Michigan Press.

Schotter, Andrew (1981) *The Economic Theory of Social Institutions*. New York: Cambridge University Press.

Sims, Christopher A. (1980) 'Macroeconomics and Reality', *Econometrica* 48(1) (Jan.): 1–48.

Snidal, Duncan (1985a) 'Coordination Versus Prisoners' Dilemma: Implications for International Cooperation and Regimes', *American Political Science Review* 79: 923–42.

Snidal, Duncan (1985b) 'The Limits of Hegemonic Stability Theory', *International Organization* 39: 579–614.

Snidal, Duncan (1991) 'Relative Gains and the Pattern of International Cooperation', *American Political Science Review* (Sept.) 85: 701–26.

Stein, Arthur (1982) 'Coordination and Collaboration: Regimes in an Anarchic World', *International Organization* 36: 299–324.

Tang, Shui Yan (1994) 'Institutions and Performance in Irrigation Systems', in Elinor Ostrom, Roy Gardner and James Walker (eds) *Rules, Games, and Common-pool Resources*, pp. 225–45. Ann Arbor: University of Michigan Press.

Wagner, R. Harrison (1986) 'The Theory of Games and the Balance of Power', *World Politics* 8: 546–76.

Wagner, R. Harrison (1993) 'What Was Bipolarity?', *International Organization* 47: 77–106.

Waltz, Kenneth N. (1979) *Theory of International Politics*. Reading, MA: Addison-Wesley.

Wold, Herman O. A. (1960) 'A Generalization of Causal Chain Models', *Econometrica* 28(2): 443–63.

4. HETEROGENEITY, LINKAGE AND COMMONS PROBLEMS

Lisa L. Martin

Introduction

Conditions of interdependence force states to cooperate if they wish to achieve desired outcomes in the international system (Keohane and Nye, 1977). Problems of market failure, such as those caused by collective-action problems and informational asymmetries, and problems of coordination, such as standardization, indicate that states may choose to construct institutions to help themselves cooperate more reliably (Keohane, 1984). These problems and potential solutions are analogous in many respects to those faced by individuals attempting to use common-pool resources (Ostrom, 1990). The analogies are particularly strong when we turn our consideration to global commons issues, such as environmental degradation, use of non-territorial ocean resources or species conservation. This paper examines the impact of heterogeneous capabilities and preferences on international cooperation and the role issue linkage plays under conditions of heterogeneity.

Although the concept of sovereignty gives every state equivalent legal status, states nevertheless vary greatly in their capabilities and interests. Such variation introduces heterogeneity into problems of international cooperation. Empirical analyses of common-pool resources seem to find that heterogeneity inhibits efforts to cooperate unless unusual conditions, such as the existence of a privileged group, are met (Johnson and Libecap, 1982;

I would like to thank Thráinn Eggertsson, Jeff Frieden, Bob Keohane, Elinor Ostrom and participants in the project on Local and Global Commons for their excellent comments.

Libecap, 1989). Indeed, within the scope of individual issues, heterogeneity can create conflicts of interest that reduce available gains from cooperation. However, similar distributional conflicts arise even in the presence of identical actors, unless norms of equity are internalized strongly. On the positive side, heterogeneity may create opportunities for gains from exchange across issue-areas, thus enhancing the scope and potential of cooperative arrangements. The first section of this paper considers the effects of heterogeneity. It examines how heterogeneity in capabilities affects resolution of cooperation problems and how heterogeneous preferences create demand for issue linkage. It suggests that some functional differentiation is necessary for the solution of cooperation problems and that this differentiation can result either from inherent actor heterogeneity or conscious institutional design.

The second section turns to the question of institutional design given a demand for issue linkages. While issue linkage creates room for mutually advantageous cooperation that states cannot achieve on single issues, it is often difficult to maintain in non-institutionalized environments. Individual actors face temptations to renege on cross-issue deals, hoping to achieve concessions on those issues of most intense interest to themselves and then back down from commitments of more benefit to their bargaining partners. Institutions, both domestic and international, can reduce temptations to renege, thus solidifying issue linkages and encouraging heterogeneous states to cooperate with one another.

On the local level, individuals attempting to solve cooperation problems sometimes have the option of turning to the state for solutions and enforcement. However, state intervention has frequently proven inefficient or even destructive of established self-enforcing cooperative solutions. Solutions organized by users themselves result in 'horizontal orderings', where patterns of behavior are organized but individuals do not rely heavily on external enforcement or other hierarchical structures. We might expect similar patterns to emerge on the international level, since international politics is a self-help system without the option of external enforcement. Influential analyses have suggested that states cannot afford the luxury of functional differentiation, which would increase aggregate benefits through specialization (Waltz, 1979).

However, considerations of institutional design in the presence of heterogeneity suggest a third pattern of cooperation. Solutions to cooperation problems may rely on self-enforcing agreements, but at the same time establish hierarchical patterns of authority and functional differentiation. States may choose to delegate authority to particular subsets of actors or to international organizations. Institutionalized patterns of international cooperation, such as those we see in the European Union (EU) or the United Nations (UN) Security Council, show that states may develop models that go beyond horizontal orderings without relying on external authority. By introducing heterogeneity into studies of decentralized cooperation, we both move the analysis closer to the actual problems states confront and suggest new challenges and possibilities for institutional design.

The Effects of Heterogeneity

Theories of cooperation often assume, for tractability, that actors have identical interests and capabilities. However, empirical studies typically find substantial heterogeneity. Studies of local commons problems find that introduction of heterogeneity, for example asymmetric interests or skills, reduces the chance that individuals will be able to design adequate systems of rules to govern utilization of common-pool resources (Libecap, 1989; Hackett, 1992). Because asymmetry adds complexity to the already difficult task of designing rules, according to these findings, it often results in inefficient or otherwise inappropriate management of resources. The problem of heterogeneity as such has received little attention from theorists of international cooperation. However, once we consider asymmetries of power and of preference intensities on different issues, we find that heterogeneity has in fact been of great interest and that some kinds of heterogeneity may have positive effects on the likelihood of cooperation.

Heterogeneous Capabilities

One reason that we might expect heterogeneity to impede cooperation is increasing conflicts of interest (Libecap, 1989; Kanbur, 1991; Libecap, 1994). However, asymmetry of interest or power does not always imply increased conflict of interest. Problems of distributing the gains of cooperation, for example, arise even when all actors have identical interests. Consider a situation where two individuals are attempting to divide a dollar between themselves. Assume each has an identical utility function, wishing to capture as much of the dollar for himself as possible. This situation maximizes conflict of interest and illustrates that such conflicts may arise even when individuals are homogeneous. An equal division of the dollar may seem an obvious focal point solution, but in fact almost any distribution can be an equilibrium, depending on the rules of the game, such as the sequence of moves. Analysis of the impact of heterogeneity cannot rest on a straightforward argument that conflicts of interest increase as heterogeneity does.

In international relations theory, one prominent type of heterogeneity is the distribution of power.[1] Power may be equally distributed, with all

---

1. I use 'power' interchangeably with 'capabilities' in this article to refer to resources that states can translate into influence over outcomes.

actors in a given issue-area possessing equivalent resources and therefore equivalent ability to influence outcomes. Many students of international politics assume that the end of the Cold War has coincided with movement from a bipolar to a multipolar security structure, with the distribution of power becoming more egalitarian.[2] At the other extreme, power may be concentrated in the hands of one major power, leading to a condition of unipolarity or hegemony. Structural theories of international cooperation have addressed the question of how the distribution of power - a particular kind of heterogeneity - might affect the patterns of cooperation we see. Snidal (paper 3 in this collection) draws our attention to heterogeneous capabilities on both the local and international levels, discussing how they may be either causes or consequences of institutional design.

Hegemonic stability theory provided an initial and straightforward statement of how the concentration of power might change the probability that states will manage to cooperate to solve problems of collective action. Kindleberger (1973), studying international monetary relations, drew on theories of public goods to argue that cooperation required a hegemon. He argued that highly concentrated power was a necessary (and perhaps sufficient, although this was not clearly specified) condition for international cooperation to produce public goods. The internal logic of his argument was simple. Only a state large enough to appropriate a significant share of the benefits of producing a public good such as international monetary stability would have incentives to perform the functions necessary to assure such stability. Similar analyses applied this logic to other areas of international economic cooperation, such as trade policy (Krasner, 1976; Keohane, 1980).

These empirical analyses and later theoretical works found that hegemonic stability theory generally did not provide a very accurate predictor of the level of international cooperation. In monetary policy, hegemony seemed only to establish the possibility of cooperation, but did not assure it and indeed contained elements of extreme instability in some periods (Eichengreen, 1989). In trade policy, hegemony seemed to have a loose relationship to the extent of openness in the international system, but the cycles of openness and of hegemony were not closely synchronized with one another. As damaging as these empirical findings, theoretical analyses poked holes in the prediction of hegemonic stability. The Kindleberger version relied on the assumption of public goods but many areas of international cooperation produce benefits that are excludable or in other ways diverge from the public goods assumption. Other theoretical work found that

---

2. However, others see an even more concentrated distribution of international power following the collapse of the Soviet Union, since the United States now has significant power in many areas, including military (see Nye, 1990). Wagner (1993) discusses the empirical problem of defining bipolarity during the Cold War.

cooperation could continue even 'after hegemony', through the effects of international institutions (Keohane, 1984) or as a single country became unwilling to supply public goods unilaterally, increasing the demand for international cooperation (Snidal, 1985b).

Despite these failings of hegemonic stability theory, considering the distribution of power seems essential if we are to understand the problem of institutional choice for international commons problems. Hegemony affects not only the problem of cooperation, or 'institutional equilibrium', but also institutional choice – 'equilibrium institutions' (Shepsle, 1986). To the degree that common-pool resources suffer from difficulties of non-excludability, some of the original insights regarding the incentives of powerful actors to provide solutions may be more relevant than in other international settings.

Arguments that show the possibility of continuing cooperation in the face of hegemonic decline do not imply that considerations of power are irrele-vant to the question of institutional design. On the international level, deci-sions about the institutions to be adopted are not made through a formalized constitutional process. Instead, they result from bargaining among the major players in an issue-area, so that the interests of the most powerful are sure to be reflected in the types of institutions chosen. States confronting conditions of instability are unlikely to be interested in constructing efficient institutions or effective systems of monitoring or dispute resolution, looking instead to exert leverage as necessary to extract maximum immediate gains. On the other hand, conditions that allow powerful states to adopt a long time horizon may allow them to develop an interest in delegating power to efficient institutions, bringing the insights of functional theories to bear (Martin, 1992b). If a hegemonic state can afford to take the long view, the institutions it helps create will promote gains from cooperation. If it is con-cerned only about the short term, it will have little interest in constructing efficient institutions.

When power is concentrated, we can expect institutional choice to reflect the interests of the most powerful. When it is diffuse, the logic of collective action in the international setting with a large number of states involved sug-gests that organizing to construct rules for the management of resources will be difficult. Attempts to solve international environmental problems involv-ing many states, for example, show the difficulties of designing systems of rules in the absence of leadership from a powerful state, i.e. the problems created by homogeneous capabilities (Haas et al., 1993). In these instances, such as the Law of the Sea process or development of codes to protect endangered species, states attempt to construct rules through complex processes of multilateral negotiations. However, adoption of these rules requires that the most powerful states accept them. In some instances, attempts to develop rules are embedded within nested institutions, so that states may overcome collective-action problems by adopting the negotiating procedures specified by an umbrella organization such as the United Nations. The process of institutional design is affected by power asymmetries, in that powerful states will choose rules that operate to their own benefit. While these rules are unlikely to be notably fair or just, they at least avoid the worst outcome of no cooperation whatsoever. If power is more evenly distributed, the process of cooperation itself may create heterogeneity through functional differentiation, providing an alternative pattern of institutional solutions. I elaborate these points below.

Heterogeneity in Collaboration and Coordination Problems

We can further assess the effects of heterogeneous capabilities by considering the role of power in different strategic situations. Theorists of international cooperation argue that two distinct types of cooperation problems confront states. States may face dilemmas of market failure, where short-term, self-interested behavior leads to suboptimal outcomes, as in the public goods problems just discussed. Such problems have been labeled *collaboration* dilemmas (Stein, 1982; Snidal, 1985a).[3] States may also disagree on which of multiple efficient equilibria they prefer. This leads to distributional conflict and results in *coordination* dilemmas.

Collaboration problems result when the individual pursuit of short-term self-interest by all states leads to suboptimal outcomes. Such outcomes are inefficient in a Pareto sense, so that others exist which would make all players better off. Analysts have typically used the Prisoners' Dilemma game to exemplify this cooperation problem. The paradigmatic 'tragedy of the commons' assumes a Prisoners' Dilemma with many players, as do many analyses of the issues involved in use of common-pool resources (Hardin, 1968). In such commons problems, each individual confronts a situation in which regardless of the behavior of others the strategy that results in the highest immediate payoff is to behave non-cooperatively, for example by extracting more of a fixed resource base than can be sustained over the long term. These perverse incentives face all actors and can lead to severe depletion of common-pool resources. Situations characterized by collaboration dilemmas involve potential market failure in that rational self-interested action may leave everyone worse off than they could be.

Solutions to such problems exist, contrary to the earliest analyses of Prisoners' Dilemma problems. On the domestic level, collaboration problems are often used as justification for state intervention, on the argument that only centralized, coercive solutions that rely on external enforcement

---

3. Martin (1992a) refers to collaboration problems as *coadjustment* dilemmas.

can overcome the inherent intense conflicts of interest (Hardin, 1968). More recent analyses, based on extensive field research and experimental evidence, illustrate that individuals can solve local commons problems without external intervention, often to the benefit of all concerned (Ostrom, 1990; Ostrom et al., 1994).

On the international level, analysts have never taken seriously the notion that only external enforcement can resolve collaboration problems. A core assumption of dominant models of international relations, one that seems a sound description of reality, is that no central authority exists. Instead, states exist in a condition of anarchy, relying on their own efforts to assure survival and prosperity in a 'self-help' system. However, this assumption does not imply that states cannot take actions to mitigate the effects of anarchy. Instead, strategies of reciprocity and far-sighted behavior can sustain cooperation among states without the construction of a central authoritative source of policy guidance and enforcement. The logic of decentralized cooperation in collaboration problems is supported by formal game-theoretic analyses, particularly the well-known folk theorem (Friedman, 1971; Abreu, 1988), and by computer simulations (Axelrod, 1984).

Resolution of collaboration problems requires iteration, so that actors care about the future, and credible punishment strategies. Actors will cooperate only so long as they believe that defection will be reciprocated, reducing their future payoffs. To make punishment threats credible, states require accurate and timely information about one another's behavior, making monitoring crucial. However, the provision of monitoring may itself be costly, bringing us back to the public goods problems just considered. Heterogeneous capabilities may facilitate solution, as very large states will have the interest and ability to undertake monitoring and enforcement. In the absence of sufficient heterogeneity, states may choose to delegate monitoring authority to an agent, turning to institutional solutions. Milgrom et al. (1990) argue that medieval traders turned to the services of the Law Merchant in situations like this. If power asymmetries do not create the conditions for self-motivated monitoring, actors must create functional differentiation – i.e. heterogeneity – through institutional design. As Snidal (paper 3 in this collection) argues, heterogeneity is often endogenous to institutions.

Institutions designed to resolve collaboration problems will tend to take on certain general characteristics. Centralized monitoring activities, or at least a central clearinghouse making available information on past patterns of cooperation or defection, will reduce temptations to exploit cooperators in the hope of immediate gain. However, decisions about whether to cooperate or to punish non-cooperators remain decentralized. In international trade regimes where the temptation for surreptitious protection exists, as in the General Agreement on Tariffs and Trade (GATT) or the EU, we see the development of dispute-resolution mechanisms that allow states to publicize and receive judgments on claims of inappropriate protection (Hudec, 1990). Members of the regime can then use such information to implement their own strategies of reciprocity. Since the temptation to cheat if one believes one can get away with it is high in collaboration dilemmas, states looking to resolve them can be expected to design institutions that provide information that allows them to punish detectors through strategies of specific reciprocity (Keohane, 1986). A certain amount of heterogeneity, whether endowed or created, is necessary for resolution of these dilemmas.

While patterns of cooperation and punishment continue to be decentralized, perhaps even characterized by a complex pattern of bilateral deals, the concept of a horizontal ordering may not capture all the dynamics of successfully resolved collaboration problems. International relations theory understands a horizontal ordering to mean that no hierarchical patterns of authority exist. Waltz has argued that 'Hierarchy entails relations of super- and subordination among a system's parts, and that implies their differentiation' (1979: 93). Delegation of authority, whether to agents like the European Court of Justice (ECJ) or powerful states as in the UN Security Council, leads to states taking on different functions as some acquire decision-making authority. Patterns of delegation and differentiation, rather than external enforcement, characterize the solutions we see to international collaboration dilemmas. States may be willing to delegate monitoring or dispute-resolution authority to a central actor since this will allow them to pursue decentralized cooperation more efficiently by providing additional information about the behavior of others. However, they are not willing to cede sovereignty to the degree necessary to create reliable, rule-bound external enforcement. Thus, while a 'statist' solution to collaboration problems is unlikely on the international level, we should expect to see the development of institutions that involve some functional differentiation and delegated authority.

Perhaps we can think in terms of a series of patterns of organization, reflecting levels of heterogeneity. At one extreme, we may have 'pure' horizontal orderings, with neither hierarchical patterns of authority nor functional differentiation among units. The demands of international collaboration problems suggest such ideal-type solutions are unlikely to be effective, at least when enough states are involved to make monitoring costly. This suggests a second category, where functional differentiation emerges without hierarchy. For example, states may set up specialized organizations to collect information without giving them decision-making authority. This is a 'Law Merchant' kind of solution, for example as found in various international human rights regimes whose major function is to provide information about states' human rights conditions. In the next category, decision-making authority is delegated to some states or bodies created by states, as in the Security Council or dispute-resolution mechanisms found in international trade agreements. Enforcement, however, remains decentralized. While the Security Council can call for economic or military sanctions, such enforcement actions are actually imposed by states, who can and do sometimes choose to disregard Security Council resolutions.

If states manage to solve a collaboration problem, they still face a further obstacle to cooperation, in that they must decide on the *form* of cooperation. This obstacle involves not joint movement to mutually preferred outcomes but bargaining over the distribution of benefits from cooperation. States, therefore, face a coordination problem, where they recognize that failure to agree will hurt all, but they frequently have strongly divergent preferences about *which* cooperative equilibrium to choose. The difficulty is that many cooperative equilibria exist, often with no obvious criteria for choosing among them.[4] Some states may favor some outcomes while others prefer different equilibria, as in a Battle of the Sexes game. In coordination games, pursuit of self-interest demands adopting strategies that are consistent with those of others, such as using similar standards for telecommunications equipment or railway gauges.

A number of authors have suggested that choosing among optimal equilibria constitutes an alternative to considering international cooperation to be primarily a problem of overcoming potential market failure and avoiding suboptimal outcomes (Krasner, 1991; Goldstein, 1993). Krasner argues that thinking about choices among efficient equilibria better fits the realist approach to international politics, as it creates an explicit role for the exercise of state power. He finds that the choice of equilibria is determined by power, with the most powerful state choosing the equilibrium that benefits it the most. Other states then have little choice but to go along with this outcome – 'the weak suffer what they must', as Thucydides put it. For example, the dominant position of US firms in some telecommunications markets may have given them the ability to choose standards most to their liking, leaving others to follow along even if this meant incurring high adjustment costs.

If international cooperation dilemmas are resolved by the unilateral exercise of power, patterns of cooperation will deviate from a purely horizontal ordering. Although all states may be formal equals both in international law and international relations theory, the most powerful will in effect take on a hierarchical role through their ability to decide on particular policies and assume that others will follow.[5] Mitchell (paper 9 in this collection), for

---

4. The equilibria may or may not be distinguished from one another by efficiency considerations. The following discussion assumes that states are choosing among equilibria that are all Pareto-optimal.

5. Such a model of cooperation suffers from the usual difficulties of power analysis, since it may become merely a tautological statement that powerful states determine outcomes because they are powerful, unless the observable components of power are specified in advance.

example, finds that the power of the United States was central to the resolution of the problem of international oil spills. He also finds, as the argument of this section implies, that functional differentiation of the actors involved in this issue was reflected in institutional design and appears to have facilitated cooperation. Hackett et al. (paper 5 in this collection) study a similar distributional problem, but in the absence of power asymmetries they find rule-based solutions embodying norms of equity. It remains questionable whether these laboratory results carry over well to the international setting.

In coordination games, asymmetries of power may facilitate rapid resolution of distributional conflict, but at the cost of an inequitable division of the benefits of cooperation, since the powerful state will choose an equilibrium it prefers. Nevertheless, all states may prefer a skewed distribution of benefits from cooperation to the delays and reduced gains that result from extensive bargaining over the choice of an equilibrium (Fearon, 1993). If power is not heterogeneous enough for one state to dictate an outcome, states may create agents to solve bargaining conflict. For example, Garrett and Weingast (1993) interpret the role of the ECJ in these terms, as it facilitates settlement of disputes among EU member states. Institutional solutions to coordination problems are likely to have several advantages over solutions imposed through the exercise of power, such as greater equity and stability, but they suffer from some of the same collective-action problems as the issues they are meant to resolve. Whether we focus on collaboration or coordination problems (and most issues involve both), we find that heterogeneity, either inherent in the distribution of power or constructed through institutional design, is central to the resolution of cooperation problems.

Heterogeneous Preference Intensities

Besides heterogeneity in the distribution of power, a common sort of heterogeneity in international negotiations involves differing preference intensities on different issues. Due to varying international economic and political positions, the vagaries of domestic political processes or a plethora of other reasons, states put different weight on different issues on their mutual agendas. In current negotiations within the EU, for example, the major state actors have different preference intensities. Germany puts high weight on achieving political union, while France puts greater stock in achieving control and stability in the area of monetary policy (Garrett, 1993). To greatly simplify a complex situation, it seems that in each dimension taken individually, a high degree of conflict of interest exists. Germany prefers the existing European monetary system, since it gives great power to the Bundesbank, while France prefers creation of a European Central Bank, which would more closely reflect French interests in macroeconomic policy. On the political dimension, Germany prefers rapid development of supranational policy-making institutions, such as increasing the powers of the European Parliament. France is reluctant to move rapidly toward political union.

However, representatives of these two states with their divergent interests reached a mutually acceptable deal in the Maastricht treaty. The permissive condition was the different weight each put on the two dimensions. Because Germany felt strongly about political union, it was willing to make compromises on monetary arrangements; the opposite condition held for France. By linking these two issues to one another, a set of mutually advantageous deals that were not available on any single dimension became possible (Martin, 1993b). Similar asymmetries in preference intensities are common in international negotiations. Some states have intense security concerns and so are willing to make concessions on economic issues to assure their security; some have intense interests in environmental protection and so are willing to make economic sacrifices. Asymmetries of preference intensity are built into most models of international bargaining, since without them little scope for agreement would exist. In spatial models, preference intensities are captured by different shapes of indifference curves, indicating the tradeoffs actors are willing to make (Mayer, 1992). In this instance, heterogeneity is in no way an impediment to cooperation; indeed, it may be a necessary condition for it.

Asymmetries of preference intensities can lead states to link issues to one another in order to further their own self-interest. Issue linkage thus becomes one of the key elements in understanding international cooperation. Sebenius (1983) and Tollison and Willett (1979) illustrate how issue linkage can create space for mutually advantageous deals on the international level. The sovereign right of any state to agree to only those international agreements it wishes makes linkage even more valuable than it is in situations where policies are decided by some version of a majority-rule process. When decisions do not require unanimity for approval, changes in policy are possible even when they are not Pareto-improving. In simple majority-rule situations, for example, just less than 50 percent of the decision-making group may be hurt by a proposal, relative to the status quo, but the proposal may still pass. When unanimity is required, as for most significant international agreements, only proposals that give something to everyone will gain approval, restricting the set of feasible changes to those that are Pareto-improving (Buchanan, 1959). In general, a unanimous decision-making requirement creates incentives for issue linkage. Within the EU, unanimity requirements have led to extensive use of side-payments during treaty revision negotiations and on other decisions requiring unanimity. On those issues now subject to qualified-majority voting, issue linkage should be less common, since members can move away from the status quo without it.

Although students of international politics often discuss issue linkage and recognize its central role in negotiations, the conditions for its success have not been explored systematically. Oye (1992: ch. 3) moves in this direction by developing a typology of issue linkage, based on the problem states are attempting to solve. *Extortion* occurs when states threaten to take steps costly to themselves if concessions on other issues are not forthcoming. This type of linkage obviously suffers from credibility problems, so that its success is dependent on measures that allow states to make credible commitments to take costly steps. *Exchange* takes place when states agree to forgo benefits on some issues in return for concessions on others and seems to be the type of linkage assumed in most discussions of international negotiations. Credibility is still a problem, as states continue to have incentives to renege, by following the course of action they had intended prior to the negotiation. Finally, states may rely on *explanation*, attempting to create the image of issues being inherently linked to one another. In this instance, linkage may not be the result of a conscious tactical choice by a state but recognition that actions have effects in many different dimensions. For example, pledges of exchange-rate stability have impacts on inflation, employment and other issues so that they cannot easily be separated from one another. Explanation involves making such inherent linkages apparent and intelligible to others. In this case, credibility only emerges as a difficulty if there is some chance that what is being presented as an 'inherent' linkage is actually a case of extortion or exchange. The next section discusses the ways in which institutions can lend credibility to linkage.

Research on local commons problems has suggested that heterogeneity creates impediments to cooperation. Work on international cooperation suggests that this insight may not travel well to the international level. Two types of heterogeneity that characterize international politics, power inequalities and asymmetric preference intensities, may actually create opportunities for cooperation. However, we should not overgeneralize to argue that all types of heterogeneity encourage cooperation. Informational asymmetries, for example, may often hinder cooperation. States also differ significantly in the nature of their political systems. Empirical work has shown quite conclusively that democratic states do not go to war with one another, while democracies fight non-democracies frequently (Doyle, 1983; Gaubatz, 1993). However, it also appears that democracies fight non-democracies at about the same rate at which non-democracies fight one another. This observation suggests that homogeneity is less important than factors that inhere in democracy, such as relatively transparent decision-making procedures, since the interaction between democracies and non-democracies is identical to that among non-democracies. Having seen that heterogeneous preferences may create demands for linkage, the next section considers institutional characteristics that make such linkages more durable.

Institutional Effects on Issue Linkage

Heterogeneity can create the conditions for international cooperation through the mechanism of issue linkage. However, linkage is usually tenuous, making its supply problematic. Opportunities proliferate for reneging on deals cut across issues in the international arena (Keohane, 1984: 91). While Germany has made concessions on monetary union in order to achieve progress on political union, for example, this deal may fall apart due to deliberate actions by Germany or other EU governments, failures on the domestic level to implement the deal or international economic pressures that change the costs and benefits of agreed policies. Problems of incomplete contracting plague all attempts at international issue linkage and states must find ways to overcome them if they are to reap its benefits. Powerful states, in particular, will find it necessary to assure bargaining partners of their credibility, since a powerful state's reneging will seriously harm others. A central problem in making linkage work to the benefit of all involves making credible commitments to deals with other countries. Here, I consider two sets of factors that influence the credibility of issue linkage: domestic ratification processes and institutional decision-making rules on the international level.

The Effects of Ratification Rules

One way in which the problem of international cooperation typically diverges from that of the local commons is in the 'two-level' nature of the cooperation process (Putnam, 1988). Agreements may be negotiated among a small number of individuals, but these individuals represent larger constituencies and are constrained to various degrees in the kinds of deals to which they can commit them by the pattern of authority existing between them and their constituency. Some have argued that negotiators with great autonomy from their domestic constituency can make commitments to other countries (Moravcsik, 1991). Negotiators with little autonomy face the problem of not being able to speak with authority. Any commitments that they make will only go into effect if accepted by their constituencies after some formal or informal ratification process.[6]

The nature of the ratification process, specifically the level of authority that has been delegated to the chief negotiator, affects the credibility of commitments to link issues in international negotiations. At the simplest level, the greater the authority the greater the negotiator's short-term credibility, assuming the negotiator is trustworthy. Negotiators who do not have to

---

6. Of course, lack of autonomy may have an offsetting advantage, in giving the negotiator more leverage to demand concessions from negotiating partners.

anticipate stringent ratification processes can make concessions to other states without considering in detail the preferences of ratifying bodies such as legislatures. Thus, we might expect that negotiators facing no specified ratification procedure, such as most authoritarian states or majority governments in parliamentary systems with strong party discipline, would have the greatest capacity to make binding commitments. At the other extreme, negotiation of treaties that will require formal ratification with supermajority requirements in the legislature and that may be subject to legislative amendment, would seem to exaggerate the credibility problem. In between these two extremes, procedures that involve legislative approval but eliminate the possibility of amendments to a negotiated agreement, such as fast-track arrangements for trade negotiations, would apparently establish an intermediate level of credibility. These hypotheses fit with some interpretations of American foreign policy that see congressional involvement as a handicap for the US ability to negotiate effectively with other countries (Crabb and Holt, 1992: 281–3).

In a world of complete information and where leadership turnover was not a variable, such simple statements might in fact hold and they suggest hypotheses possibly worth testing. However, when we adopt a longer-term view and ask about the credibility of commitments under conditions of incomplete information, these hypotheses seem suspect. Incomplete information about the preferences of the negotiator or of groups involved in ratification and implementation may produce outcomes strikingly different from what we would expect in a simpler world of common knowledge.

First, consider the position of the head of government.[7] If this individual is unconstrained, his/her negotiating partners are aware of his/her preferences, preferences are stable and the negotiator is expected to remain in office for a significant length of time, others should be able to calculate in a straightforward way the chance that he/she will live up to the deals they negotiate with him/her. Commitments to linkage should therefore gain credibility, since states will not sign on to deals that they know will be violated. However, it is unlikely that all – if any – of these conditions will hold. Even heads of government not constrained by formal ratification procedures typically have to satisfy the demands of a 'selectorate' (Shirk, 1993) and opacity of the identity and interests of the selectorate create constraints of a type for which it is difficult to account in international negotiations. An unconstrained head of government also may be the most difficult to read, from the perspective of knowing his/her preferences, since he/she is not

---

7. I assume here, for simplicity, that the chief negotiator is appointed by the head of government and accurately reflects his/her principal's interests, so that the distinction between the chief negotiator and the head of government is not an interesting one.

chosen through any formal mechanism and the head of government is usually there on a temporary basis, even in non-democratic systems. Even if the head of government remains in place, if the observation of international commitments takes place at his/her whim, the stability of his/her own preferences becomes a matter of grave concern. Taking such factors into account suggests that requiring a formal ratification process, which implies public assent from a broader spectrum of society, may actually enhance the credibility of deals.

Second, consider the problem of the preferences of the ratifying body. As just mentioned, such a body nearly always exists, even if its participation in the ratification process is informal. If these preferences are known, calculation of credibility under alternative ratification procedures may be straightforward and other states can take account of it during the negotiation process. However, if other states initially lack information about the ratifying body's preferences (or if perhaps its own government does!), the costs of a formal, open ratification process may in fact reveal valuable information, thus preventing heads of government from committing themselves to deals that they will not be able to implement. Cowhey (1993), for example, argues that the United States has been more successful in committing itself to multilateral arrangements than has Japan because of the open, transparent nature of US domestic approval processes.

Although negotiators often complain about the difficulties of doing their jobs when they are subject to constant public scrutiny, such scrutiny may actually enhance the durability of inherently fragile international deals. Keohane (1984: 95) makes a similar point regarding the relative reliability of states that have transparent decision-making processes. A government that has gone through a public procedure of gaining approval of its foreign policy commitments will bear domestic costs in addition to international ones if it reneges on these commitments. In the area of economic sanctions, for example, such 'audience costs' seem to have a positive impact on the credibility of threats and promises and so on the level of cooperation (Martin, 1993a). An extremely stringent ratification process, such as one that requires formal legislative approval and allows the legislature to make amendments to international agreements, may constrain negotiators to the point that they become ineffective. However, an intermediate level of stringency, such as fast-track requirements that mandate a formal approval process but eliminate the possibility of amendment, may provide an optimal level of credibility through their role in revealing information.

The Interaction of Heterogeneity and Decision-making Rules

Domestic institutional features can enhance the credibility of issue linkage. Likewise, the characteristics of international institutions can affect such deals. Arguments about reputational effects as well as empirical evidence suggest that linkage is more credible when it takes place within an institution than in an uninstitutionalized environment (Keohane, 1984; Martin, 1992a). We are likely to find variation in the effects of different *types* of institutions on credibility. Some institutional characteristics, such as those that allow for diffuse reciprocity or create long time horizons, may increase the value of reputation or otherwise enhance the demand for credibility. Other characteristics, such as revelation of information about preferences, may facilitate efforts of states to establish credible commitments, enhancing the supply of credibility.

Linkage and international institutions are not alternatives to one another. States wishing to influence one anothers' behavior do not have to choose between relying on issue linkage and on rule-structured interaction. Instead, institutions often incorporate, facilitate and demand issue linkage. The formalization of strategies of specific reciprocity that many organizations undertake enhances the value of linkage. For example, the GATT incorporates reciprocity by demanding that key trading partners make mutual concessions. Although the GATT deals only with trade issues, the mutual concessions that states make often cover quite diverse areas of traded goods and services. The GATT provides a framework for negotiation of such deals, publicizes their content, provides dispute-settlement mechanisms and in other ways enhances the reliability of linked concessions by raising the costs of reneging. In general, institutions that reveal information about preferences and increase the probability of retaliation for defection will allow states to make more credible commitments.

The formal decision-making processes of organizations can create demands for linkage even if they do not formalize reciprocity. In particular, unanimity rules create demands for linkage, as discussed previously (see also Weber and Wiesmeth, 1991). Under unanimity, policies can move away from the status quo only if such movement is in the interest of all members of the institution; any proposed policy change will only pass the stringent unanimity approval requirement if it is Pareto-superior to the status quo. Taking issues in isolation, this is an extremely difficult standard to meet. For example, consider the EU, where treaty revisions continue to require unanimous approval although day-to-day decisions often have only to meet a lower threshold of qualified-majority voting. On any single issue, such as monetary union, change of the status quo will only be approved if the status quo is undesirable from the perspective of all members. Change is thus difficult.

However, the EU deals with many issues. At the Maastricht summit in 1991, for example, two of the major issues on the table were monetary union and political union. When such issues are linked, as they were at Maastricht, the scope for Pareto-improving changes to the status quo increases significantly. As discussed above, asymmetry in the intensity of preferences created scope for a deal. Because all EU members had to approve any changes to the existing Treaty of Rome, linkage was a necessary component of any bargain. While the Maastricht example of linkage is clear and recent, the history of the EU suggests that such cross-issue deals are at the heart of EU policy. Unanimity requirements will, in general, necessitate issue linkage if states wish to change the status quo.

Thus, heterogeneity of preferences interacts with institutional structure to create varying demands for issue linkage. Figure 1 summarizes the expected effects. It shows, in highly simplified form, the probability that adoption of new joint patterns of behavior will involve issue linkage. Heterogeneity of preference intensities, combined with unanimity rules, generate a high demand for linkage. Of course, attempts to cooperate to move away from the status quo may fail, in which case we will not see successful linkage. This figure summarizes the conditions under which linkage is a necessary component of cooperation.

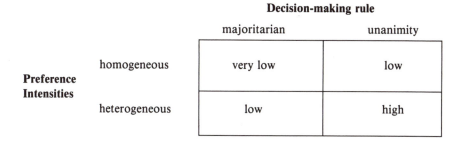

Decision-making rule

		majoritarian	unanimity
Preference Intensities	homogeneous	very low	low
	heterogeneous	low	high

Figure 1. Probability that movement away from status quo will involve issue linkage.

International institutions that rely on consensus for policy change, rather than accepting some form of majority voting, will provide fertile grounds for cooperation as long as they incorporate a number of issues on which participants have different preference intensities. Along a single dimension, consensus requirements are often a recipe for paralysis. However, asymmetric actors can design institutions that create demands for linkage and cover issue-areas that can be profitably linked, thus enhancing the scope for cooperation. We should expect to see less scope for linkage in institutions that rely on majoritarian procedures for decision making and may therefore expect that heterogeneous actors will be reluctant to commit themselves to cooperate within such a framework. This analysis thus suggests that more heterogeneity in actors' preferences will lead to the construction of institutions that cover a number of issues and make decisions using unanimity or other supermajority rules. It suggests a way to begin specifying the conditions for linkage, a continuing research problem in international relations.

Issue linkage often creates scope for mutually advantageous agreements where none would exist on individual issues, providing that states can make credible commitments. Both domestic and international institutions affect the ability of states to make such commitments. On the domestic level, stringent ratification procedures restrict the government's autonomy but may, through revealing information and making policies difficult to change, actually enhance the credibility of commitments over the long term. On the international level, similar effects of institutions on the symmetry of information enhance credibility, reducing incentives to renege on commitments. Additionally, institutional rules that demand unanimity (or something approaching it) for policy change, rather than relying on majoritarian procedures, increase the demand for issue linkage, and we should expect heterogeneous states to favor such rules.

Conclusion

Studies of common-pool resources have shown that individuals do not need to rely on external enforcement to avoid the tragedy of the commons. Strong analogies exist between decentralized patterns of cooperation on the local level and patterns of international cooperation, where no external enforcement agency is generally available. For analytical simplicity, empirical and deductive studies of decentralized cooperation have generally assumed homogeneous actors. Heterogeneity has been considered a major hindrance to the pursuit of cooperative solutions. However, heterogeneity of capabilities and of preference intensities may themselves lead to cooperative solutions, often through the mechanism of issue linkage.

Heterogeneity of capabilities and preference intensities was explored here. Concentrated patterns of power facilitate the solution of public-goods problems. If power is not sufficiently concentrated, states may have to create functional differentiation through institutional design. In addition, if heterogeneity takes the form of differing preference intensities on different issues, it creates the potential for mutually advantageous issue linkage, thus increasing the probability of successful cooperation. However, successful issue linkage requires that states be able to make credible commitments to one another. Stringent domestic ratification requirements, while apparently putting the chief negotiator in a more difficult position, can actually enhance the long-run stability of linkages. On the international level, rules that require unanimity, or something close to it, mean that issue linkage will be an important aspect of decision making, thus further increasing the demand for it.

Heterogeneity thus has systematic effects on the form of cooperation, but does not inevitably make it less likely on the international level. States with heterogeneous preference intensities will take their differences into account when designing the institutions through which they wish to pursue gains from cooperation. If they are heterogeneous, they are likely to require something close to unanimity on important institutional decisions, anticipating that other decision-making criteria will often leave them worse off. This will, in turn, lead to issue linkage. However, the analysis in this paper suggests that states will be less reluctant to delegate authority at the operational level, since without functional differentiation cooperative agreements are unlikely to be upheld. Thus, we are led to expect that heterogeneous states will create institutions with more extensive delegation at the operational than at the decision-making level.

REFERENCES

Abreu, Dilip (1988) 'On the Theory of Infinitely Repeated Games with Discounting', *Econometrica* 56: 383–96.

Axelrod, Robert (1984) *The Evolution of Cooperation*. New York: Basic Books.

Buchanan, J. M. (1959) 'Positive Economics, Welfare Economics, and Political Economy', *Journal of Law and Economics* 2: 124–38.

Cowhey, Peter F. (1993) 'Domestic Institutions and the Credibility of International Commitments: Japan and the United States', *International Organization* 47: 298–326.

Crabb, Cecil V. and Pat M. Holt (1992) *Invitation to Struggle: Congress, the President, and Foreign Policy*. Washington, DC: Congressional Quarterly.

Doyle, Michael (1983) 'Kant, Liberal Legacies, and Foreign Affairs', *Philosophy and Public Affairs* 12: 205–35.

Eichengreen, Barry (1989) 'Hegemonic Stability Theories of the International Monetary System', in Richard N. Cooper, Barry Eichengreen, Gerald Holtham, Robert D. Putnam and C. Randall Henning, *Can Nations Agree? Issues in International Economic Cooperation*, pp. 255–98. Washington, DC: Brookings Institution.

Fearon, James D. (1993) 'Cooperation and Bargaining Under Anarchy', mimeo. Chicago: University of Chicago.

Friedman, James (1971) 'A Noncooperative Equilibrium for Supergames', *Review of Economic Studies* 38: 1–12.

Garrett, Geoffrey (1993) 'The Politics of Maastricht', *Economics and Politics* 5: 105–23.

Garrett, Geoffrey and Barry Weingast (1993) 'Ideas, Interests, and Institutions: Constructing the EC's Internal Market', in Judith Goldstein and Robert O. Keohane (eds) *Ideas and Foreign Policy: Beliefs, Institutions, and Political Change*, pp. 173–206. Ithaca, NY: Cornell University Press.

Gaubatz, Kurt Taylor (1993) 'Democratic States and Commitment in International Relations', mimeo, Stanford University.

Goldstein, Judith (1993) 'Creating the GATT Rules: Politics, Institutions, and American Policy', in John Gerard Ruggie (ed.) *Multilateralism Matters: The Theory and Praxis of an Institutional Form*, pp. 201–32. New York: Columbia University Press.

Haas, Peter M., Robert O. Keohane and Marc A. Levy, eds (1993) *Institutions for the Earth: Sources of Effective Environmental Protection*. Cambridge, MA: MIT Press.

Hackett, Steven C. (1992) 'Heterogeneity and the Provision of Governance for Common-Pool Resources', *Journal of Theoretical Politics* 4: 325–42.

Hardin, Garrett (1968) 'The Tragedy of the Commons', *Science* 162: 472–81.

Hudec, Robert E. (1990) 'Dispute Settlement', in J. Schott (ed.) *Completing the Uruguay Round*, pp. 180–204. Washington, DC: Institute for International Economics.

Johnson, Ronald N. and Gary D. Libecap (1982) 'Contracting Problems and Regulation: The Case of the Fishery', *American Economic Review* 72: 1005–22.

Kanbur, Ravi (1991) 'Heterogeneity, Distribution and Cooperation in Common Property Resource Management', mimeo. Washington, DC: The World Bank.

Keohane, Robert O. (1980) 'The Theory of Hegemonic Stability and Changes in International Economic Regimes, 1967–1977', in Ole R. Holsti, Randolph M. Siverson and Alexander L. George (eds) *Change in the International System*, pp. 131–62. Boulder, CO: Westview Press.

Keohane, Robert O. (1984) *After Hegemony: Cooperation and Discord in the World Political Economy*. Princeton, NJ: Princeton University Press.

Keohane, Robert O. (1986) 'Reciprocity in International Relations', *International Organization* 40: 1–27.

Keohane, Robert O. and Joseph S. Nye (1977) *Power and Interdependence*. Boston, MA: Little, Brown.

Kindleberger, Charles P. (1973) *The World in Depression, 1929–1939*. Berkeley: University of California Press.

Krasner, Stephen D. (1976) 'State Power and the Structure of International Trade', *World Politics* 28: 317–43.

Krasner, Stephen D. (1991) 'Global Communications and National Power: Life on the Pareto Frontier', *World Politics* 43: 336–66.

Libecap, Gary D. (1989) 'Distributional Issues in Contracting for Property Rights', *Journal of Institutional and Theoretical Economics* 145: 6–24.

Martin, Lisa L. (1992a) *Coercive Cooperation: Explaining Multilateral Economic Sanctions*. Princeton, NJ: Princeton University Press.

Martin, Lisa L. (1992b) 'Interests, Power, and Multilateralism', *International Organization* 46: 765–92.

Martin, Lisa L. (1993a) 'Credibility, Costs, and Institutions: Cooperation on Economic Sanctions', *World Politics* 45: 406–32.

Martin, Lisa L. (1993b) 'Domestic and International Institutions in the EMU Process', *Economics and Politics* 5: 125–44.

Mayer, Frederick W. (1992) 'Managing Domestic Differences in International Negotiations: The Strategic Use of Internal Side-payments', *International Organization* 46: 793–819.

Milgrom, Paul R., Douglass C. North, and Barry R. Weingast (1990) 'The Role of Institutions in the Revival of Trade: The Law Merchant, Private Judges, and the Champagne Fairs', *Economics and Politics* 2(1): 1–23.

Moravcsik, Andrew (1991) 'Negotiating the Single European Act: National Interests and Conventional Statecraft in the European Community', *International Organization* 45: 19–56.

Nye, Joseph S., Jr. (1990) *Bound to Lead: The Changing Nature of American Power*. New York: Basic Books.

Ostrom, Elinor (1990) *Governing the Commons: The Evolution of Institutions for Collective Action*. New York: Cambridge University Press.

Ostrom, Elinor, Roy Gardner and James Walker (1994) *Rules, Games, and Common-pool Resources*. Ann Arbor: University of Michigan Press.

Oye, Kenneth A. (1992) *Economic Discrimination and Political Exchange: World Political Economy in the 1930s and 1980s*. Princeton, NJ: Princeton University Press.

Putnam, Robert D. (1988) 'Diplomacy and Domestic Politics: The Logic of Two-level Games', *International Organization* 42: 427–60.

Sebenius, James K. (1983) 'Negotiation Arithmetic: Adding and Subtracting Issues and Parties', *International Organization* 37: 281–316.

Shepsle, Kenneth A. (1986) 'Institutional Equilibrium and Equilibrium Institutions', in Herbert Weisberg (ed.) *Political Science: The Science of Politics*, pp. 51–81. New York: Agathon.

Shirk, Susan L. (1993) *The Political Logic of Economic Reform in China*. Berkeley: University of California Press.

Snidal, Duncan (1985a) 'Coordination versus Prisoners' Dilemma: Implications for International Cooperation and Regimes', *American Political Science Review* 79: 923–42.

Snidal, Duncan (1985b) 'The Limits of Hegemonic Stability Theory', *International Organization* 39: 579–614.

Stein, Arthur A. (1982) 'Coordination and Collaboration: Regimes in an Anarchic World', *International Organization* 36: 299–324.

Tollison, Robert D. and Thomas D. Willett (1979) 'An Economic Theory of Mutually Advantageous Issue Linkage in International Negotiations', *International Organization* 33: 425–49.

Wagner, R. Harrison (1993) 'What Was Bipolarity?', *International Organization* 47: 77–106.

Waltz, Kenneth N. (1979) *Theory of International Politics*. New York: Random House.

Weber, S. and H. Wiesmeth (1991) 'Issue Linkage in the European Community', *Journal of Common Market Studies* 29: 255–67.

Part II

Evidence from the Laboratory

5. HETEROGENEITIES, INFORMATION AND CONFLICT RESOLUTION: EXPERIMENTAL EVIDENCE ON SHARING CONTRACTS

Steven Hackett, Dean Dudley and James Walker

Sharing Rules and Distributional Conflict

Consider a situation in which a group is making allocation decisions that determine the size and distribution of a commonly held surplus. Prior to the allocation decision, individuals make capital investments. The ultimate value of the investments is assumed to depend on the group's ability to resolve conflicts arising over the distribution of joint surplus. Examples include the construction of water injection wells by those who own mineral rights in a common oil field, investments in maintenance of a commonly held irrigation system or the construction of product-specific manufacturing facilities by parties to a joint venture. What will be the linkage between these individual capital investments and group-devised sharing rules? To what extent is this linkage affected by the degree to which information on investments is public or private? What are the broader implications of

Financial support from the National Science Foundation (Grants SES-8820897, SES-8921884 and SBR-9222656) is gratefully acknowledged. Data are available upon request from the authors. Send inquiries to Professor James M. Walker, Department of Economics, Ballantine 901, Indiana University, Bloomington, IN 47405, USA or Professor Steven Hackett, School of Business and Economics, Humboldt State University, Arcata, CA 95521–8299, USA.

heterogeneous investments and imperfect information for joint surplus? In this paper we investigate these issues using laboratory methods from two related economic applications: the study of input allocation rules for common-pool resources (CPRs) in the natural resources literature and the study of ex post negotiation of surplus shares in incomplete contracts in the literature on contracting and the firm.

A growing body of field and experimental literature provides considerable evidence that individuals may evolve and adopt self-governing institutions that enable conflict resolution. A principal focus of this paper is the question of whether heterogeneities in individuals' production capabilities and in past investments act as an obstacle to conflict resolution. The literature provides several arguments that point to heterogeneity as a deterrent to cooperation (Hardin, 1982; Johnson and Libecap, 1982; Libecap and Wiggins, 1984; Wiggins and Libecap, 1987; Ostrom, 1990; Kanbur, 1991; Hackett, 1992). For example, Kanbur (1991) argues:

> ... theory and evidence would seem to suggest that cooperative agreements are more likely to come about in groups that are homogeneous in the relevant economic dimension, and they are more likely to break down as heterogeneity along this dimension increases (1991: 21–2).

The task of making and sustaining agreements is considered more difficult when individuals are heterogeneous in production capabilities and investments because of the distributional conflict associated with alternative sharing rules.[1] In heterogeneous settings, different sharing rules may produce different distributions of earnings across individuals. While all individuals may be made better off by cooperating, some may benefit more than others. Consequently, individuals may fail to cooperate on the adoption of a sharing rule because they cannot agree upon what would constitute a fair distribution of benefits.[2] Further, information asymmetries often exist in

---

1. Sharing rules can be in the form of agreements regarding inputs or outputs. We use the term 'input allocation' to refer to the decision to allocate inputs to the production process of appropriating from the CPR. We use the term 'appropriation' to refer to the actual level of output resulting from this production process. Note, if users are homogeneous in technologies employed (as is the case in the experiments reported here), then identical input allocations imply identical appropriation. In the field, where technologies may differ, this may not be case.

2. These issues have recently been investigated in a theoretical context by Hackett (1992). His work suggests that heterogeneous resource endowments can lead to disagreement over the supply and implementation of rules that allocate access to CPRs. For example, consider two allocation rules commonly found in the field - equal appropriation and appropriation proportionate with capacity or historic use. The interests of large-endowment appropriators are served by proportionate allocations, while the interests of small-endowment appropriators are better served by equal-sized appropriation rights allocations. When self-governing CPR groups are heterogeneous, rule supply involves a tradeoff between the cost of investing in the 'social capital' necessary to reach consensus on an allocation rule and the added costs of monitoring and enforcing agreements opposed by some subset of appropriators.

heterogeneous settings. For example, Libecap (paper 7 in this collection) offers examples of contractual failures that can be tied to information asymmetries regarding individuals' gains or losses from adopted sharing rules.

This paper presents results from two ongoing experimental research programs that are relevant to these issues. In the first study, parties make up-front investments in inputs that can be applied to a production process, while in the second study, parties make up-front investments in value enhancement or cost reduction. These investments lead to heterogeneities in individuals' abilities to affect the size of potential surplus and their relative shares of the surplus. Moreover, the information individuals have about each others' capabilities and prior investments and the role this information plays in the resolution of conflict over sharing rules are key research issues. The studies differ in terms of emphasis. The first study focuses on the allocation of inputs to a CPR production process and on the use of face-to-face negotiations to resolve conflicts at the level of individual appropriation from the resource. In contrast, the second study focuses on tests of bargaining theory in a more structured negotiation setting where negotiation occurs after parties have made transaction-specific investments that impact the magnitude of jointly held surplus.

Heterogeneities and CPRs

Common-pool resources are natural or human-made resources in which (a) exclusion is non-trivial (but not necessarily impossible) and (b) yield is subtractable (Ostrom et al., 1992). Individuals jointly using a CPR are assumed to face a social dilemma – commonly referred to as the tragedy of the commons – in which individual resource users ignore the external harm they impose on other users, leading to outcomes that are not optimal from the perspective of the group. Policy proposals for resolving CPR dilemmas often follow one of two approaches – privatizing the resource or centralizing its management within the state.

Building on the experimental research of Walker et al. (1990) and Hackett et al. (1994), this section examines a decision setting where individuals make input allocation decisions between a CPR and an outside alternative with a fixed marginal return. Heterogeneity in appropriation capabilities is introduced by allocating different input endowments across subjects. The allocation of endowments is achieved through an auction process that leads to heterogeneities in subjects' investments in inputs. Two distinct auction mechanisms are used to generate two different information settings. In the first case, auction prices are common (public) information. In the second, they are private information. The principal question is to what degree do the heterogeneities and differences in information affect individuals' abilities to coordinate their use of the CPR? In this experimental setting, coordination of input use and the evolution of self-governing rules of use are examined by allowing subjects to discuss the decision problem in face-to-face communication sessions.

The Game-theoretic Decision Setting

Assume a fixed number n of appropriators with access to the CPR.[3] Each appropriator i has an endowment of inputs e_i that can be allocated to the CPR or allocated to an outside activity with a constant marginal return, w. Endowments allocated to the CPR can be viewed as inputs applied to harvesting from the CPR. The payoff to an individual appropriator from allocating inputs to the CPR depends on aggregate allocations to the CPR and on the appropriator's allocation as a percentage of the aggregate. Let x_i denote appropriator i's allocation to the CPR, where $0 \leqslant x_i \leqslant e_i$. The group return to allocations to the CPR is given by the production function $F(\Sigma x_i)$, where F is a concave function, with $F(0) = 0$, $F'(0) > w$, and $F'(\Sigma e_i) < 0$. Initially, allocating inputs to the CPR pays better than the opportunity cost $[F'(0) > w]$, but at some level of allocation $(x_h < \Sigma e_i)$ the outcome is counterproductive $[F'(x_h) < 0]$. Thus, the yield from the CPR reaches a maximum net level when individuals allocate some but not all of their endowments to the CPR. More specifically, CPR rents are maximized (where rents per unit of input allocation are defined to be the average revenue product of allocations to the CPR less the average revenue product of allocations to the outside option) where the marginal return from the last input allocated to the CPR equals the marginal return from the outside option. In summary, overallocation of endowed inputs to the CPR implies excessive effort applied to harvesting, reducing rents earned from the CPR.

Let $x = (x_1, \ldots, x_n)$ be a vector of individual appropriators' input allocations to the CPR. The payoff to an appropriator, $u_i(x)$, is given by:

$$
\begin{array}{ll}
we_i & \text{if } x_i = 0 \\[2ex]
w(e_i - x_i) + \left[x_i \middle/ \Sigma x_i\right] F\left(\Sigma x_i\right) & \text{if } x_i > 0.
\end{array}
\tag{1}
$$

Equation (1) reflects the fact that if an appropriator allocates all of their endowment in the outside alternative, they get a sure payoff (we_i), whereas if they allocate some of their endowment to the CPR, they get a sure payoff $w(e_i - x_i)$, plus a payoff from the CPR. An appropriator's payoff from the CPR depends on the yield from total allocations, $F(\Sigma x_i)$, multiplied by their

---

3. We rely significantly on the discussion in Ostrom et al. (1992) and Hackett et al. (1994) for the discussion of the decision setting.

share of overall group allocations $(x_i/\Sigma x_i)$.[4] Previous studies have simplified the analysis of the CPR game by using designs that yield fully symmetric non-cooperative equilibria. To see this, let the payoffs in (1) be the payoff functions in a symmetric, non-cooperative game. Then each player allocates x_i^* in the CPR such that:

$$-w + (1/n)F'(nx_i^*) + F(nx_i^*)((n-1)/x_i^*n^2) = 0. \qquad (2)$$

The focus of this paper, however, is on appropriator heterogeneity. In particular, the experimental design allows for two levels of input endowments. One subset of appropriators have large endowments, e_i^l, $i = 1,2, \ldots, M$; the remaining appropriators have small endowments, e_j^s, $j = M + 1, M + 2, \ldots, n$, and $e_i^l > e_j^s$ (superscripts refer to endowment size). Parameters are chosen so that the Nash equilibrium is symmetric within appropriator type, but asymmetric across type; large appropriators allocate more inputs to the CPR than small appropriators.[5] This is accomplished by letting the small players' endowment be a binding constraint in equilibrium. Allocations at the Nash equilibrium satisfy:

$$-w + (x_i^*/(Z + Mx_i^*))F'(Mx_i^*) +$$
$$F(Mx_i^*)[Z + (M-1)x_i^*]/(Z + Mx_i^*)^2 = 0 \qquad (3a)$$

for $i = 1,2, \ldots, M$ large-endowment players, and

$$x_j^* = e_j, \qquad (3b)$$

for $j = M + 1, M + 2, \ldots, n$ small-endowment players ($Z \equiv \Sigma x_j^*$). Group allocations to the CPR at this asymmetric Nash equilibrium are greater than optimal, but not all rents from the CPR are dissipated. To see this, compare this deficient equilibrium to the optimal solution. Summing across individual payoffs $u_i(x)$ for all appropriators i yields the group payoff function $u(x)$,

$$u(x) = w\Sigma e_i - w\Sigma x_i + F\left(\Sigma x_i\right), \qquad (4)$$

that is to be maximized subject to the constraints $0 \leqslant \Sigma x_i \leqslant \Sigma e_i$. Given the

---

4. If total input allocation is held constant, one token allocated to the CPR yields the same return regardless of the identity of the player making the investment. Thus heterogeneity is in endowments, not in appropriation skills.

5. The Nash equilibrium can be made symmetric even with large- and small-endowment appropriators. In particular, a symmetric Nash equilibrium results as long as the small-endowment level is greater than or equal to that required for equilibrium play. In such a case, small-endowment appropriators simply have a lower input allocation level in the outside market than large-endowment appropriators.

above conditions on F, the group maximization problem has a unique solution characterized by the condition:

$$-w + F'\left[\Sigma x_i\right] = 0. \tag{5}$$

According to (5), CPR rents and total group earnings are maximized when the marginal return from a CPR equals the opportunity cost of the outside alternative for the last input unit allocated to the CPR. While the asymmetric Nash equilibrium depends critically on the endowment parameter e_i, the group payoff maximizing level of allocation does not. There are many different rules that can distribute individual allocations to the CPR such that total rents from the CPR are maximized. Since endowments are heterogeneous, different rules (e.g. equal allocation to the CPR versus CPR allocations proportionate with endowment) imply different wealth distributions. Such inequities may lead to disagreement over the type of sharing rule and ultimately a reduction in CPR rents.

The experimental setting is designed for the subjects to play the CPR game a finite number of times with a publicly announced end point. Denote the CPR game by X.[6] If the game has a unique equilibrium, then the finitely repeated game has a unique subgame perfect and subgame consistent equilibrium (Selten, 1971). Thus, equation (3) characterizes a finite sequence of equilibrium outcomes.

Face-to-face communication represents an interesting empirical anomaly from the perspective of game theory. If the games implemented in the laboratory setting accurately induce the valuations corresponding to the payoff function of equation (1) and the parameters we control in our experimental setting, then finitely repeated, complete information, non-cooperative game theory ascribes no strategic content to non-binding communication.[7] Face-to-face communication (and resulting verbal commitments), however, may change subjects' expectations of other players' responses. In particular, if subjects believe a cooperative play will induce cooperation from others, then cooperating can be sustained as rational play in the framework of incomplete information regarding player types.

---

6. Typically, the repeated game has many equilibria. Two equilibrium refinement principles are subgame perfection and subgame consistency. An equilibrium is subgame perfect if it prescribes equilibrium play on every subgame. An equilibrium is subgame consistent if it prescribes identical play on identical subgames.

7. When the game X has a unique equilibrium x^*, neither finite repetition nor communication creates new equilibrium outcomes. Let c denote a communication strategy, in the communication phase C, available to any player. As long as saying one thing and doing another has no payoff consequences, then any strategy of the form (c, x^*) is an equilibrium of the one-shot game (C, X) and finitely repeated x^* is a subgame perfect equilibrium outcome of repeated communication $(C, X, C, X, \ldots, C, X)$. In this situation, subgame perfection is independent of communication.

The Laboratory Setting and Design

The experiments used subjects drawn from undergraduate economics classes at Indiana University. All experiments were conducted on the NovaNET computer system. At the beginning of each experimental session, subjects were told that (1) they would make a series of allocation decisions, (2) all individual allocation decisions were anonymous to the group and (3) they would be paid their individual earnings (privately and in cash) at the end of the experiment. Subjects then proceeded at their own pace through a set of instructions summarized as follows:[8]

> Subjects faced a series of decision rounds in which they were endowed with a specified number of tokens, which they allocated between two markets. Market 1 was described as an allocation opportunity that yielded a fixed (constant) rate of output per token and that each unit of output yielded a fixed constant monetary return. Market 2 (the CPR) was described as an allocation opportunity that yielded a rate of output per token dependent upon the total number of tokens allocated by the entire group. The rate of output at each level of group allocation to Market 2 was described in functional form as well as tabular form. Subjects were informed that they would receive a level of output from Market 2 that was equivalent to the percentage of total group tokens they allocated. Further, subjects knew that each unit of output from Market 2 yielded a fixed (constant) rate of monetary return.

Subjects knew with certainty the total number of decision makers in the group, their own token endowment, the total number of tokens in the group and the number of decision rounds in the current treatment condition. After each round, subjects were shown a display that recorded their profits in each market, total group token allocations to Market 2 and a total of their cumulative profits for the experiment. During the experiment, subjects could request, through the computer, this information for all previous rounds for the current treatment condition. Subjects received no information regarding other subjects' individual allocation decisions.

Parameters and Predictions. The decision setting is operationalized with eight appropriators ($n = 8$) and quadratic production functions $F(\Sigma x_i)$ for Market 2, where:

$$F\left(\Sigma x_i\right) = a\Sigma x_i - b\left(\Sigma x_i\right)^2 \tag{6}$$

with $F'(0) = a > w$ and $F'\left(\Sigma e_i\right) = a - 2b\Sigma e_i < 0.$

For this quadratic specification, one has from (5) that the group optimal token allocation satisfies $\Sigma x_i = (a - w)/2b$. Further, the CPR yields 0% of

---

8. A copy of the instructions is available from the authors upon request. In the instructions, the term 'token investment' was used instead of 'token allocation'.

optimal rents when token allocation is twice as large as optimal.

The Nash equilibrium for a finite game with complete information (based on an individual's payoff function as shown in equation (1)) for large and small appropriators is given by:

$$\Sigma x_i = (M/(M+1))(a - w - bZ)/b, \; i = 1,2, \ldots, M, \text{ and}$$
$$\Sigma x_j = Z \equiv \Sigma e_j, \; j = M+1, M+2, \ldots, n. \tag{7}$$

The following constraints were placed on the choice of parameter values for a, b, c, d, e and w in this study. First, to preserve equilibrium uniqueness, Nash equilibrium x_i and x_j must be integer-valued, a constraint imposed by software design. Second, in order for heterogeneity in endowments to create a heterogeneous Nash equilibrium, the small players' endowments had to be sufficiently small to be a binding constraint in non-cooperative play.

The experiment parameters are shown in Table 1. Each small player was endowed with 8 tokens per round, each large player with 24. Further, each player was charged an endowment fee of $0.02 per token per period to lower the cost of the experiments. This fee is a sunk cost, thus having no effect on Nash equilibrium or optimal allocation levels. There exists a unique Nash equilibrium where total tokens allocated to Market 2 equals 96: (i) small-endowment players each allocate all 8 of their tokens in Market 2 and (ii) large-endowment players each allocate 16 tokens in Market 2 and 8 tokens in Market 1. At the Nash equilibrium, subjects earn approximately 49% of

Table 1. Experimental Design Baseline: Parameters for a Given Decision Period

Subject type	Low endowment	High endowment
Number of subjects	4	4
Individual token endowment	8	24
Production function: Market 2*	$33(\Sigma x_k) - .25(\Sigma x_k)^2$	$33(\Sigma x_k) - .25(\Sigma x_k)^2$
Market 2 return/unit of output	$0.01	$0.01
Market 1 return/unit of output	$0.05	$0.05
Earnings per subject at group maximum (evaluated at benchmark conventions)		
Equal allocation	$1.23	$1.70
Equal absolute reduction	$0.66	$2.26
Equal proportionate reduction	$0.94	$1.98
Earnings/subject at Nash equilibrium	$0.56	$1.33
Earnings/subject at zero net yield	$0.24	$0.72

*Σx_k = the total number of tokens allocated by the group in Market 2. The production function shows the number of units of output produced in Market 2 for each level of tokens allocated in Market 2. All payoffs include a per-period fee of $0.02 per token.

the maximum rents from Market 2, the CPR. Computing earnings from both Market 1 and Market 2 at this equilibrium, small players receive a per-period payoff of (8 × $0.09) − (8 × ($0.02) = $0.56. Large players receive a per-period payoff of (8 × $0.05) + (16 × $0.09) − (24 × $0.02) = $1.36, with a total group payoff per period of $7.68.

In order to maximize group earnings, 56 tokens must be allocated to Market 2, yielding a group per-period payoff of $11.78. Various allocation rules can be used to achieve the group optimum of 56 tokens allocated to Market 2. Different allocation rules, however, generate meaningful differences in individual payoffs (displayed in Table 1). Under the rule of *equal allocation*, each player allocates 56/8 = 7 tokens at the group optimum. Each small player receives a net payoff of $1.23, while each large player receives a net payoff of $1.70. Using the non-cooperative Nash allocation level as the reference point, *equal absolute reductions* in tokens allocated to Market 2 require that each player remove 40/8 = 5 tokens from Market 2. Each small player allocates 3 tokens in Market 2, with a net payoff of $0.66. Each large player allocates 11 tokens in Market 2, with a net payoff of $2.26. (Note that small players are still better off with this rule relative to the Nash equilibrium.) Again using the Nash equilibrium as the reference point, an *equal proportionate reduction* in tokens allocated to Market 2 requires the group to cut token allocations to Market 2 by 42%. Each small player allocates 5 tokens in Market 2, with a net payoff of $0.94. Each large player allocates 9 tokens in Market 2, with a net payoff of $1.98.

Treatment Sequences.   Subjects participated in two (consecutive) 10-round sequences of the asymmetric game.[9] In the first 10 rounds, subjects were not allowed to communicate. In the final 10 rounds, the subjects were informed that prior to each decision round they would have the opportunity to discuss the allocation problem (10 minutes prior to the first decision round and 3 minutes prior to each subsequent round). No physical threats or side payments were allowed.[10] Thus, the structure of the experiment can be summarized as follows:

Sequence 1	Sequence 2
$X, X, \ldots, X$	$C - X, C - X, \ldots, C - X.$

---

9. After completing the instructions, subjects had the opportunity to participate in a series of five salient reward decision rounds with identical endowments of 20 tokens each. Otherwise, the parameters were identical to those in Table 1. These 'trainer' rounds were implemented to give the subjects initial experiences with the logistics of the experiment.

10. Each person was identified with a badge. This facilitated player identification in our transcripts. If unanimous, players could forego discussion.

Prior to each 10-round treatment sequence, four subjects were assigned the 'large' token endowment (24 tokens each), while the remaining four subjects were assigned the 'small' endowment (8 tokens each). Subjects had to make costly investments in order to secure one of the large-endowment positions. Two distinct auction mechanisms were used to generate information settings where auction prices were common (public) or private information.

Treatment 1: Common Price Auction

The first auction mechanism used for assigning endowment positions was a multiple unit ascending price auction. Prior to the ten decision rounds with no-communication and again prior to the ten decision rounds with communication, the subjects received a set of instructions summarized as follows:

> For each of the next 10 rounds, four subjects will be assigned 8 tokens, while the other four will be each assigned 24. Tokens will be assigned using an auction in which each subject bids for the right to have 24 tokens. The auction will begin with each subject raising their right hand. The auctioneer will call out bids that increase every 5 seconds, in $0.25 intervals. When the auctioneer reaches a bid that is the highest total amount a subject is willing to pay to have 24 tokens rather than 8 tokens each round, the subject should lower their hand. This means the subject is out of the auction. When there are only 4 persons left with their hands raised the auction stops. Each of the 4 persons remaining in the auction is allocated 24 tokens each round for the next 10 rounds, paying a one-time auction price equal to the last bid that was called by the auctioneer when the auction stopped. The 4 persons who drop out of the bidding process are allocated 8 tokens each round.

This '*common price*' auction mechanism was chosen for several reasons: (1) the price paid for the large-endowment position should theoretically correspond with the maximum value placed on this position by the subject with the fourth highest valuation – the four subjects who won the auction should be those who placed the highest value on having the large endowment; (2) the price paid for the large-endowment position was common to all auction winners – simplifying the decision setting; and (3) the price paid for the large-endowment position was common knowledge to all subjects.

An overview of results from the experiments utilizing the common price auctions is organized around two design cells: (1) No-Communication – Common Price Auction Assignment (NC-CP) and (2) Communication – Common Price Auction Assignment (C-CP). The discussion focuses first on individual token allocations to Market 2, followed by a summary of rent accrual as a percentage of optimum. This overview will be followed by a discussion of agreements to specific allocation rules, adherence to these agreements and auction prices.

Individual Decisions. Figure 1 displays frequency distributions of individual Market 2 decisions for both design cells. As seen in the no-communication condition, NC-CP, the modal Market 2 allocation is 8 tokens. Recall that low-token endowment subjects had an endowment of 8 tokens. The high frequency at 8 can be attributed primarily to those subjects allocating their entire endowments in the CPR in numerous decision rounds (consistent with the Nash prediction). Focusing on specific decision rounds, however, the pattern of allocations at the individual level is not strictly consistent with the Nash prediction of 8 tokens for low-endowment subjects and 16 tokens for high-endowment subjects. To illustrate this result, consider the 10th round of experiment 3 of the NC-CP design. The four large-endowment subjects allocated 16, 11, 16 and 21 tokens to Market 2, while the four small-endowment subjects allocated 8, 7, 8 and 8 tokens to Market 2. The results from this decision round are representative of decision rounds in other NC experiments. A high percentage of low-endowment subjects allocate their entire endowment of 8 tokens to Market 2, while Market 2 allocations by high-endowment subjects is quite varied, falling primarily in the range of 14 to 24 tokens.[11]

The opportunity to communicate led to a noticeable change in Market 2 allocations. With the allocation rules agreed upon in communication

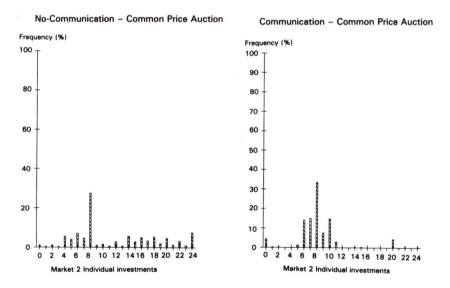

Figure 1. Individual Investments – Market 2 Frequencies Across Design Conditions.

---

11. Walker et al. (1990) also found little support for the Nash equilibrium prediction at the individual decision level.

rounds, subjects concentrated their aggregate Market 2 allocations near the optimal allocation of 56 tokens. In the C-CP condition, individual Market 2 allocations were clustered in the range of 6–10 tokens.

Rents. Rents could be dissipated through an excessive allocation of tokens to Market 2 and/or by the bidding competition for token endowments. First consider rent dissipation from overallocation to Market 2. Table 2 displays summary information regarding the level of rents generated across the two design conditions. In the no-communication condition, mean rent accrual was 45.8%, relatively close to that predicted by the Nash equilibrium (48.9%). The opportunity to communicate led to a noticeable shift toward optimality. In condition C-CP, overall rents increased to an average of 96.1%. Thus, even in an environment of extreme heterogeneity in subject endowments, communication remains a powerful mechanism for promoting coordination.

Table 2. Rents as a Percentage of Optimum: Common Price Auction

	No-communication rounds (%)		Communication rounds (%)	
Experiment no.	1–5	6–10	11–15	16–20
1	61	54	91	90
2	31	29	98	98
3	58	68	98	98
4	34	30	97	100

Auction Prices. One would expect auction prices to be dependent upon subjects' expectations of the value of having 24 tokens rather than 8. One possible source of these expectations is the value of the 16 additional tokens at the Nash equilibrium in the CPR game. The expected payoff for subjects with the small endowment is $0.56 per round, while that for large-endowment subjects is $1.36, a difference of $0.80 per round. Because auction winners were endowed with an additional 16 tokens in each of 10 rounds, this leads to a prediction of $8.00 as the auction price. On the other hand, auction prices could be consistent with other expectations. For example, in conditions allowing for face-to-face communication one might conjecture that subjects might be forward looking in the sense that they anticipate group cooperation with an allocation to Market 2 of 64 tokens (the level of Market 2 allocations that they seem to perceive to maximize earnings). This conjecture yields a wide range of possible payoffs ($4.80 to $24.00) depending upon the distribution of tokens one anticipates for allocations to Market 2.

As displayed in Table 3, auction prices were similar across the eight com-

Table 3. Common Price Auctions: Prices and Effects on Potential Earnings

No-communication		Communication	
Auction price	Earning as % of optimum	Auction price	Earnings as % of optimum
$5.25	53	$8.00	66
$7.75	26	$7.25	74
$9.50	43	$9.75	65
$8.25	26	$7.00	75

mon price auctions. The four NC-CP auctions generated prices of: (1) $5.25, (2) $7.75, (3) $9.50 and (4) $8.25 for an average of $7.69. The four C-CP auctions generated prices of: (1) $8.00, (2) $7.25, (3) $9.75 and (4) $7.00 for an average price of $8.00. The competitive bidding for obtaining the large-endowment position dissipated rents beyond that due to overappropriation to Market 2. This point is illustrated in Table 3, where actual earnings (net of auction prices) are reported as a percentage of maximum possible earnings.

Allocation Rules: Summary. In all experiments in the C-CP design, subjects adopted allocation rules that explicitly attempted to equalize net payoffs (net of auction price), while achieving close to optimal allocation in Market 2. A few representative comments illustrate the nature of the discussion process:

> 'We have to decide which is the best number . . . I think the best number is 64. . . .'
> 'Obviously we want to maximize our group return, right? . . . that's at 64.'
> 'We need to allow the people who bid for the 24 to make up their bid price.'[12]

In 36 of the 40 decision rounds, rules designed to equalize net payoffs resulted in subjects choosing allocation rules that allowed large appropriators to allocate more to Market 2 than the small appropriators. The most commonly agreed-to allocation rule was a Market 2 allocation of 10 tokens by each large-endowment subject and 6 by each small-endowment subject. Under this rule, large-endowment subjects had 62.5% of the total token allocation to Market 2, compared to their 75% share of total token endowment. Thus, this most commonly used rule is weakly proportionate with endowment shares.

---

12. Why 64? The summary table subjects received for payoff returns from Market 2 shows possible levels of Market 2 allocations (and resulting total, average and marginal returns) for allocation levels beginning at 6 tokens and ending with 128 – with intervals of 6 or 7 tokens. Sixty-four tokens is the level of allocation shown on the table to maximize group returns from Market 2. Thus, as observed in many experiments, subjects tended to ignore marginal returns and focus on a total return instead.

Defections. The occurrence of defections on agreed-upon allocation schemes was relatively minor across the set of four experiments. Agreements were reached in all 40 decision rounds. At least one subject defected in 6 of these 40 decision rounds and the overall defection rate was 7 out of 320 individual allocation decisions (2.2%). In all but 3 instances, however, the magnitude of the defection was no more than 2 tokens above the agreement. Further, defection did not lead to a breakdown of subjects' ability to adopt agreements in any of the four experiments.

Treatment 2: Discriminative Price Auction

The results from the four common price auction experiments illustrate the power of face-to-face communication as a mechanism to facilitate cooperation, even with heterogeneous agents. The second treatment condition was designed to investigate the robustness of this result. As noted, in the common price auction treatment condition agreements were designed so that 'auction winners' – the subjects who were assigned the large endowment – were able to recoup their auction investment. We conjectured that this rule selection was facilitated by using a mechanism that yielded a single, publicly known, price.

Experiments utilizing a second auction mechanism were designed to investigate this conjecture. A discriminative price sealed-bid auction was used. Prior to the ten decision rounds with no-communication and again prior to the ten decision rounds with communication, the subjects received a set of instructions summarized as follows:

> For each of the next 10 rounds four subjects will be assigned 8 tokens, while the other four will be assigned 24. Tokens will be assigned using an auction in which each subject bids for the right to have 24 tokens. In the auction, each subject will privately submit a bid stating the amount they are willing to pay to receive 24 rather than 8 tokens each round for the next 10 rounds. None of the bids will be announced. The 4 subjects with the 4 highest bids will be allocated 24 tokens each round for the next 10 rounds. They will pay a one-time fee equal to their bid. The 4 persons with the 4 lowest bids will be allocated 8 tokens each round and pay no fee. If two persons tie with the fourth highest bid, the auctioneer will randomly choose which of the subjects with the tied bids will pay the fee and receive 24 tokens and which will receive 8 tokens.

The '*discriminative*' auction mechanism was chosen for two reasons: (1) it increased the complexity of the decision setting – subjects with winning bids paid different prices for endowment positions; and (2) it added a form of incomplete information in the decision setting, since individuals paid different prices that were not publicly reported.

Three experiments were conducted using the discriminative price (DP) auction. Results are reported for two design cells: (1) No-Communication – Discriminative Price Auction Assignment (NC-DP) and (2) Communication –

Discriminative Price Auction Assignment (C-DP). Because the results from these three experiments are similar to those obtained using the common price auction, the focus will be primarily in terms of summary observations.

Rents.   Table 4 displays information regarding the level of rents generated across the two design conditions. In the no-communication condition, rent accrual was 57.1%, somewhat higher than that predicted by the Nash equilibrium (48.9%). As with the CP design, the opportunity to communicate led to a noticeable shift toward optimality. In condition C-DP, overall rents increased to an average of 93.16%. Thus, even in this environment of heterogeneity in subject endowments and incomplete information regarding costly investments, communication remained a powerful mechanism for promoting coordination.

Table 4. Rents as a Percentage of Optimum: Discriminative Price Auction

	No-communication rounds (%)		Communication rounds (%)	
Experiment no.	1–5	6–10	11–15	16–20
1	67	76	98	98
2	67	46	94	88
3	46	45	85	96

Auction Prices.   The discriminative price auction allows the observation of both 'winning' and 'losing' bids, as well as heterogeneity in bids. The bid results from the three NC-DP and C-DP conditions are summarized in Table 5. The heterogeneity in bids is considerable, with low bids in the neighborhood of $0.02 and high 'winning' bids as high as $15.00. As with the CP condition, the winning bids represent significant losses in rents, as shown in Table 5.

Table 5. Discriminative Price Auctions: Price and Effects on Potential Earnings

No-communication		Communication	
Auction prices range	Earnings as % of optimum	Auction prices range	Earnings as % of optimum
$3.01–$9.03	60	$4.80–$9.60	73
$5.50–$12.00	45	$6.00–$15.00	59
$5.00–$10.80	37	$6.00–$11.00	64

Allocation Rules and Defections: Summary.   We conjectured that the heterogeneity in auction prices and limited information generated by the discriminative price auction would yield (a) sharing rules that were more complex than those observed with the common price auction and/or (b) an increased frequency of breakdown in agreements. In particular, we conjectured that since auction prices and endowments were private information, subjects might strategically misrepresent their situation in order to bargain for a more favorable sharing rule. In actuality, subjects tended to reveal their situation truthfully or remain silent in communication sessions in discussions related to endowment size and auction prices. Because of this behavior, asymmetric information had very little impact on the form of agreements, but did appear to increase defections somewhat.

Parallel to the common price experiments, in all three experiments the subjects tended to focus on a group allocation of 64 tokens allocated to Market 2. In experiments 1 and 2, the agreements were primarily an allocation of 6 tokens by small-endowment subjects and 10 by large-endowment subjects. In experiment 3, the early agreement was an allocation of 8 tokens by all subjects, later modified to an allocation of 9 tokens and 8 tokens by large- and small-endowment subjects, respectively. Similar to the common price experiments, sharing rules were weakly proportionate with endowment shares.

Agreements were reached in 30 of 30 decision rounds. In 15 of 30 decision rounds – 33 of 240 (13.8%) individual decisions – at least one subject was observed to have defected. Most defections were small, one or two additional tokens allocated to Market 2. In a few instances, however, large-endowment subjects allocated as many as 14 tokens over the agreed-upon level. In all instances, groups were able to overcome such defections and maintain Market 2 allocation levels closer to optimum than observed in the no-communication decision rounds.

Incomplete Contracting in the Laboratory

Consider incomplete contracting from the perspective of international relations, for example a military alliance. Countries can initially expend resources in adapting their military structures or technologies to complement those of other alliance members. The situation can result in a potential 'free rider' problem, however, where countries strategically underinvest in adaptation, relying on others to make alliance-improving investments. In particular, this free rider problem arises because the costs of adaptation are private, but the benefits are joint. This underinvestment dilemma can be somewhat attenuated by crafting rules that link shares of the benefits created by the alliance to alliance-specific investments.

This section examines the private investment and benefit-sharing process in incomplete contracts, building on the experimental research of Hackett (1993, 1994). The theoretical research by Grossman and Hart (1986) and others has led to what can be viewed as the standard incomplete contracting model.[13] The model describes a one-shot game with two stages, an investment stage and a negotiation stage.

The incomplete contracting decision problem is implemented in our experiments as a product-improving innovation. A buyer and seller have agreed to a vertical joint venture in which they will trade a fixed quantity of some good in the future, after which the relationship will be terminated.[14] The parties are assumed to have already agreed on a basic design for the good, the value and cost of which are normalized to zero. All decisions are therefore related to implementation of a quality-enhancing product innovation. The innovation is in the works at the time the parties agree to contract, but the value and the cost associated with this improvement have a stochastic component that is not realized until after the buyer and the seller have made independent investments in value and cost, respectively.

While contracting parties may fix a price up front, the circumstance of interest is one in which price is (re)negotiated after stochastic shocks to demand and cost are realized.[15] Given the simple nature of the model, ex post price determination is zero sum – equivalent to determining a surplus-sharing rule.

The Laboratory Incomplete Contracting Process

The laboratory incomplete contracting process is outlined in Figure 2. In the first stage, the buyer's induced value (V) of the product improvement is

---

13. Accessible versions of this model are presented in Hart and Holmstrom (1987), Tirole (1988), and Holmstrom and Tirole (1989). While this is one of the most influential incomplete contracting models, there certainly are others, such as those described in Wiggins (1991).

14. The example that follows frames incomplete contracts in the context of a vertical relationship between a buyer and seller, as is also done in the experiments. As in Grossman and Hart (1986), however, incomplete contracts can equivalently be framed in the context of lateral or horizontal relationships, such as professional partnerships.

15. It is also possible that extensive terms are fixed up front, but contract incompleteness occurs because the parties cannot prevent future renegotiations of terms. Grossman and Hart (1986) argue that ex post contract negotiations occur when one party can credibly threaten to withhold deployment of assets required to transact exchange if price is not (re)negotiated. This credible threat is made feasible in the laboratory experiments below by giving both parties the capacity to prevent implementation of the product improvement. Preventing ex post contract negotiations may be either undesirable (e.g. terms are intentionally left incomplete because the value of ex post adjustment outweighs the cost) or infeasible (e.g. it is very difficult to fashion renegotiation-proof contracts). Factors that lead to ex post negotiation include stochastic shocks to demand and cost, and unobservable attributes of the other contracting parties such as their tastes for opportunism, their norms of distributive justice or their preferences toward absolute versus relative payoffs. The focus of this experimental study is on behavior within a particular contract structure; the question of what factors influence subject's choice of contract structure is addressed in Hackett et al. (1993).

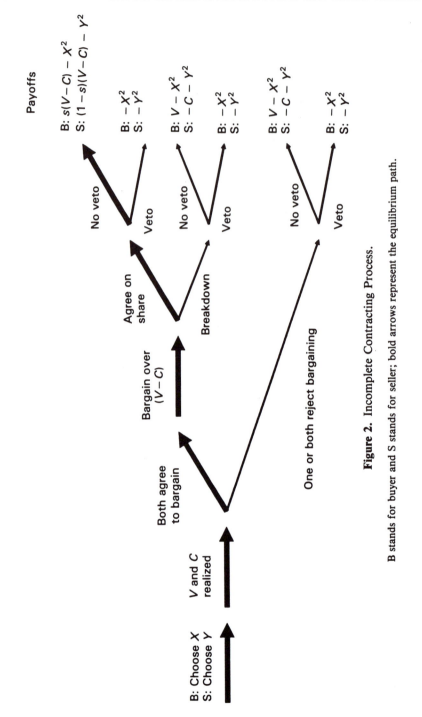

Figure 2. Incomplete Contracting Process.

B stands for buyer and S stands for seller; bold arrows represent the equilibrium path.

uncertain and can either be 'high' (V_h) with probability X or 'low' (V_l) with probability $(1 - X)$. Similarly, the seller's induced cost (C) of the product improvement is uncertain and can either be 'low' (C_l) with probability Y or 'high' (C_h) with probability $(1 - Y)$. The process begins with the buyer and seller independently making investments that increase expected value and decrease expected cost, respectively. To simplify the investment decision, buyers choose X, the probability that value is high, by choosing a number $0 \leq X \leq 1$ at (sunk) cost X^2. Likewise, the seller chooses the likelihood that cost is low by choosing a number $0 \leq Y \leq 1$ at (sunk) cost Y^2. In the experiments described below, a 2-cell treatment design is utilized where X and Y are information common to both buyer and seller (CI), and where X and Y are private information (PI).

After the buyer and seller choose X and Y in the first stage, the second stage begins with the realization of value and cost. Value is determined by comparing X to a random number drawn from a uniform distribution over the unit interval; if X is greater than or equal to the random number then value is high, otherwise value is low. Cost is determined in a similar manner by comparing Y to a random number. V and C then become common knowledge. Once value and cost are realized, buyers and sellers are confronted with a bargaining decision and a veto decision. First, a buyer and seller must decide whether to bargain over the rule used to divide realized surplus $(V - C)$.[16] Second, and regardless of whether any bargaining actually occurs, each buyer and seller must decide whether to veto (terminate) the joint venture, which has the effect of causing value and cost to become zero.

In equilibrium, the incomplete contracting model features a successfully negotiated surplus-sharing rule and implementation of the product improvement (no veto).[17] Further, parties foreseeing the outcome of second-stage bargaining compute their optimal first-stage investment. If V and C are independent random variables and if the buyer and the seller are risk-neutral and capable of perfect foresight, then the buyer will choose X^* to maximize:

$$s[X(Y(V_h - C_l) + (1 - Y)(V_h - C_h))$$
$$+ (1 - X)(Y(V_l - C_l) + (1 - Y)(V_l - C_h))] - X^2 \qquad (8)$$

where s is the buyer's (fully anticipated) share of ex post surplus determined through ex post bargaining. The first term is simply the buyer's share of the

---

16. The step allowing subjects to skip bargaining can be omitted with no violence to the properties of the model, as it is equivalent to a breakdown of bargaining in terms of the seller's dominant strategy to veto. This step was added for laboratory investigation so subjects not wanting to bargain would not hold up the others.

17. For a more detailed derivation of this equilibrium see Hackett (1994).

expected value of $(V - C)$. The seller will similarly choose Y^* to maximize

$$(1 - s) [Y(X(V_h - C_l) + (1 - X) (V_l - C_l))$$
$$+ (1 - Y) (X(V_h - C_h) + (1 - X) (V_l - C_h))] - Y^2 \qquad (9)$$

where the first term is the seller's share of the expected value of $(V - C)$. Maximizing equations (1) and (2) with respect to X and Y yields:

$$X^* = [s(V_h - V_l)]/2 \qquad (10)$$

$$Y^* = [(1 - s) (C_h - C_l)]/2. \qquad (11)$$

Ex ante investments in this equilibrium depend on anticipated ex post surplus shares, but these surplus shares are independent of ex ante investments.

The laboratory bargaining setting is based on a variant of the alternating offer protocol developed by Rubinstein (1992) and Stahl (1972). In this procedure the parties alternate making proposals indefinitely until a proposal is accepted or the negotiations break down. Some mechanism is required to give parties an incentive to reach early agreement. The particular mechanism used here is a probability of forced breakdown upon the rejection of a proposal, as described in Binmore et al. (1991). Upon rejection of a proposal, a random move determines whether another round of negotiations will be allowed or whether bargaining will end. The possibility of forced breakdown causes bargainers to discount future payoffs and so creates a motive for reaching immediate agreement.

Subjects and the Decision Setting

Subjects were recruited from economics courses at Indiana University and had no prior experience with the experiment. The experimental setting was computerized. An experimental session consisted of two practice rounds of the two-stage incomplete contracting game followed by eight rounds played for cash payoffs. Each session was played under *one* of the two information conditions.[18] Four experiments were conducted in each treatment condition. Eight subjects were used in each experiment, except in two cases in which poor turnout required the use of six subjects.

The order of events in a given decision round was as described in Figure 2 and is summarized as follows:[19]

---

18. The programming that enforces the information and message constraints of the experiment and which performs record-keeping, is written in FORTRAN and operates on a VAX mainframe computer.

19. To help subjects become familiar with the experimental procedures, without experiencing loss exposure and following Binmore et al. (1991), decisions were made without cash reward in the first two rounds.

Subjects were first randomly and anonymously matched and randomly assigned a buyer or seller status. Next they independently chose a level of investment (X and Y). At the beginning of the second stage, V and C were determined after the random number n was realized and compared to X and Y. To maintain complete privacy in the private information (PI) condition described below, independent draws of n were performed for buyers and sellers.[20] The values of n drawn for buyers in each of the ten rounds were: .04, .65, .38, .38, .02, .60, .72, .12, .87, .21 while the values of n drawn for sellers in each of the ten rounds were: .21, .62, .14, .11, .85, .71, .04, .56, .83, .50.

V and C were then revealed to both parties.[21] Under information condition CI, X and Y were also revealed to both parties. Each subject then chose whether to enter the process of bargaining over ($V - C$). If both parties agreed to bargain, they proceeded into the bargaining phase, alternating offers. Offers were computerized and contained only a proposal for a percentage sharing rule for the joint surplus. In odd-numbered contracting rounds, buyers made the first offer, while in even-numbered rounds, sellers made the first proposal. Rejection of a share offer led to a chance that negotiations would exogenously be ended with no surplus sharing. Following Binmore et al. (1991), the number of allowed rejections before forced breakdown was set in advance.[22] The maximum number of rejections allowed in each of the ten rounds of an experimental session were:

$$9, 2, 11, 2, 10, 7, 7, 16, 12, 8.$$

This is the same set used by Binmore et al. (1991). One cannot statistically reject the hypothesis that upon rejection of the first proposal, a breakdown occurs independently with probability 0.1. Finally, subjects privately and non-cooperatively decided whether to veto. After the veto decision, each subject had their payoff for the round added to their cash account.

Parameters, Treatment Conditions and Predictions

Parameters.   Induced buyer and seller investment incentives were symmetric: V could take on the values of $5.00 or $3.00, while C could take on the values of $2.50 or $0.50. Thus, both buyers and sellers could increase surplus by up to $2.00 with their investment. One advantage of this parameterization was that bargainers could not use investment incentives to infer anything about relative investment levels when investments were

---

20. Only one random number sequence was used in the CI experiments, as the inference problem was eliminated by directly revealing investments.

21. The draws were fixed in advance. Given the samples one cannot statistically reject the hypothesis that n was randomly drawn from the unit interval for either set. Subjects were told that the values of V and C would be made known to both parties. By randomizing whether subjects were buyers or sellers in a given period, it would become clear to the subjects that the announced common knowledge of these parameter values is in fact true.

22. Specifically, subjects were told that '[t]he total number of share offers that can be made by you and the other party is limited and has been fixed in advance. . . . You should reckon that there is a 90 percent chance (33 percent chance in the high discount rate treatments) that at least one more share offer can be made'. Binmore et al. (1991) report initial difficulty in communicating breakdown probabilities to subjects, which led them to fixing them in advance.

unobservable. As noted above, buyer investment (X) occurs at cost X^2, while specific seller investment (Y) occurs at cost Y^2. For example, if a buyer chooses $X = 70$, there is a 70% chance that $V = \$5.00$ and a 30% chance that $V = \$3.00$ and as a consequence the buyer incurs a sunk cost of $0.49.

Treatment Conditions. When investments are common information (CI), X and Y, along with V and C, are shown to the buyer and the seller prior to negotiation. In contrast, when investments are private information (PI), the buyer is not informed of the seller's investment and the seller is not informed of the buyer's investment.

Sharing Rule Predictions. Predictions about behavior and outcomes in this setting depend on the solution theory used. Two theories appropriate to this setting are subgame perfect equilibrium theory and equity theory. First, consider the predictions of a perfect equilibrium model. Let the induced payoffs be the payoffs to a non-cooperative game. Then the 'forced breakdown' sequential bargaining protocol has a unique subgame perfect bargaining equilibrium, where the prediction for buyer and seller surplus shares depends on which party is the first proposer.[23] If the buyer is the first proposer, then the buyer's predicted equilibrium surplus share $s^* = 1 - [\delta/(1 + \delta)]$, while the seller's predicted equilibrium surplus share $(1 - s^*) = [\delta/(1 + \delta)]$, where $\delta = (1 - d)$, and d is the common discount rate. These shares are reversed when the seller is the first proposer. The predictions of the perfect equilibrium benchmark bargaining model can be summarized as follows:

1. All first proposals will be accepted.
2. Given an induced discount rate of 10%, surplus-sharing agreements will feature a first proposer premium of 2.6 percentage points: the first mover is predicted to get 52.6% of surplus and thus the first decider is predicted to get 47.4% of surplus.
3. Surplus shares will be independent of the parties' transaction-specific investment.

An alternative 'equity' theory can also be used in this game setting. As discussed by Adams (1963), Homans (1974), Selten (1978), and Levinthal (1980), among others, traditional equity theory is based on the notion that humans believe that rewards and punishments should be distributed proportionate with recipients' inputs or contributions. Güth (1988, 1992) extends traditional equity theory by developing a behavioral model of distributive justice in which the allocation rule arrived at from bargaining is predicted to depend on the information content of the bargaining setting. The

---

23. See Schelling (1960) for a pioneering discussion of first mover advantages and other strategic moves.

predictions of the equity-theoretic benchmark bargaining model can be summarized as follows:

1. There is no reason why first proposals will not be accepted.
2. No first proposer premia are predicted.
3. In condition PI, where bargainers cannot observe others' investments, the fair allocation rule is based on an *individual equality* rule, in which case surplus is predicted to be divided equally. In condition CI, however, where bargainers can observe each others' investments, bargainers can allocate surplus in proportion to investments. With this additional information, a *strictly proportionate* rule would set the buyer's surplus share $s = X^2/(X^2 + Y^2)$, and the seller's share $(1 - s) = Y^2/(X^2 + Y^2)$. Note that these equity-theoretic predictions are independent of discount rate.

In addition to the predictions that are derived from perfect equilibrium bargaining theory and equity theory, some researchers have argued that bargaining outcomes may reflect the fact that bargainers have different conceptions of what constitutes a fair allocation (Levinthal, 1980; Bolton, 1991; Güth, 1992; Rabin, 1992). Moreover, an individual's 'fairness' type is private information that is costly to credibly transmit to other bargaining parties (Kennan and Wilson, 1993). If bargainers have different fairness types that are private information, then first proposals will not always be accepted, since proposal rejection is a signal of fairness type.

Predictions Related to Investments.   The nature of the surplus-sharing agreements anticipated by contracting parties is a central determinant of their incentives for investment. The perfect equilibrium benchmark model described above predicts a first proposer premium in surplus-sharing agreements. If parties anticipate these premia, the first proposer will have incentive to invest more than the first decider. In contrast, if parties anticipate surplus-sharing rules indexed to shares of investment, this indexing scheme can lead to stronger investment incentives for both parties, and thus enhance contractual efficiency. As a consequence, the following investment predictions are given:

1. Under the perfect equilibrium benchmark model, the first proposer receives a larger share of surplus. Thus, the contracting party to be the first proposer will invest more than the party to be the first decider.
2. Under the equity-theoretic benchmark model, surplus shares are allocated proportionately with shares of transaction-specific investment when these investments are observable. Thus, making investments observable may increase overall investment as both parties attempt to gain greater shares of joint surplus.

Results

There are two interrelated issues of interest: surplus-sharing rules and buyer and seller investments. Given that the incomplete contracting model is solved backwards, surplus-sharing rules are discussed first, in particular the comparative-static predictions regarding each bargainer's information on investments. One of the central predictions that follows from the incomplete contracting model is that investment incentives derive from the surplus-sharing rules anticipated by the contracting parties. Following the discussion of sharing rules, the buyer and seller investment decisions are considered. The analysis utilizes all 8 periods in which subjects received cash payments for their decisions.

Frequency of Successful Agreements in Surplus-sharing Rules. Only about 25% of first proposals were accepted (25.8% under CI and 21.7% under PI). These results are consistent with the notion that parties have heterogeneous fairness types and that these types are private information. Parties use proposal rejection to signal their type. In contrast, the rate of successful bargaining outcomes was 85.8% under CI and 87.5% under PI.[24] It is important to point out that of the 32 instances in which a pairing did not result in a successful agreement, the seller subsequently vetoed in 31 of the 32 cases, a 94% veto rate. Further, of the 208 pairings that resulted in successful agreements, sellers vetoed in only 2 cases, a 1% veto rate. These results for seller veto behavior are generally consistent with the behavioral predictions supporting the equilibrium path in the incomplete contracting model, as shown in Figure 2.

First Proposer Advantage in Surplus-sharing Rules. Mixed evidence is found for a first proposer advantage in agreements. In the CI condition, the difference in mean buyer surplus shares in two samples, differentiated by whether buyers or sellers were first proposers, was only 1.9 percentage points (54.6% vs 52.7%, respectively, significant at the 6% level). In the PI condition, this difference is an insignificant −0.4 percentage points. These

---

24. In a recent survey of alternating-offer bargaining experiments, Ochs and Roth (1989) report that on average between 10% and 29% of first proposals were rejected in the various experimental studies that they surveyed. Moreover, Binmore et al. (1991) found that about 15% of first proposals were rejected using the same bargaining protocol as the present study. These findings stand in sharp contrast to the 75% first proposal rejection rate reported here. Ochs and Roth (1989) found that at least a majority of counterproposals were disadvantageous (the counterproposer's share was higher in the original rejected proposal) in all of the studies that they surveyed. Their findings stand in sharp contrast to the findings reported in the present study. Of 168 pairings in which both parties made at least one proposal, only 6 instances of disadvantageous counterproposals were observed, a 3.6% rate. These findings reinforce the argument that context (framing) is an important determinant of bargaining behavior.

results offer only limited support for predictions of first mover advantage with the discount rate used here.

Evidence of attempts to exercise a first proposer advantage can be examined by exploring whether some proposers offering first proposals that were weighted to their advantage had their proposals rejected or whether proposers did not attempt to extract large first mover premia. This question is investigated with a two-sample comparison of accepted and rejected first proposals across all CI and PI data.[25] First, consider data in which sellers were first proposers. In this case, the mean buyer surplus shares in first seller proposals that were accepted was 50.1%, while mean buyer surplus shares in rejected first seller proposals was 45.2%. This difference is significant at the 2% level (*t*-test). Now consider data in which buyers were first proposers. Mean buyer surplus shares in first buyer proposals that were accepted was 54.3%, while mean buyer surplus shares in *rejected* first buyer proposals was 63.7%. This difference is significant at the 1% level (*t*-test). These results support the notion that first deciders are willing to risk contractual failure in order to limit first proposer premia in sharing rule agreements. The analysis lends force to the argument that there are substantial fairness effects influencing surplus sharing in incomplete contracts.

Buyer and Seller Investments.   The effects of common versus private information on investments is examined by comparing surplus-sharing agreements using ordinary least squares (OLS).[26] The dependent variable is the surplus-share agreement, expressed in terms of the buyer's share. In addition to an intercept and a variable designating the decision period, the independent variables include 'BFP Dummy' (which is zero unless the buyer was the first proposer, in which case it is one), and 'Buyer Investment Cost Share,' which is $X^2/(X^2 + Y^2)$. As shown in Table 6, OLS estimates an intercept coefficient of 40, implying a minimum buyer surplus share of 40%. The coefficient on Buyer Investment Cost Share is 23.67, which means, for example, that if $X^2/(X^2 + Y^2) = 0.6$, then on average the buyer's surplus share will be $40 + 0.6 \times 23.67 = 54.02$. Other variables are not different

25. Treatment effects are tested for in the following way. First, two samples are constructed from the two treatment conditions. Statistical techniques are then used to test the hypotheses that (i) the two samples derive from the same underlying stochastic processes and (ii) the mean values of the two samples are the same. The Wilcoxon test is used for (i) and the *t*-test for differences in sample means is used for (ii). The analysis uses the convention of reporting the surplus-sharing rule using the buyer's surplus share; in all cases the seller's surplus share is simply 100% minus the reported buyer surplus share.

26. Note that since individual surplus shares must fall between 0 and 100%, one might conjecture that two-limit censoring occurs, in which case OLS estimates will be inconsistent. In fact, Tobit estimation yields the same coefficient estimates as OLS, as there are no limit observations on the dependent variable in the sample.

Table 6. Surplus-sharing Agreements Regression (Ordinary Least Squares)

Dependent variable: Surplus-sharing agreement expressed in terms of buyer surplus share
(out of 100%)

Independent variable*	Estimated coefficient	Standard error	t statistic
Intercept	40.00	2.38	16.80
BFP Dummy	1.40	0.927	1.51
Buyer Investment Cost Share	23.67	3.09	7.65
Period	−0.03	0.18	−0.17

*'BFP Dummy' is 1 when buyers were the first proposers and 0 otherwise; Buyer Invest-
ment Cost Share is $X^2/(X^2 + Y^2)$; 'Period' refers to the decision round in the relevant
experimental session. White test: chi-square value = 7.41; maintain H_0 of homoskedasticity
$p > \chi^2 = 0.49$). F statistic: 21.03; reject H_0 that all coefficient estimates are 0 Adjusted
$R^2 = 0.37$

from zero at the 10% level or lower. These results are not consistent with
either the perfect equilibrium or the equity theoretic hypotheses. The perfect
equilibrium benchmark predicts a 0 weight on Buyer Investment Cost Share,
while the equity theory benchmark predicts a 0 intercept and a coefficient of
1.0 for Buyer Investment Cost Share. The analysis suggests that both bargaining power and equity considerations are at work, which is consistent with the
heterogeneous fairness types/private information argument. Those who
invest more tend to get greater surplus shares – a potential source of proportionality between investments in surplus-enhancement and surplus shares.

Recall that somewhat limited evidence of a first proposer advantage was
found in the CI treatment. If these first proposer premia were anticipated,
then the premium gives the first proposer an increased investment incentive
and the first decider a decreased investment incentive. This can be
investigated by constructing two samples based on whether the buyer or the
seller was the first proposer and then comparing buyer shares of overall
investment ($X^2/X^2 + Y^2$). In general, first proposers tended to invest more
than first deciders, but this effect is not significant at the 10% level or below
in either the CI or the PI treatment.

Recall the OLS coefficient estimate on buyer investment as a percentage
of overall investment shows that surplus-sharing agreements placed a 24%
weight on investment cost shares on average in the CI treatment. Thus, the
party who made the relatively larger transaction-specific investment tended
to receive a relatively larger share of joint surplus, despite the fact that these
investments were sunk. While this relationship has a natural fairness interpretation, it may also serve overall contractual efficiency. The linkage between investments and surplus shares identified in the regression provides
buyers and sellers with an increased incentive to invest and as a consequence
enhances the expected joint surplus of the contract. Important to this result

is whether buyers and sellers make significantly greater investments in the CI condition, where investments are common information. Strong support is found for the hypothesis that contracting parties anticipate the linkage between observable investments and surplus-sharing agreements and increase their investment accordingly. Making investments observable raised the mean value of X from 55.2% to 65.9% and the mean value of Y from 52% to 59.8%. Both of these differences are significant at below the 1% level (t-test).

These elevated investments in the CI treatment condition increase the expected joint surplus generated by the incomplete contract. To see this, note first that under the laboratory parameterization used here, the expected *individual* surplus-maximizing investments (under the subgame perfect benchmark assumptions, including surplus-sharing rules independent of specific investments) are that investments equal surplus shares, which from equations (10) and (11) *sum* to 100. Thus expected joint surplus is $2.00. In contrast, the expected *joint* surplus-maximizing investments are $X = Y = 100$, yielding expected joint surplus of $2.50. Evaluating expected joint surplus at the mean X and Y values of 65.9 and 59.8, expected joint surplus is $2.22, which represents an 11% increase in expected joint surplus over the subgame perfect benchmark level of $2.00, and which captures 98% of the maximum available expected joint surplus.

Summary Comments

Using evidence from two illustrative experimental research programs, this paper has explored the role of heterogeneity in individuals' production capabilities and past investments, under varying information conditions, as an obstacle to conflict resolution. Individuals appropriating from a commonly held resource that was subtractable in units of appropriation (1) significantly dissipated rents (reduced efficiency) when placed in a 'stark' institutional setting that did not allow face-to-face communication and (2) successfully crafted sharing rules that coordinated appropriation and increased efficiency when face-to-face communication was possible, despite heterogeneities in input endowments. Individuals negotiating surplus-sharing rules in the context of an incomplete contract successfully negotiated contracts in 86.7% of the total cases and while individuals attempted to negotiate a first proposer premium, proposals with large premia were systematically rejected. Relative to the joint optimum, these individuals underinvested in joint surplus enhancement as predicted.

Both research programs examined common versus private information on individual attributes as a factor affecting sharing agreements and investments. In the CPR decision setting, face-to-face communication generally led to the truthful revelation of information on individual attributes, thus effectively eliminating the private information treatment condition. In the incomplete contract setting, individuals were limited to proposing, accepting or rejecting share offers. This very limited message space led to outcomes sensitive to the information condition. Specifically, when individuals had only private information on investments, the modal sharing rule was 50–50. When investment information was commonly known, individuals linked surplus shares to investments. As a consequence, surplus-enhancing investments were significantly increased.

In both the CPR setting and the incomplete contract setting with common information, individuals negotiated sharing rules that were consistent with broad notions of fairness – in particular, rules were adopted that effectively reduced differences in net payoffs. Such rules had important consequences for efficiency enhancement. In the CPR settings, agreements were structured so as to minimize net payoff differentials, subject to appropriating at a level that maximized group income. In this context, such agreements increased the earnings for all subjects relative to earnings without such agreements. Thus, minimizing net payoff differentials was used as the foundation for creating group commitment to near optimal resource use. Such rules effectively created a cost for cheating since cheating could imply a reversion back to non-agreement behavior. In the incomplete contracting setting, linking surplus shares to investments had the dual effect of reducing net payoff differences and providing stronger incentives for surplus-enhancing investments.

In the CPR study, individuals purchased the rights to larger input-endowment positions and sharing rules were crafted so that these individuals earned a greater proportion of surplus. Likewise, in the contracting study, individuals who made greater surplus-enhancing investments received a larger share of surplus. Field studies of CPRs and long-term contracts often report rule configurations that are proportional to some characteristic of the contracting parties, such as capital holdings or joint surplus-enhancing investments. The evidence from this paper suggests a possible fairness-based behavioral foundation for proportionality in sharing rules.

In summary, the results from the two experimental studies reported above suggest that heterogeneities across individual capabilities and prior investments lead to only a limited constraint on the abilities of parties to craft and adopt joint surplus maximizing agreements. These results stand somewhat in contrast to the field examples described by Libecap (paper 7 in this collection). We offer three possible explanations for these differences.[27] First, in

---

27. A fourth possibility is related to the differences in magnitudes of potential payoffs associated with commons dilemmas in the laboratory versus most field settings.

the experimental settings described here, it was feasible for subjects to craft sharing rules that ensured each person a payoff gain relative to that earned at the status quo. In the field studies reported by Libecap, exogenously imposed sharing rules or restrictions appear to have, in some cases, made it likely that some parties would be made worse off under proposed sharing agreements. Second, in the laboratory, subjects know with certainty the size of their endowment, prior investment, the linkage between investments and outputs, and the value of outputs. In the field, there is considerable incomplete information both within and across bargainers. Finally, in the laboratory settings investigated here, the surplus generating resource does not feature irreversibilities. As Libecap discusses, however, in many field situations learning and negotiation occur as the resource is depleted, without reversibility.

REFERENCES

Adams, J. (1963) 'Toward an Understanding of Inequity', *Journal of Abnormal and Social Psychology* 67: 422–36.

Binmore, Ken, Peter Morgan, Avner Shaked and John Sutton (1991) 'Do People Exploit Their Bargaining Power? An Experimental Study', *Games and Economic Behavior* 3: 295–322.

Bolton, Gary (1991) 'A Comparative Model of Bargaining: Theory and Evidence', *American Economic Review* 81: 1096–136.

Grossman, Sanford and Oliver Hart (1986) 'The Costs and Benefits of Ownership: A Theory of Vertical and Lateral Integration', *Journal of Political Economy* 94: 691–719.

Güth, Werner (1988) 'On the Behavioral Approach to Distributive Justice – A Theoretical and Experimental Investigation', in S. Maital (ed.) *Applied Behavioural Economics*, pp. 703–17. New York: New York University Press.

Güth, Werner (1992) 'Distributive Justice: A Behavioral Theory and Empirical Evidence', EFI Research Paper no. 6461, Stockholm School of Economics, Sweden.

Hackett, Steven (1992) 'Heterogeneity and the Provision of Governance for Common-pool Resources', *Journal of Theoretical Politics* 4: 325–42.

Hackett, Steven (1993) 'Incomplete Contracting: A Laboratory Experimental Analysis', *Economic Inquiry* 31: 278–93.

Hackett, Steven (1994) 'Is Relational Exchange Possible in the Absence of Reputations and Repeated Contact?', *Journal of Law, Economics and Organization* (10): forthcoming.

Hackett, Steven, Edella Schlager and James Walker (1994) 'The Role of Communication in Resolving Commons Dilemmas: Experimental Evidence with Heterogeneous Appropriators', *Journal of Environmental Economics and Management*, forthcoming.

Hackett, Steven, Steven Wiggins and Raymond Battalio (1993) 'The Endogenous Choice Between Contracts and Firms: An Experimental Study of Institutional Choice', mimeo. Bloomington, IN: Indiana University.

Hardin, Russell (1982) *Collective Action*. Baltimore, MD: Johns Hopkins University Press.

Hart, Oliver and Bengt Holmstrom (1987) 'The Theory of Contracts', in Truman Bewley (ed.) *Advances in Economic Theory: Fifth World Congress*, pp. 168–202. New York: Cambridge University Press.

Holmstrom, Bengt and Jean Tirole (1989) 'The Theory of The Firm', in Richard Schmalensee and Robert Willig (eds) *Handbook of Industrial Organization*, pp. 61–133. Amsterdam: North-Holland.

Homans, George (1974) *Social Behavior: Its Elementary Forms*. New York: Harcourt Brace Jovanovich.

Johnson, Ronald and Gary Libecap (1982) 'Contracting Problems and Regulation: The Case of the Fishery', *American Economic Review* 72: 1005–22.

Kanbur, Ravi (1991) 'Heterogeneity, Distribution and Cooperation in Common Property Resource Management'. Washington, DC: World Bank.

Kennan, John and Robert Wilson (1993) 'Bargaining with Private Information', *Journal of Economic Literature* 31: 45–104.

Levinthal, Gerald (1980) 'What Should Be Done with Equity Theory?', in Kenneth Gergen, Martin Greenberg, and Richard Willis (eds) *Social Exchange: Advances in Theory and Research*, pp. 27–55. New York: Plenum Press.

Libecap, Gary and Steven Wiggins (1984) 'Contractual Responses to the Common Pool: Pro-rationing of Crude Oil Production', *American Economic Review* 74: 87–98.

Ochs, Jack and Alvin Roth (1989) 'An Experimental Study of Sequential Bargaining', *American Economic Review* 79: 355–84.

Ostrom, Elinor (1990) *Governing the Commons: The Evolution of Institutions for Collective Action*. New York: Cambridge University Press.

Ostrom, Elinor, James Walker and Roy Gardner (1992) 'Covenants With and Without a Sword: Self-governance is Possible', *American Political Science Review* 86(2): 404–17.

Rabin, Matthew (1992) 'Incorporating Fairness Into Game Theory and Economics', mimeo. Berkeley, CA: University of California.

Rubinstein, Ariel (1982) 'Perfect Equilibrium in a Bargaining Model', *Econometrica* 50: 97–110.

Schelling, Thomas (1960) *The Strategy of Conflict*. Cambridge, MA: Harvard University Press.

Selten, Reinhard (1971) 'A Simple Model of Imperfect Competition Where 4 Are Few and 6 Are Many', *International Journal of Game Theory* 2: 141–201.

Selten, Reinhard (1978) 'The Equity Principle in Economic Bebavior', in H. Gottinger and W. Leinfellner (eds) *Decision Theory and Social Ethics*, pp. 289–301. Dordrecht, Holland: Reidel.

Stahl, Ingomar (1972) *Bargaining Theory*. Stockholm: Economics Research Institute.

Tirole, Jean (1988) *The Theory of Industrial Organization*. Cambridge, MA: MIT Press.

Walker, James, Roy Gardner and Elinor Ostrom (1990) 'Rent Dissipation in a Limited-access Common-pool Resource: Experimental Evidence', *Journal of Environmental Economics and Management* 19: 203–11.

Wiggins, Steven (1991) 'The Economics of the Firm and Contracts: A Selective Survey', *Journal of Institutional and Theoretical Economics* 147: 603–61.

Wiggins, Steven and Gary Libecap (1987) 'Firm Heterogeneities and Cartelization Efforts in Domestic Crude Oil', *Journal of Law, Economics, and Organization* 3: 1–25.

Part III

Evidence from the Field

6. CONSTITUTING SOCIAL CAPITAL AND COLLECTIVE ACTION

Elinor Ostrom

The importance of physical capital to economic growth and development is generally accepted. The importance of social capital, particularly local institutions, has not generally been recognized. Focusing primarily on the technology of constructing physical capital and ignoring social capital formation has been, however, a misplaced strategy in both domestic and international affairs. Substantial sums have been spent on the construction of unsustainable infrastructure due to the lack of appropriate institutions (Harral and Faiz, 1988; Israel, 1987; E. Ostrom et al., 1993; Repetto, 1986; World Bank, 1988).

All forms of capital are created by spending time and effort in transformation and transaction activities. Physical capital is the arrangement of material resources to improve flows of future income (Lachmann, 1978). Social capital is the arrangement of human resources to improve flows of

Earlier versions of this paper were presented at the conference on 'Heterogeneity and Collective Action', Indiana University, Bloomington, Indiana, 14–17 October 1993, the conference on 'Hierarchies, Markets, Power in the Economy: Theories and Lessons from History', Castellanza (Varese), Italy, December 15–17 1993 and at the Harvard–MIT Joint Research Seminar on International Environmental Affairs: Institutions, Politics, and Policies, Cambridge, Massachusetts, 3 February 1994. Comments by participants in the above and by Steven Hackett, Robert Keohane, Myungsuk Lee, Lisa Martin, Robert Putnam, Kenneth Shepsle and James Walker on earlier drafts are appreciated. The support of the Ford Foundation (Grant no. 920-0701) is gratefully acknowledged.

future income.[1] Human capital is the knowledge and skills that individuals bring to the solution of any problem. Social capital is created by individuals spending time and energy working with other individuals to find better ways of making possible the 'achievement of certain ends that in its absence would not be possible' (Coleman, 1966: S98).

The presence of physical capital is usually obvious to external onlookers. School buildings, roads and engineering works are not hard to see. Social capital, on the other hand, may be almost invisible unless serious efforts are made to inquire about the ways that individuals organize themselves and the rights and duties that they follow – sometimes with little conscious thought. If external agents of change do not expect that villagers in developing countries have effective ways of relating to one another, they may easily destroy social capital without knowing what they have done.

Walter Coward (1988) describes, for example, the efforts of government engineers to improve the operation of a water system in Indonesia by removing an old log that served as a 'primitive' water divider and replacing it with a modern, concrete division box. The modern device, however, did not enable the farmers to allocate water consistent with the water rights of farmers on the two channels. Their indigenous structure had done this allocation automatically. The property rights of the farmers along the branches were embedded in the way that the physical structure divided the water. In this instance, the construction of new physical capital without consulting the farmers did not permanently destroy the productive way that farmers related to one another. Soon after the engineers modernized the system, the farmers simply rejoined the two channels below the modern box and reinstalled a traditional device that allocated water between the two branches according to the property rights of those farming on each branch. This story has a happier ending than many efforts to improve irrigation systems by external investments in physical capital alone. The investment in modern engineering works was wasted and farmers had to invest more time and effort in rebuilding the physical works to conform to their social capital. The farmers' organization, however, was not destroyed and it was able to rebuild a structure to allocate water consistent with the rights and duties of farmers as locally understood.

Other efforts to construct physical capital have not had such happy

---

1. All forms of capital can be used to improve the flow of future income for at least some individuals. For a pattern of social relationships or a set of institutions to be considered as capital, it does not need to achieve optimality for all participants – simply an improvement in the benefits of those who create the social capital. All forms of capital can be used by some groups to gain advantage over other groups or even to harm others while benefitting from the harm. Tle physical capital involved in any one country's missile sites has the potential of generating vast destruction in achieving the 'benefit' of national defence.

endings. Billions of dollars have been spent building highways, irrigation systems, power generation and transmission facilities and providing technical assistance to the governments of developing countries related to the use of the new high-tech physical capital put in place. The overall dismal record is well known. Many of the projects have not been sustainable (E. Ostrom et al., 1993). That is, after the project has been completed, the net flow of costs has exceeded the net benefits of the project. Further, the massive loans assumed by developing countries have proved to be more of a burden to long-run development than the desired stimulus to further capital investment and economic growth.

In this paper, I first develop the concept of social capital. Then I focus on one type of social capital, that of local institutions designed in extended trial and error processes by participants within a larger political structure provided by higher level governments. Building on the work of Jack Knight (1992) and others, I represent the process of selecting rules as a bargaining process. I start with a setting where the parties are relatively homogeneous in all regards. Then, I analyze how heterogeneity of capabilities affects the process of bargaining over rules under circumstances where those with lesser capabilities have or do not have resources of value to those with greater capabilities. While most of the paper is theoretical in nature, a short overview of recent findings from a study of irrigation systems in Nepal is presented in support of the theoretical results. The last section of the paper begins to address how crafting rules is embedded in layers of action situations that have complex feedback loops when viewed as a dynamic process.

Creating Physical and Social Capital

Physical capital opens up some opportunities while restricting others. The purpose of physical capital is to increase the flow of future benefits achieved by a group of beneficiaries beyond those achievable without the presence of the capital. Social capital also opens up some opportunities while restricting others. Crafting institutions – sets of rules that will be used to allocate the benefits derived from a physical facility and to assign responsibility for paying the costs of the facility – is one form of investing in social capital (E. Ostrom, 1990, 1992).[2] Rules open up some opportunities, while restricting others. Without enforceable rules that allocate both rights and duties, some individuals would be tempted to free ride on the efforts of others or to take more than their share of water.

---

2. Other forms of social capital may also exist – networks, norms and social beliefs that evolve out of processes that are not investment activities (Putnam, 1993a).

Creating the social capital that makes physical capital operational over the long run is something that individuals who successfully use physical capital repeatedly do, but it is not as well understood as the technology of constructing physical capital. Given the multitude of nested collective-action problems involved in the creation of institutions, explaining how individuals overcome these problems is not easy. Further, the diverse sources of asymmetries among participants make it even more difficult to explain how individuals solve thorny distribution problems (see Johnson and Libecap, 1982; Hackett, 1993; Hackett et al., 1994; and papers 5 and 7 in this collection).

Processes that create social capital do occur, however, in thousands of disparate local settings. Similar processes occur at the international level (Young, 1982; Keohane, 1989; Dasgupta and Mäler, 1992; McGinnis and Ostrom, 1993; Haas et al., 1993). An extensive literature including many case studies describes institutions that have been constituted by those affected in all corners of the world.[3] The lack of theories of institutional change and development based on firm microfoundations has limited the capacity of scholars to develop cumulative understanding of how individuals develop their own social capital in the form of rules used by self-governing communities.[4] Recent work on institutional analysis and institutional change begins to provide a solid theoretical foundation for understanding the conditions needed for individuals to craft or evolve their own institutions and enforce these institutions themselves (see Bates, 1988; Calvert, 1994; Libecap, 1989; North, 1990; E. Ostrom, 1990; E. Ostrom et al., 1994; V. Ostrom et al., 1993).

Substantial progress has been made in the explanation of how institutions evolve to solve repeated coordination problems where most of the participants are symmetric in regard to relevant attributes (Lewis, 1969; Sugden, 1986).[5] These theoretical accounts are useful and important in explaining the evolution of institutions in the types of settings specified where the primary problem is selecting one out of multiple equilibria that have relatively similar distributional effects. Once an equilibrium is selected, it is self-enforcing in the sense that all participants are motivated to select strategies consistent with that equilibrium (Telser, 1980).

---

3. See F. Martin (1989/1992), *Common-Pool Resources and Collective Action*, Vols. 1–2 for an extensive bibliography of case studies describing institutions related to the use of common-pool resources (CPRs). Volume 3 of the bibliography by C. Hess is forthcoming in 1994. In June 1994 these bibliographies will be mounted on the IU-B Libraries Gopher under the menu 'Workshop in Political Theory and Policy Analysis'. To access the gopher via the Internet, gopher to: lib-gopher.lib.indiana.edu (129.79.34.15) port 70.

4. Self-consciously created rules are not the only form of social capital. When Putnam (1993b) refers to social capital, for example, he means patterns of relationships many of which have come about without much self-conscious design.

5. See also Field (1979) for a critique of this work and L. Martin (1994).

While substantial progress has been made, puzzles remain. How individuals who differ substantially from one another agree to sets of rules with major distributional consequences is not yet fully understood. In an important recent study, Jack Knight (1992) presents a more general theory of institutional change based on the relative bargaining power of participants to account for the evolution or design of institutions. Knight is able to account for a wide diversity of locally evolved social institutions where outcomes are distributed asymmetrically. The 'most important resources' in Knight's account of the bargaining over rules 'are those available to the actors in the eventuality that bargaining is either lengthy and costly or ultimately unsuccessful' (Knight, 1992: 132). Knight places most of his emphasis on explaining the outcomes of rule negotiation processes on the differential status quo position of participants. The 'breakdown point' in a bargaining process is obviously one of the important dimensions affecting the choice of rules to emerge from such a process. It is not, however, the only source of bargaining power that participants can bring to the negotiating table when constituting an organization to overcome collective-action problems (see Elster, 1989).

In this paper, I use a similar theoretical approach to that of Knight for analyzing the process of constituting a self-governing farmers' association to construct and maintain an irrigation system. This example provides a setting in which to examine (1) the process of negotiating rules among both homogeneous and heterogeneous participants, (2) how physical variables affect the relative bargaining power of participants and (3) how external interventions may create disruptive asymmetries as an unintended effect of financial assistance.

While the application is focused on one kind of collective action, many aspects of more general processes involved in creating social capital in the form of rules – particularly those related to other kinds of jointly used physical capital – are captured in the analysis. None of the simple models capture the full richness of the considerations facing participants in field settings. Only two rules are considered at one time, for example, when the number of rules that could be introduced into discussions is much larger. Only pure strategies are considered when mixed strategies could also be analyzed. The models starkly illustrate, however, the major underlying problems that participants face. The purpose of the models is intended to be illustrative of the coarse structure of the types of situations farmers face in homogeneous versus heterogeneous settings rather than being a complete analysis of the full range of situations and strategies that could be undertaken.

Underlying Assumptions

For farmers to seriously consider constituting themselves into even a loose form of association to construct an irrigation system, they would need to share the following:

1. Sufficiently secure land tenure to presume they will reap the longer term benefits of their collective action.

2. The capacity to repeatedly communicate with one another on a face-to-face basis.

3. A common understanding that they would each be able to increase their agricultural yields enough through the provision of an irrigation system potentially to compensate each of them – depending on the sharing formula agreed upon – for the costs of their immediate and long-term investments.

4. A common understanding that they would have to enforce their own rules on a day-to-day basis but could count on external authorities not to interfere in their rule-making, rule-following and rule-enforcement activities.[6]

5. A common understanding of a repertoire of rules that, if enforced, can effectively counteract perverse, short-term incentives.

6. A common understanding that if they agree to a set of rules and follow accepted procedures to signify their agreement, then each participant would be precommitted to follow these rules or be sanctioned by the others for non-conformance.

7. Trust that most of the farmers, who agreed to a set of rules and denoted their agreement in an accepted way, would actually follow these rules most of the time so that the effort to monitor and enforce these rules would not be itself extremely costly.

Thus extensive common knowledge (Aumann, 1976) about the structure of incentives they face, the types of individuals with whom they would be interacting over the long run and alternative ways of structuring their relationships are prerequisites for constituting associations to undertake major, long-term collective action.[7] Those involved also need to switch levels of action from that of a day-to-day operational situation to a rule-making situation. In an operational situation, farmers make decisions about alternative actions to be taken within a set of rules. In a rule-making situation, farmers make decisions about rules that affect the alternative actions

---

6. Earlier non-cooperative game-theoretic models have demonstrated that it is possible for farmers to undertake self-monitoring and self-sanctioning responsibilities even though it is not possible to reduce stealing rates to zero (Weissing and Ostrom, 1991, 1993).

7. The assumptions about common knowledge are *strong* assumptions. If participants had asymmetric and incomplete information, the results would frequently be different.

available in future operational situations.[8] The farmers may meet informally in a tea house, someone's home or at the stream where they plan a
diversion. The procedures used may be quite informal. The essential aspect,
however, is that they have switched from taking actions to making decisions
about rules that constrain and open up opportunities for future actions. If
they can agree to a set of enforceable rules that distribute expected benefits
to each participant greater than expected costs, they are likely to craft a constitutional agreement and start on the long-term process of providing such
a system.

If the set of beliefs previously outlined is not altered by experience so as
to destroy the assessment made by each about the beliefs that others share
and the likely strategies that others will adopt, such a set of farmers would
be able to construct a system and operate it for a long period of time. If the
precommitment that they make by signaling their agreement is followed by
behavior consistent with that precommitment, each farmer's beliefs become
more certain that others will follow the agreement, including sanctioning
non-conformers (see Elster, 1979; Schelling, 1960). Given the dual precommitments and behavior consistent with these precommitments, it is then in
each farmer's interest to conform to the agreed-upon rules most of the
time.[9] In other words, a constitutional agreement is successful not simply
because it creates joint benefits. It is successful when those who contribute
to its continuance expect net benefits for themselves and their families that
are greater than the alternatives available to them.

Nothing is automatic or deterministic about such a process.[10] What is
crucial is that the farmers believe that their individual long-term benefits will
exceed their long-term costs, that they find a set of rules upon which they
can agree and that they adopt strategies that do not constantly challenge the

---

8. There are two broad types of rule-making situations: constitutional-choice and collective-
choice situations. In a constitutional situation, the decision is made whether or not to constitute
some form of association including who is a member, what are the initial operational rules to
be followed and the procedures to be used in the future to make collective choices for the
association. In a collective-choice situation, decisions are made in an ongoing association about
policies to be adopted and operational rules to be changed. These are discussed in the last section
of the paper.

9. It is almost impossible for farmers to follow allocation rules in all instances. Given the
stakes involved, the temptation to shirk or steal can be very large in some circumstances. Even
on systems that have survived for centuries, consistent evidence shows that some shirking and
some stealing is a fact of life (see E. Ostrom, 1990; Weissing and Ostrom, 1991, 1993).

10. Even though it is possible to discover the structure of these situations and array them as
diverse games, which is done in the next section, most of these games have multiple equilibria.
Which of the many equilibria is selected in a particular situation is therefore dependent on many
factors – including the shared beliefs and conceptions held by the participants – that are
localized in time and space.

delicate balance of mutual expectations that they have to maintain to keep the system going over the long run. Some farmers may be left much better off than others. The less advantaged must feel, however, that they receive a positive gain from participation or they will not voluntarily participate.

If experience generates information that they were incorrect in their beliefs about benefits, monitoring effectiveness or the likelihood of others following rules, then the mutual understanding that is necessary for success begins to come unglued. Similarly, if those who are less favored come to feel that they are being taken advantage of by those better favored by the rules, their low but positive economic assessment may be offset by negative feelings engendered by unfair rules. If they are unable to gain better economic returns, change rules again and/or change the frequency with which rules are broken, then a successful operating system at one time may slip into becoming a poorly operating system at another time. Thus, individual incentives depend on farmers' expectations, the viability of the rules they have established, their consequent beliefs concerning overall net benefits and the distribution of benefits and costs.

Homogeneous Situations

Let us assume that 10 farmers own equal-sized plots of land on an alluvial plain. One of the farmers (who has a reputation for designing prudent and well-conceived community works) has proposed a plan to divert a previously untapped mountain stream to their area. If allocated carefully, the source could provide water for three crops for all 10 farmers. The plan involves the construction of a short main canal and two branch canals that each serve five families. The farmers can obtain a low-interest loan in order to purchase some of the needed materials and they have the skills needed to do the actual construction themselves. Figure 1 is a stylized version of the type of irrigation system under consideration. A diversion works at the source sends water

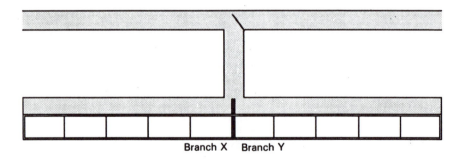

Branch X   Branch Y

Figure 1. A Simple Symmetric Irrigation System.

into a relatively short and uncomplicated canal which is then divided into an X Branch and a Y Branch each serving five plots of equal size.

In order to start the project, the farmers need to agree about the rules that they will use to (1) allocate expected annual benefits from the project and (2) allocate expected annual costs. No one will voluntarily contribute funds and/or hard work to construct an irrigation system unless they believe that their own, discounted flow of future expected net benefits is larger than their share of the costs of construction. For purposes of analysis, we will treat all farmers on each branch as if they formed a single team player facing all farmers on the other branch (also conceptualized as a single team player) in a two-player bargaining game.[11] If they do not reach an agreement about the set of rules they will use, the farmers continue their practice of growing rain-fed crops. The yield that they receive from rain-fed agriculture thus constitutes the 'breakdown' value for each player – what they can expect if no agreement on constructing a new system is achieved.

The general structure of the bargaining situation they face is presented in Figure 2. In this situation, there are two rules being considered: Rule I and Rule J. Both players – Branch X and Branch Y – have to agree to either Rule I or Rule J, or they will not construct the system. If they do not agree, they

Branch Y

		Rule I	Rule J
	Rule I	$(e^I B - f^I C)$, $(g^I B - h^I C)$	SQx, SQy
Branch X			
	Rule J	SQx, SQy	$(e^J B - f^J C)$, $(g^J B - h^J C)$

Figure 2. General Structure of Bargaining Game Over Rules.

---

11. In other words, we will not consider any within-team differences. One could think of the mechanism for achieving this as being of several kinds: (1) a random device picks one farmer from Branch A to bargain with one farmer from Branch B and whatever these two farmers agree (or don't agree) upon binds everyone else on the branch, (2) each set of five families is part of a larger extended family and they each send the head of the family to represent them or (3) each set of five families creates a branch organization to represent them in all decision making and select a branch representative in an annual election. The advantages of using a 2-player bargaining game for this series of models are substantial in terms of the array of questions that can be analyzed using this very simple mechanism. Also I wish to ignore, for the time being, divisions among the players on Branches A and B so I can concentrate on the effect of various changes in physical, economic or social variables on the structure and outcome of the 2-player game.

continue with their current rain-fed agriculture and obtain the status quo yield (SQ_x, SQ_y) from growing one crop a year. In the symmetric situation, the status quo yield is equal for both branches. If both players agree on one of the rules, they will receive each year some combination of the total annual expected benefits (B) and costs (C) associated with providing this system. Both benefits and costs are expressed in crop units.[12] Let us assume that total annual expected benefits exceed total annual expected costs as well as the status quo yield of each branch:

$$(B - C) \geq SQ_x + SQ_y \tag{1}$$

Each branch would most prefer a situation where they obtained all of the benefits and none of the costs. But the other branch would never agree to such a distribution. Without agreement, no one will contribute to the construction of the systems. Rules used to allocate benefits and costs affect the proportion of benefits and costs that each obtain. The proportion of the expected annual benefits received by Branch X will be e^I if Rule I is agreed upon and e^J if Rule J is agreed upon. Similarly, the proportion of expected annual benefits received by Branch Y players is given by g^I or g^J depending on the rule selected. If they agree on Rule I and it assigns 60% of the benefits to Branch X and 40% of the benefits to Branch Y, then $e^I = .60$ and $g^I = .40$.

$$1 \geq e^I, e^J, g^I, g^J \geq 0 \tag{2}$$

$$e^I + g^I = 1 \text{ and } e^J + g^J = 1. \tag{3}$$

Similarly, the coefficients, f^I, h^I, and f^J and h^J are the proportion of costs assigned to the two branches under different rules.

$$1 \geq f^I, f^J, h^I, h^J \geq 0 \tag{4}$$

$$f^I + h^I = 1 \text{ and } f^J + h^J = 1. \tag{5}$$

Let us assume that all farmers are risk-neutral (neither orientated toward taking risks nor avoiding them) and have equal and low discount rates that are omitted from the analysis since their inclusion would not change the results.

Rules to Allocate Benefits.   Let us focus on the authority rules that the farmers could use for allocating water. For our initial consideration of the authority rule related to benefit distribution, we will temporarily assume that the cost of construction and maintenance is equally divided. Let us suppose they consider two rules:

---

12. Alternatively, they could be expressed in labor units as in E. Ostrom and Gardner (1993). In either case it is the basic production function between labor input and crop yields that enables one to use a single metric when denoting both benefits and costs. In a fully monetized economy, one would simply denote benefits and costs as a monetary unit.

Rule 1: All water from the main canal is allocated to Branch Y for one week and Branch X for the next week.

Rule 2: Construct a dividing weir that permanently divides the water in half so that half of the flow of the main canal automatically flows into each branch at all times that water is present in the main branch.

The structure of this game related to these two rules (or any similar rule of equal division) is presented in Figure 3. Since we are assuming for now that their share of the benefits minus the costs of the irrigation system is greater than the status quo yield for both branches (Eq. 1), they face a benign coordination situation. There are two pure strategy equilibria in this game: both choose Rule 1 or both choose Rule 2.[13] Since communication is possible, it can be used to solve this coordination problem. Some of the discussion may relate to variables not taken into account in the above simplified payoffs, if there are any. If one of the farmers is well known for his or her capability and honesty in constructing dividing weirs so that everyone can trust them to divide the water exactly in half,[14] the two branches might be more likely to agree upon Rule 2 because it involves the least continued effort in shifting the water every week from one canal to the other. If none of the farmers knows how to construct an exact dividing weir, they would prefer Rule 1 as it is unambiguous and easy to monitor. Which rule is finally chosen, if they come to an agreement, depends on a variety of situation-dependent variables including the costs of implementing different rules or

Branch Y

		Rule 1	Rule 2
	Rule 1	$(.5B - .5C), (.5B - .5C)$	SQx, SQy
Branch X			
	Rule 2	SQx, SQy	$(.5B - .5C), (.5B - .5C)$

Figure 3. An Initial Illustration.

---

13. In this paper, I am considering only pure strategy equilibria. A mixed strategy does not make sense when the alternative is a rule. One can model rule-breaking behavior using mixed strategies (see Weissing and Ostrom, 1991, 1993). Rules that use one allocation formula during one season and another allocation formula during a second season will be considered as separate rules.

14. Some irrigation systems in Nepal use dividing weirs like this to allocate the flow of a canal according to the agreed-upon proportions (see E. Martin and Yoder, 1983).

whether similar rules have been tried on neighboring systems and worked well in practice.

Rules to Allocate Costs.   Now, let us focus on a second type of rule – one related to how the farmers allocate responsibilities for providing labor during construction and for the annual maintenance efforts. The rules proposed may or may not be quite so symmetric in their effect. If there were one adult son in each of the families on Branch X and no adult sons on Branch Y, someone on Y might well propose the following rule:

Rule 3: Each family is required to send all adult males in the household for each labor day devoted to the irrigation system.

Someone in Branch X might, however, propose the following rule:

Rule 4: Each family is required to send one adult male for every labor day devoted to the irrigation system.

Assuming that either Rule 1 or Rule 2 had already been agreed upon, these proposals would result in a bargaining game like that of Figure 4.

Assuming that the increased yield exceeds the costs that would be imposed on Branch X under Rule 3 ($.5B - .67C > SQx$) both branches would be better off agreeing to either rule as contrasted to having no system. But Rule 3 assigns a higher proportion of net benefits to Branch Y, while Rule 4 treats both branches equally. Consequently, the debate between the two branches over these two rules might be considerable. Branch Y could argue that the irrigation system was providing benefits for all households and that all adult males should pitch in. Branch X could argue that they should not have to contribute twice as much labor as Branch Y simply because they had more sons. There are again two pure strategy equilibria to this game: both choose Rule 3 or both choose Rule 4. Since the results are asymmetric, however, which rule is chosen depends on the relative bargaining strength of the participants. For Branch Y to get its way, it would have to precommit

| | | **Branch Y** | |
		Rule 3	Rule 4
Branch X	Rule 3	$(.5B - .67C), (.5B - .33C)$	SQx, SQy
	Rule 4	SQx, SQy	$(.5B - .5C), (.5B - .5C)$

Figure 4. A Second Illustration.

itself in a credible manner to this rule being an essential precondition to obtaining its agreement to the plan for the irrigation system.

On the other hand, Branch Y could recognize the importance of establishing a good continuing relationship and that if Branch X resented being forced to agree to a rule due to a weak bargaining situation, Branch Y might face trouble later getting Branch X to abide by the agreement on a continuing basis. Even though Branch Y really thinks it is inappropriate for one-third of the adult males, who are benefitted by the system, to sit at home while the other two-thirds do all the work, its members might recognize that one male per household is considered a fair rule in this setting and not push this proposal to the point of breakdown of negotiations. Further, it is unlikely that the set of rules brought forward for consideration will include only Rule 3 and Rule 4 when one branch is disadvantaged by one of the rules under consideration.

Branch X could, for example, propose Rule 5 that would make Branch Y change its absolute preference for Rule 3 over Rule 4:

Rule 5: All water from the main canal must be allocated to a branch in proportion to the amount of labor that the branch provides for construction and annual maintenance.[15]

Now whether Branch Y prefers Rule 3 or Rule 4 depends on whether it is combined with Rule 5 or Rule 1 (ignoring Rule 2, which has an identical outcome function). If the expected benefits of building the system were 100 and the expected costs were 60, the results of different configurations of rules would be as shown in Table 1.

Table 1. Results of Different Configurations of Rules

Rules	Branch X	Branch Y
1 and 3	$.50B - .67C = 10$	$.50B - .33C = 30$
1 and 4	$.50B - .50C = 20$	$.50B - .50C = 20$
5 and 3	$.67B - .67C = 27$	$.33B - .33C = 13$
5 and 4	$.50B - .50C = 20$	$.50B - .50C = 20$

15. This is a proportional distribution rule and would be considered an example of a 'fair rule' according to many criteria such as the one proposed by Selten (1978). A fair rule would be characterized as one where $e = f$ and $g = h$ even though $e \neq g$ and $f \neq h$. Examples of such rules abound in regard to irrigation. The Constitution for the Andhikhola Multipurpose Water Users' Association (a relatively large FMIS located in the Syangja and Papal Districts of Nepal) provides an example of such a rule. In its constitution, a 'share' of the first stage of the project is defined as: '1/25,000 proportion of the water that flows out of the head gate. The initial value of a stage-one share is fixed at five days of labour' (AKWUA Constitution, Section 3c). In this system, some farmers own more shares than others and thus receive more benefits than others. But since every share involves an obligation to contribute five days of labor annually, they also pay costs in the same proportion as they receive water.

Once Rule 5 is introduced into the rule-making situation, Branch Y no longer finds Rule 3 essential to its interests. If combined with Rule 5, Rule 3 leaves it with the worst, rather than the best, payoff.[16]

The process of negotiating about rules is complex and not determined by a small number of factors. While it is useful to model the process as a succession of choices between two rules, the impact of each rule depends on the other rules that have already been agreed upon or are to be discussed in the future. In most constitutional processes, initial agreements to specific rules are tentative. Eventually, the participants must agree to the entire configuration of rules embodied in some form of agreement. The overall effect of one rule may change radically depending on the other rules in the set.

Heterogeneous Situations

Many variables potentially create asymmetries among the players in a choice of rules game. In the previous analysis, we addressed the possibility that the amount of labor available per household could vary among the players. Let us now examine differences in outcomes that result if the assumption of equality in the status quo situation of both branches is changed. This is the major focus of Knight's theory of institutional change. If the farmers on Branch Y are able to obtain a higher yield on their farms depending only on rainfall than the farmers on Branch X ($SQy > SQx$), they could use this asymmetry to their advantage in bargaining over rules. In Figure 5 we illustrate how an asymmetry in the status quo yields of the two players affects their bargaining position. If the status quo yields of both players were equal to A, and I and J represent the net benefits that would be distributed under Rule I and Rule J, any rule that distributed net benefits to the two players along the line connecting I and J could be agreed upon by both players. If, however, Branch Y had a higher status quo yield, then the initial status quo position of the two players could be represented by B on the diagram. Branch Y would no longer agree to Rule I nor to any rule that did not distribute net benefits at least equal to I'. Branch Y's bargaining position is so substantially stronger that it might even be successful in demanding J as the final rule. Exactly which agreement will be reached depends on the norms of fairness shared by participants and their bargaining skills – factors that are not fully taken into account in this simple analysis. The key point is, however, that rules that could be agreed upon if the status quo yields

---

16. This is an example of the linkage of issues discussed by Lisa Martin (paper 4 in this collection).

of both players were equal, are infeasible if the status quo yields were different.[17]

But now let us introduce a substantial asymmetry related to physical location on a canal.[18] Instead of a canal that divides into two small branches, let us assume that the canal enters from one side. Now, the first five plots receive water before the last five plots. Water is sufficient to provide an ample supply for the head-enders, but not for the tail-enders. Irrigators located at the head end of a system have differential capabilities to capture water and may not fully recognize the costs others bear as a result of their actions. In addition, farmers located at the head end of a system receive proportionately less of the benefits produced by keeping canals (located next to or below them) in good working order than those located at the tail. These asymmetries are the source of considerable conflict on many irrigation systems – substantial enough at times to reduce the capabilities of farmers to work together.

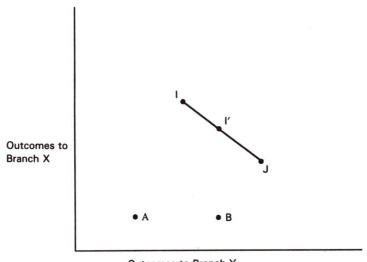

Figure 5. The Effect of Status Quo Positions on the Range of Acceptable Rules.

---

17. In general, if $g^IB - h^IC > g^JB - h^JC = SQy$, Branch Y will only agree to Rule I. If instead, $g^IB - h^IC > g^JB - h^JC > SQy$, Branch Y will strongly prefer Rule I, but could agree to Rule J if placed in a weak bargaining situation. A similar set of conditions exists for Branch X.

18. Another source of heterogeneity among farmers is inequality in the amount of land owned (Lam, 1994).

Yoder (1991) reports on a conversation held in one system where the farmers had difficulties keeping their system in good repair. When the farmers at the head end of a long canal were asked about how they undertook system maintenance, they replied: 'Last year the farmers down there (pointing toward fields lower in the system) used water from the canal but when the canal was blocked by a landslide they refused to help clean the canal even when we called them' (Yoder, 1991: 53). Yoder indicates that the head-end farmers complained bitterly that the tail-end farmers were neglectful and refused to help repair the canal. When one farmer lower in the system was asked similar questions about maintenance, he answered: 'Why should I repair the canal? The farmers with fields up there use all the water anyway' (Yoder, 1991: 53). Why, indeed! This conversation illustrates, from the farmer's perspective, the close interrelationship among the willingness to invest in maintenance, farmers' expectations about obtaining water, their expectations about the contributions others will make and the tensions that can exist among head-end and tail-end farmers. These asymmetries create differences in the relative bargaining power among farmers when debating about the relative merits of different rules.

Farmers at the head end of a system would prefer a set of rules that allowed them to take water first and to take as much water as they needed. Farmers at the tail end of a system would oppose such an authority rule and prefer a set of rules that would enable them to take water first and as much water as they needed. Both rules are used in practice. Frequently, modified versions of these two rules are used in combination. One version of the combined rule is that in one year (or season) a rotation system starts at the head and in the next year (or season) the rotation system starts at the tail.

Farmers at the head end of a system would also prefer rules that required each farmer to maintain only that part of the canal that passed by their own land. Farmers at the tail end of a system would oppose such an authority rule for allocating maintenance responsibilities because head-end farmers are not likely to take into account the cumulative nature of the process of water loss along a stretch of a watercourse. Farmers at the tail end of a system would most prefer rules that assign responsibilities for maintenance in the same proportion as the amount of water that farmers obtain. That way, if the farmers at the head end receive more water, they would have to contribute more resources to maintenance.

To the extent that head-end farmers depend upon the resources that tail-end farmers mobilize to keep a main canal in good working order, the initial bargaining advantage of the head-end farmers is reduced. In other words, if the amount of resources needed to maintain the system is large, farmers at the tail end have more bargaining power in relationship to the farmers at the head end than if the amount of resources needed for maintenance is small.

Several physical factors affect the amount of resources needed to keep a system operating. Let us first assume that the water source serving the system is a perennial spring and that very little work is needed at the headworks to keep such a system operating. We can then posit three kinds of systems depending on the length of the main canal as illustrated in Figure 6. In Figure 6a there is no distance between the water source and the head-enders. In Figure 6b there is a short distance between the water source and the head-enders. In Figure 6c there is a long distance between the water source and the head-enders. The costs of maintaining these three systems will be lowest for a 6a type of system (C'), higher for a 6b type of system (C'') and highest for a 6c type of system (C''').[19]

The bargaining advantage of head-enders in systems like those shown in Figure 6a is much stronger than in systems like those shown in Figure 6b or 6c. Let us illustrate this with a numerical example of the choice of rules game. Let us continue to assume that the expected benefit of the water made available regardless of the length of the canal is 100 units (denoted in labor productivity units) and that the labor costs of maintaining systems like 6a are 25 units, systems like 6b are 50 units and like 6c are 75 units. Thus in all three systems, the expected annual benefits of water obtained are greater than the expected annual labor costs. Let us further assume that two rules were being considered in such a situation:

Rule 6: The head-end farmers are authorized to take as much water as they can put to beneficial use prior to the water being made available to the tail end and farmers contribute labor to maintain the system voluntarily (head-enders have prior-rights rule).

Rule 7: Half of the water is allocated to the head and half of the water to the tail and the labor needed to maintain the system is based on the proportion of water assigned each set of farmers (equal-split rule).

If Rule 6 were agreed upon, let us assume the head-enders would take 65 units of water per year. All labor would be contributed by the head-enders. If Rule 7 were agreed upon, the head-enders would only obtain 50 units of water per year, but would only have to put in one-half of the labor costs per year. Both head-enders and tail-enders would receive zero units of value in

---

19. Labor 'contributions' can be considered a form of taxation. Contributing several weeks of hard physical labor is rarely accomplished unless there is a general agreement to the formulae embedded in the rules of a farmers' system that determine how much labor each farmer is responsible for providing and what collective-choice procedures should be used to determine the total amount of labor needed for any particular season. Once a decision is made that all farmers shall contribute a particular number of days of labor, labor itself becomes a resource to be allocated for the benefit of the commons.

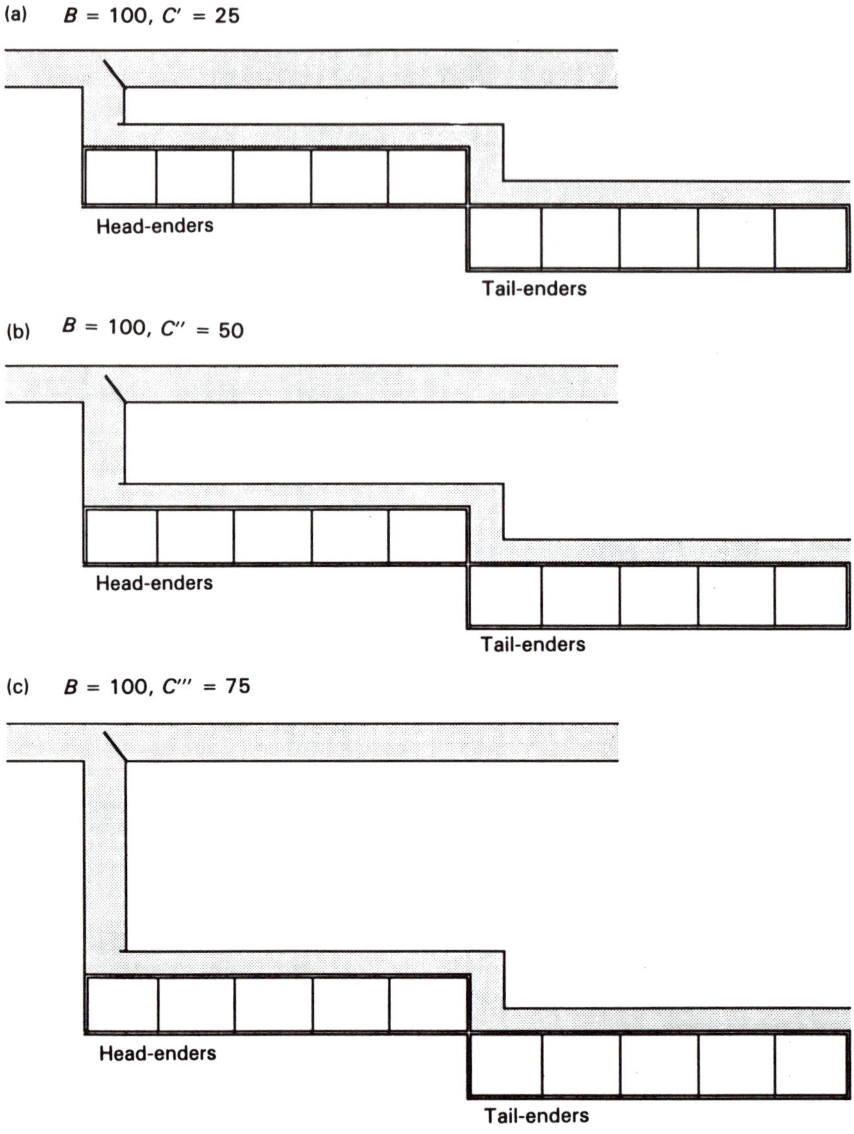

(a) $B = 100$, $C' = 25$

(b) $B = 100$, $C'' = 50$

(c) $B = 100$, $C''' = 75$

Figure 6. Three Irrigation Systems With Increasing Costs of Maintenance.

the situation of a breakdown. The payoffs for the three games are shown in Figure 7.

In systems where the cost of labor input is the lowest ($C' = 25$), there are two equilibria as shown in Game 7a: both choose Rule 6 or both choose Rule 7. The head-enders would prefer Rule 6 and the tail-enders would prefer Rule 7. In 7a, the head-enders would try to make a credible assertion that they will agree to Rule 6 and no other rule and refuse to engage in any further bargaining with the tail-enders. While tail-enders prefer Rule 7, Rule 6 does not leave them as disadvantaged as appears to be the case if one were to examine only the impact of the rule allocating water. Tail-enders would not contribute to the maintenance effort of the headworks. The head-enders would expect an annual return of $65 - 25 = 40$. The tail-enders receive only 35 units, rather than the 37.5 ($100/2 - 25/2 = 37.5$) they could receive under an equal split. But since the tail-enders do not contribute at all to maintenance, they might even be accused of free riding in such a situation. They could, however, point to their willingness to work if and only if they obtained an equal split of the water.

The same two pure strategy equilibria are present in Game 7b where labor costs are 50 units, but the preferences of the players are now reversed. Now the head-enders prefer Rule 7 while the tail-enders prefer Rule 6. In addition, the bargaining power of the tail-enders has improved markedly over Game 7a. The tail-enders can credibly assert that the extra water is not worth the labor contribution. Some head-enders might end up agreeing to Rule 6. Under Rule 6, the tail-enders gain considerable advantage from their 'free riding' on the work of the head-enders (head-enders $65 - 50 = 15$ and tail-enders $35 - 0 = 35$).[20] In situations such as this, the final outcome depends not only on the bargaining strength of the parties but on their ingenuity in crafting a series of rules that yield a final bargain to which they can agree.[21]

In systems where the need for labor input is the highest ($C''' = 75$), head-enders cannot afford to agree to a rule that allocates them prior rights. They would receive a net loss ($65 - 75 = -10$) if Rule 6 were used. Consequently, Rule 7 is the only equilibrium for a choice of rules game involving only Rule 6 and Rule 7 in a high-cost environment. To get the labor input from the tail-enders, the head-enders would be willing to guarantee that the tail end received a full half of the water. Thus the payoff to both segments under the high-cost condition would be 12.5 units.

In order to illustrate how the agreements about rules – and their impacts –

---

20. This is an example of the 'weak' exploiting the 'strong' (see Olson, 1965).

21. As Lisa Martin and David Genovese have pointed out to me, if there were well-developed markets in the setting the head-enders might well assert claims to all of the water, sell the units they do not need to tail-enders and purchase the labor they need to keep the system in good repair.

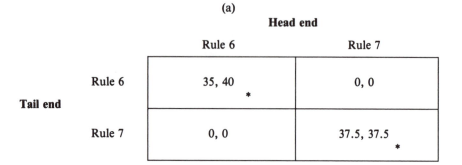

Figure 7. The Choice of Rules Games for the Irrigation Systems With Increasing Costs of Maintenance. (* = game equilibria)

are affected by differences in physical environments, the above analysis focusing on only two rules is blatantly sparse. In a more general analysis examining the effect of several parameters, including that of the status quo, one would find a variety of rules likely to be agreed upon in different physical environments. One would expect that the rules that are negotiated in systems like that of Figure 6a will authorize head-enders to take a larger proportion of the water than those negotiated in systems like that of Figure 6c.[22] Holding the size of the systems constant, one should observe a greater disparity in performance between the head and tail in systems like 6a than in systems like 6c. In systems where the costs of maintenance are moderate, like those of Figure 6b, the outcome is less clear. If tail-enders are fully symmetric with head-enders in regard to all other variables that would affect bargaining strength (such as size of farm plots and caste), then one would expect proportionately more water to be allocated to head-enders and labor contributions to be voluntary (see E. Ostrom and Gardner, 1993).

The previous analysis was based on an assumption that the overall cost of maintaining the system is relatively low. If instead of this situation the farmers had to construct new diversion works each year that required substantial resources, head-end farmers in all three types of systems would have less bargaining power. Consequently, the 'equalizer' in many farmer-organized systems is a substantial need for the contributions of resources each year by the tail-enders to keep the system well maintained. The need may stem from several physical factors including the yearly reconstruction of the headworks or the clearing and cleaning out of a long canal or both. In those farmer-organized systems where substantial resources are needed on a regular basis to cope with maintenance, we should observe rules that assign water in about the same proportion as resources are mobilized, more water allocated to the tail and higher productivity (see McKean, 1992; E. Ostrom, 1992).

---

22. An example of such a system is Thambesi, a farmer-organized system in Nepal where the headworks is a simple brush and stone diversion works that can be adjusted each year with only a few farmers doing the work. 'The members with holdings in the tail cannot force those with land above theirs to deliver water to them equally by not participating in maintenance and other system activities' (Yoder, 1986: 179). Head-enders have clearly established prior rights to water and 'fill their fields with water first before those further down the secondary are able to take water' (Yoder, 1986: 292). During the water-scarce months, farmers at the head of the system grow water-intensive crops while those at the tail do not irrigate at all.

Why External Assistance Does Not Always Improve Performance

The previous analysis provides a potential answer to the puzzle of why many effective, farmer-organized systems collapse soon after their systems have been modernized using funds provided by international donors. Project evaluations usually consider any reductions in the labor needed to maintain a system as a project benefit. Thus, investments in permanent headworks and lining canals are justified because of the presumed increase in agricultural productivity and the reduction in annual maintenance costs. The possibility that greatly reducing the need for resources to maintain a system would substantially alter the bargaining power of head-enders versus tail-enders is not usually considered in project evaluations. As indicated in the introduction, social capital is rarely taken into account in policy analyses.

Let us assume that an external donor plans to invest in a system with a physical structure and benefit–cost ratio like that of Figure 6c. Prior to investment, total benefits minus maintenance costs are equal to 25 units. The donor assumes that it is possible to raise the benefit level to 200 by teaching the farmers new agricultural techniques and by lowering the maintenance cost to 25 units through a one-time investment where the annualized value to the donor is also 25 units. Thus, the benefit–cost analysis leads the donor to make the investment since an annual benefit of 150 (200 − 25 − 25) is substantially above the 25 net annual benefits achieved prior to the planned improvement. The payoff matrix implicit in the benefit–cost analysis is illustrated in Figure 8a where the only outcome projected is an equal distribution of a higher agricultural yield. The donor assumes the farmers will somehow work out a scheme to share benefits as shown.

What frequently happens in practice is, however, illustrated in Figure 8b. Instead of increasing benefits to 200, the system stays at 100 and the head-end farmers now grab 90 units and make no investment in maintenance. Neither the head-enders nor the tail-enders are required to pay the annualized cost of the donor's investment. The tail-end farmers also do not invest in maintenance and receive only 10 units of water. Rule 6 has become the default 'might is right' rule that is not agreed upon but rather imposed on the tail-enders by head-enders who simply grab the water. They can ignore the contribution of the tail-enders to maintenance because for a few years the concrete structures will operate well without any maintenance. Of course, at some time in the future, the productivity of the system will fall below what it was prior to outside help. The tail-enders may initiate violence against the head-enders due to their perception that the water rights they had achieved with their hard labor had been taken from them (see Ambler, 1990). The end result can easily be that a community which had been knitted together by their mutual dependence dissipates into a setting of considerable conflict and low overall productivity.

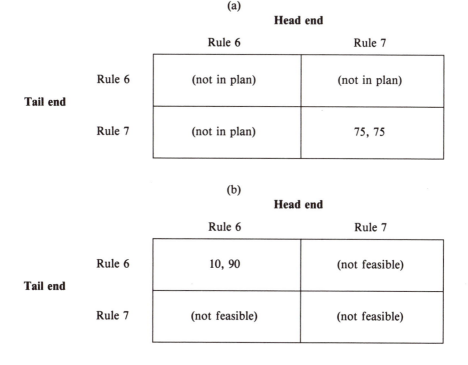

Figure 8. Planned and Actual Results of Some Types of Donor Assistance.

If the farmers were expected to pay back the costs of the investment made in physical capital (or to pay taxes to keep the system well maintained), tail–end farmers would again find themselves in a better bargaining relationship with head-enders. A very disruptive aspect of external assistance is that it is 'free' to the farmers involved in most developing countries. Without any need for resources from tail-enders, head-enders can ignore the interests of the less advantaged and take a larger share of the benefits.

What the previous analysis has shown is that there are many sources of heterogeneity among participants facing collective-action problems.[23] These asymmetries affect the bargaining strength of participants and resulting outcomes. Further, rules have distributional consequences. To

---

23. An important source of asymmetries not discussed in this paper relates to that of information (see Rasmusen, 1989).

ignore these distributional effects leads to an incomplete analysis. However, how asymmetries affect the distribution of outcomes depends on the configuration of (1) attributes of participants, (2) attributes of physical systems and (3) rules designed by participants. In other words, knowing about one asymmetry without knowing the full configuration of attributes about participants, physical systems and rules can lead to false conclusions about overall outcomes.

Those who are rich in terms of human capital (having two sons rather than one) may find themselves disadvantaged if a rule requiring all males to contribute labor is agreed upon. The effective 'counter' to this outcome is the rule that water will be allocated using the same formula as labor input. Those located at the head end of a physical system may be strongly advantaged unless they need the labor input of those lower in the system. In collective-action settings where individuals can generate substantial improvements in the flow of future benefits by agreeing upon a full configuration of rules, it is frequently possible to design the overall configuration so that participants can agree on a final set that is perceived to be fair.

Quantitative Evidence[24]

Given the previous analysis, one should expect to observe a wide diversity of outcomes in field settings regarding the distribution of net benefits between the head and tail portions of irrigation systems. Some systems will not be maintained over time and will collapse. Others will operate at lower efficiency than feasible and some farmers will gain a disproportionate share of water. An example of this type of settlement occurs on the Kamala Irrigation Project in Nepal where:

> Water allocation is primarily first come, first served. Thus, farmers at the head . . . tend to get all the water they need, while farmers at the tail often receive inadequate and unreliable amounts of water. This situation has often led to conflict between head and tail farmers. Sometimes hundreds of farmers from the area near the middle village of Parshai will take spears and large sticks and go together to the head village of Baramajhia to demand that water be released. At Baramajhia, farmers are often guarding their water with weapons. If water is released, Parshai farmers have had to maintain armed guards to assure that the minor canal remains open (Laitos et al., 1986: 147).

Still others will operate at a higher efficiency and net benefits will be more equitably shared. Given the number of variables that affect system performance and its distribution, it is difficult to conduct empirical tests of these

---

24. This section draws on a portion of E. Ostrom and Gardner (1993).

kinds of theoretical findings.[25] Until the development of the Nepal Institutions and Irrigation Systems (NIIS) database, no large-scale data set with the appropriate variables existed that could be used for this purpose. The NIIS database contains information on 127 irrigation systems (see E. Ostrom et al., 1992).

Nepal has an area of about 141,000 square kilometers, slightly larger than England. Its 18 million inhabitants are engaged largely in agriculture. Of the approximately 650,000 hectares of irrigated land, irrigation systems operated by farmers – called Farmer Managed Irrigation Systems (FMIS) – irrigate about 62% or 400,000 hectares (Small et al., 1986). The remaining irrigated land is served by a variety of Agency Managed Irrigation Systems (AMIS), many of which have been constructed since 1950 with extensive donor assistance.

In Nepal, FMIS achieve a high average level of agricultural productivity. Of the 127 systems in the NIIS, we have productivity data for 108. The 86 FMIS average 6 metric tons a year per hectare (6 MT/ha); the 22 AMIS, 5 metric tons a year per hectare ($p = .05$). FMIS tend also to achieve higher crop intensities[26] (see E. Ostrom et al., 1992). Agricultural yields and crop intensities depend on whether farmers can be assured of water during the winter and spring seasons when water becomes progressively scarcer. A higher percentage of FMIS in Nepal are able to get adequate water to both the head and the tail of their systems across all three seasons. During the spring, when water is normally very scarce, about 1 out of 4 FMIS are able to get adequate water to the tail of their systems, while only 1 out of 12 AMIS get adequate water to the tail of their systems. Even in the summer monsoon season, only about half of the AMIS system get adequate water to the tails

---

25. Many empirical studies do provide evidence concerning other types of asymmetries. Shui Yan Tang (1992), using our earlier CPR database, found a negative relationship between the variance in the average annual family income among irrigators and the degree of rule conformance and level of maintenance. Wai Fung Lam (1994), in his dissertation based on the Nepal Institutions and Irrigation Systems database, finds a negative relationship between inequalities of land holding and irrigation system performance. Easter and Palanisami (1986), in their study of 10 irrigation reservoirs in India, found that the smaller the variance in farm size among farmers, the more likely farmers were to form water user associations that coped with collective-action problems. Jayaraman (1981) found a similar relationship between egalitarian community structures and effective organization of farmers (see also Wade, 1987; Bandyopadhyay and von Eschen, 1988; Kanbur, 1991; Bardhan, 1993). Singh and Ballabh (1993) do not, however, find that homogeneity among participants is a necessary condition for the achievement of better performance.

26. It should be pointed out that FMIS are on average smaller than AMIS, but the size of the system is not significantly related to agricultural productivity when we control for the type of governance and for other physical attributes such as the presence of permanent headworks and at least partial lining (see Lam et al., 1994).

while almost 90% of the FMIS get water to the tail of their system (E. Ostrom et al., 1992).

To begin to address the impact of physical capital on the distribution of water between head and tail, we analyze how physical variables and type of governance structure combine to affect the difference in water availability achieved at the head and the tail of irrigation systems. The *difference in water availability* is a crude indicator of how well an appropriation process gets water to the tail end of a system. We have estimated the following equation:

Water Availability Difference = f (Headworks, Lining, Terrain, Length, Labor Input, Type of Governance)

where

Water Availability Difference is the difference in the score (adequate = 2, limited = 1, scarce or non-existent = 0) achieved at the head of a system minus the score achieved at the tail of a system averaged across three seasons,[27]
Headworks is coded 1 if the headworks are permanent and 0 if otherwise,
Lining is coded 1 if the canals are partly or fully lined and 0 otherwise,
Terrain is coded 1 if the system is located in the Terai and 0 otherwise,
Length is the length in meters of the canals of a system,
Labor Input is the number of labor days devoted to regular maintenance per year divided by the number of households served,
Type of Governance is coded 1 if a FMIS and 0 otherwise.

The result of a multiple regression analysis for the 76 irrigation systems for which we have complete data is:

Water Availability Difference = .64** + .34**Headworks − .14 Lining − .10* Terrain + 0 Length + 0 Labor Input − .32** Type of Governance
$F = 5.92$, Adjusted $R^2 = .28$, **$p < .05$, *$p < .10$.

The difference in water availability achieved at the head and the tail of

----

27. Thus, a score of zero indicates that for all three seasons, the level of water adequacy was the same in the head and tail sections of the system. A score of .33 indicates that in one season, the head received adequate water and the tail received limited water or that the head received limited water and the tail received scarce water. For the 118 systems for which we have data, the difference score ranges from −0.66 to 1.66. The regression presented in the text is based on data for 76 systems for which we had data on all variables in the regression equation. A parallel analysis using multinomial probit estimates yields parallel findings concerning the direction and significance of permanent headworks and type of system, but the negative relationship between terrain and the difference score does not reach statistical significance. Myungsuk Lee's assistance in undertaking the regression and probit analysis is deeply appreciated.

these Nepali irrigation systems is significantly and negatively related to being in the Terai as expected – meaning it is greater in the hills. The presence of a permanent headworks – frequently considered as one of the hallmarks of a modern, well-operating, irrigation system with channel lining – is positively related to an inequality between the water availability achieved at the head and the tail. The difference in water availability is significantly reduced at the tail of a FMIS as compared to that of an AMIS.

Constructing a permanent headworks is related to increased inequality between water availability at the head and at the tail of irrigation systems. As discussed previously, such headworks have frequently been funded by external sources, with farmers not required to repay the cost of this investment. This type of external 'help' substantially reduces the short-term need for mobilizing labor (or other resources) to maintain the system each year. The calculations in the design plans, however, do not always match the results achieved. Without a realistic requirement to pay back capital investments, farmers and host government officials are motivated to invest in rent-seeking activities and may overestimate previous annual costs in order to obtain external aid (Repetto, 1986). Further, such help can change the pattern of relationships among farmers within a system, reducing the recognition of mutual dependencies and patterns of reciprocity between head-enders and tail-enders that have long sustained the system. By denying the tail-enders an opportunity to invest in the improvement of infrastructure, external assistance may also deny those who are most disadvantaged from being able to assert and defend rights to the flow of benefits (see Ambler, 1990, 1991).[28]

Thinking About Rule-making Situations

The empirical evidence previously presented supports the argument that both the structure of physical works and the social capital that is used to operate physical capital affect the outcomes that are achieved. The models, however, are extremely sparse and simplistic representations of far

---

28. The interpretation of the empirical findings is consistent with many recorded case studies that describe farmer-managed irrigation systems that prior to an intervention required very high levels of labor from farmers, but achieved very high levels of agricultural performance. These same systems in many instances failed to sustain their organizational vigor and maintenance activities after donor agencies funded the construction of permanent headworks. Thus, overall performance was less after the intervention than before. Several cases are cited in E. Ostrom and Gardner (1993). There are, of course, rival hypotheses that we are currently exploring. It is possible, for example, that agency systems that normally have permanent headworks were constructed in less desirable locations than those that the farmers had already developed. Wai Fung Lam (1994) addresses these competing hypotheses in his dissertation.

more complex and rich phenomena. One limitation is that the choice of rules was presented as if it were a one-layered bargaining game. Expected outcomes are presented as if they were received automatically depending on the bargain made over rules. If farmers have accurate information about potential benefits and costs and about the equilibrium strategies that they will all use in the day-to-day operation of the system, this is a good first approximation of the problem they face.[29] It simply aggregates the total expected annual benefits and costs from the ensuing series of games. For participants to actually obtain net benefits in any year, however, they face a series of repeated games to be played within whatever rules are chosen. In addition, if there are multiple equilibria in the ensuing games, the initial representation needs considerable additional elaboration.

Now that we have introduced the problem of agreeing upon rules, let us view the choice of rules as a choice among games that will be played repeatedly until the rules (or the physical variables that also affect game structure) are changed to create a revised game or the players stop interacting. Further, in most systems, rules create games in which the outcomes are rules for still further games. In other words, many layers of rules and games are stacked upon one another. For purposes of analysis, it is useful to divide rule-making games into two broad types: constitutional rule-making games and collective-choice rule-making games.

The results of decisions made in a constitutional-choice rule-making game are the rules that are used for making initial agreements about constituting an enterprise and deciding on the key initial rules to be used in that enterprise. In the models presented previously, the rule of unanimity was used in the constitutional rule-making game. Unless everyone agreed, the status quo continued. For the initial consideration of whether to constitute a system or not, unanimity is frequently used in practice by participants engaged in microconstitutional-choice processes to create or not create a long-term association. Since more than two players are usually engaged in these processes, a subset of the initial group involved in discussions may all agree on a set of rules even though other players do not. But the success of such agreements depends on the benefits of the project being great enough that even if the subset of players who reach an agreement pays all the costs, the

---

29. Because the game involves a long series of future benefits, the loss of not reaching an agreement is usually far larger than the loss involved in keeping the status quo in a one-shot bargaining situation. Further, farmers need the continued contributions of each other to operate the system over time. In agreeing on rules, farmers are establishing a system of mutual dependence. They are dependent on each other not to steal and not to shirk (the two strong short-term incentives they are trying to surmount). In choosing rules, more attention is paid by all participants to rules that are both efficient and fair than would be paid in one-shot decisions about actions.

net benefits are still positive. In most such situations, the subset also agrees to exclude anyone who did not initially agree (or does not agree at a later point). A farmer who did not sign or affix a thumbprint on an agreement is under no obligation to provide inputs and may be totally excluded from receiving water.[30] Thus, an important decision made in the initial micro-constitutional process is how membership is defined and how someone who had not agreed to the initial document could become a member.

A major part of the constitutional process is determining the set of collective-choice rules to be used to add to, refine and change the day-to-day rules used in practice. Some decisions may be reserved for consideration by everyone. Some type of council and other official position will usually be created (through electoral or other means) that continues to revise rules related to the operation of the system as well as coping with the day-to-day contingencies of operating the system. Operational-choice rules directly affect the decisions that individuals make in the physical world and are primarily made in collective-choice games but are initially sketched out in the constitutional game.

In addition to the stacked series of rule-making games, there is also a stacked series of operational games. In an irrigation setting, one could simplify this series as represented in Figure 9. In this figure, I have returned to the assumption of two players who are now faced with a secret election in which they must both cast a ballot to agree or not agree to the final con-figuration of rules discussed in their negotiation process. Only if both of them agree to this microconstitution will they avoid the continuance of the status quo. But the annual expected net outcomes that were used in the previous series of models as the outcomes of the rule-making game are achieved only after three more games are played – the construction game, the maintenance game and the allocation of water game.

In two previous papers, Weissing and Ostrom (1991, 1993) have explored the structure and equilibria of 2-person and *n*-person allocation of water games. In these games, multiple equilibria exist and many are inefficient. The shapes of the equilibrium regimes depend delicately on the configura-tion of rules used to reward monitoring and punish stealing as well as the costs of monitoring and stealing and the detection probabilities involved.

---

30. Whether anyone can be excluded depends very much on the physical layout of the system and on whether exclusion will be sustained by external authorities if challenged by those who are excluded. If the soil is porous and those who refuse to contribute are located lower in the system than those who agree, they may receive substantial subsurface, usable flows of water without any need to contribute at all. Thus, while many farmer-organized systems do end up being able to exclude non-participatory farmers, this is a very difficult process to achieve and most self-organizing systems try hard to involve all of those who are in a physically interrelated system in the social system they create.

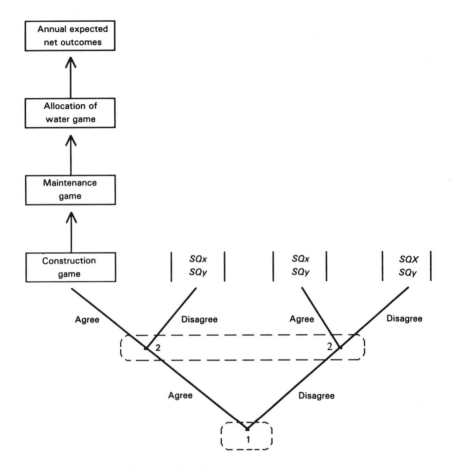

Figure 9. The Extended Series of Games.

Knowing how complex the allocation of water game is, I can only presume that the annual maintenance game is also relatively complex and contains multiple equilibria. Thus, the representation of rule-making games presented in the prior sections of this paper must be looked upon as a crude first approximation to a series of stacked games. The outcomes in the simplified view are the expectations of a series of outcomes in future games based on an estimation of the likely equilibrium in each of these stacked games.

A fuller representation of the linkage and feedback among the stacked games – including now the collective-choice rule-making game – is presented in Figure 10. Once a constitution is agreed upon and construction is completed, one can think of an annual cycle. The annual cycle contains: (1) a maintenance game in which farmers decide whether to comply with the

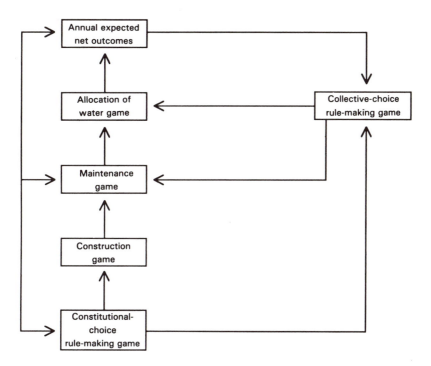

Figure 10. Operational, Collective-choice, and Constitutional-choice Situations and Their Relationships.

rules specifying how resources are to be mobilized for maintenance and whether to monitor and punish rule-infractions, (2) an allocation of water game in which farmers decide whether to comply with the rules specifying how much water they are allocated and whether to monitor and punish rule infractions, (3) annual net returns are achieved (resulting from individual agricultural production decisions as well as the two annual games) and (4) a collective-choice rule-making game in which decisions are made to change or keep rules structuring the maintenance and allocation of water games after information is obtained about annual net returns to farmers. Most farmer-organized systems have annual meetings open to all members in which they do discuss whether their current operating rules are satisfactory or whether they want to change these.

Since not all individuals involved in the process of choosing rules are as far-sighted as others and since there are many heterogeneities involved in field settings, crafting a full set of rules that work together to generate efficient and fair outcomes over a long time in a changing environment is a challenging task. The initial rules established in some systems are likely to be ill-matched to the problems they face. If the farmers are unable after some time to come to a better agreement about their rules, their system will not be as productive as those of others who have developed more effective social capital.[31] They will face problems such as unpredictability of water and inadequate maintenance. Deep resentments can develop among individuals who have invested in hard work only to watch their mutual understandings come unglued. Other farmer associations who start off poorly may continually adjust their agreements until they arrive at a set of rules that fit their local circumstances well and are considered efficient and fair by most participants. Some systems will react to changing circumstances faster than others.

It is the continual adjustment of operational rules (and perhaps even the constitutional agreement itself) at their annual meetings – combined with relatively clear-cut annual performance indicators – that allows a group of farmers to adjust their rules (and their norms of behavior) so that eventually they may approach some of the better potential outcomes that are feasibly achieved given their physical endowments. Thus, the first approximation presented above will need to be expanded in future work by modeling the annual processes that are sketched in Figure 10.

Conclusion

This paper has addressed how individuals invest time, effort and resources in physical, human and social capital in efforts to increase future flows of net benefits. The investment in social capital frequently takes the form of bargaining over which rules will be adopted to allocate benefits and costs

---

31. The amount of time and experimentation involved in actually finding a set of rules that will work effectively on a particular system can be substantial. Giri and Aryal (1989) provide an interesting description of the time it has taken for the farmers in the Gadkhar Irrigation System (a jointly managed system where the farmers have been given the task of allocating water on the system) to develop only one of the rules they use – the rule allocating water as between the two major branches of the system. As they state:

Rotation has been in effect in Gadkhar since the very beginning of water delivery, however, with limited successes. After experimenting with a number of water distribution rules, the Gadkhar Committees' persistence in finding a rotation pattern that allows water to be distributed equitably finally bore fruits when they decided on the present 96 and 120 hours rotation for a group of two canals on the basis of the aggregate command area and to appoint *pani pales* to make sure that water was available to each farm unit in the command area. The provision of *pani pales* providing services for making each and every plot of land within the command starting from the tail and penalizing landowners if their farms were found wet when they were not supposed to be, has been a remarkable innovation (1989: 33).

of collective action. When participants are characterized by substantial heterogeneities of capabilities and interests, the rules that are adopted substantially affect the distribution of outcomes. If participants are faced with crosscutting and off-setting differences, however, a configuration of rules can enable participants to generate mutually productive outcomes over time. If external agents of change do not take into account the delicate balance of interests embedded in social capital, when investments in physical capital are undertaken efforts to improve productivity can have the opposite effect. Institutions that are slowly developed through many years of tough bargaining and trial and error processes may be quickly destroyed by insensitive overemphasis on physical technology.

REFERENCES

Ambler, John (1990) 'The Influence of Farmer Water Rights on the Design of Water-proportioning Devices', in Robert Yoder and Juanita Thurston (eds) *Design Issues in Farmer-managed Irrigation Systems*, pp. 37–52. Colombo, Sri Lanka: International Irrigation Management Institute.

Ambler, John (1991) 'Bounding the System: Precursors to Measuring Performance in Networks of Farmer-Managed Irrigation Systems', paper presented at the International Workshop on Performance Measurement of Farmer Managed Irrigation Systems, Mendoza, Argentina, November.

Aumann, Robert J. (1976) 'Agreeing to Disagree', *Annals of Statistics* 4(1): 236–9.

Bandyopadhyay, S. and D. von Eschen (1988) 'Villager Failure to Cooperate: Some Evidence from West Bengal, India', in Donald W. Attwood and B. S. Baviskar (eds) *Who Shares? Cooperatives and Rural Development*, pp. 112–45. New Delhi: Oxford University Press.

Bardhan, Pranab (1993) 'Analytics of the Institutions of Informal Cooperation in Rural Development', *World Development* 21(4): 633–9.

Bates, Robert H. (1988) 'Contra Contractarianism: Some Reflections on the New Institutionalism', *Politics and Society* 16: 387–401.

Bottrall, Anthony (1992) 'Fits and Misfits Over Time and Space: Technologies and Institutions of Water Development for South Asian Agriculture', *Contemporary South Asia* 1(2): 227–47.

Calvert, Randall L. (1994) 'Rational Actors, Equilibrium, and Social Institutions', in Jack Knight and Itai Sened (eds) *Explaining Social Institutions*. New York: Cambridge University Press.

Coleman, James S. (1966) *Equality of Educational Opportunity*. Washington, DC: US Government Printing Office.

Coleman, James S. (1996) 'Social Theory, Social Research, and a Theory of Action', *American Journal of Sociology* 91(1): 309–35.

Cornes, Richard and Todd Sandler (1994) 'Are Public Goods Myths?', *Journal of Theoretical Politics*, 6(3): 369–85.

Coward, E. Walter, Jr (1998) 'Property, Persistence, and Participation: The State and Traditional Irrigation Systems', in John W. Bennett and John R. Bowen (eds) *Production and Autonomy: Anthropological Studies and Critiques of Development*, Monographs in Economic Anthropology, no. 5, pp. 329–42. Lanham, MD: University Press of America.

Curtis, Donald (1991) *Beyond Government: Organizations for Common Benefit*. London: Macmillan.

Dasgupta, Partha and Karl Göran Mäler (1992) *The Economics of Transnational Commons*. Oxford: Clarendon Press.

Easter, K. William and K. Palanisami (1986) 'Tank Irrigation in India and Thailand: An Example of Common Property Resource Management', Staff paper, University of Minnesota, Department of Agricultural and Applied Economics, August.

Elster, Jon (1979) *Ulysses and the Sirens: Studies in Rationality and Irrationality*. Cambridge: Cambridge University Press.

Elster, Jon (1989) *The Cement of Society*. Cambridge: Cambridge University Press.

Field, Alexander J. (1979) 'On the Explanation of Rules Using Rational Choice Models', *Journal of Economic Issues* 13(1) (March): 49–72.

Giri, Khadka and Murari M. Aryal, (1989) *Turnover Process of Agency-managed Irrigation Systems in Nepal*. Kathmandu, Nepal: Department of Irrigation, Irrigation Management Project.

Haas, Peter, Robert O. Keohane and Marc A. Levy (1993) *Institutions for the Earth: Sources of Effective International Environmental Protection*. Cambridge, MA: MIT Press.

Hackett, Steven (1993) 'Incomplete Contracting: A Laboratory Experimental Analysis', *Economic Inquiry* 31: 278–93.

Hackett, Steven, Edella Schlager and James Walker (1994) 'The Role of Communication in Resolving Commons Dilemmas: Experimental Evidence with Heterogeneous Appropriators', *Journal of Environmental Economics and Management*, forthcoming.

Harral, Clell G. and Asif Faiz (1988) *Road Deterioration in Developing Countries: Causes and Remedies*. Washington, DC: The World Bank.

Israel, Arturo (1987) *Institutional Development: Incentives to Performance*. Baltimore, MD: Johns Hopkins University Press.

Jayaraman, T. K. (1981) 'Farmers' Organizations in Surface Irrigation Projects: Two Empirical Studies from Gujarat', *Economic and Political Weekly* (Bombay) 16 (26 Sept.): A89–A98.

Johnson, Ronald N. and Gary D. Libecap (1982) 'Contracting Problems and Regulation: The Case of the Fishery', *American Economic Review* 72(5) (Dec.): 1005–22.

Kanbur, Ravi (1991) 'Heterogeneity, Distribution and Cooperation in Common Property Resource Management', mimeo. Washington, DC: World Bank.

Keohane, Robert O. (1989) *International Institutions and State Power: Essays in International Relations Theory*. Boulder, CO: Westview Press.

Knight, Jack (1992) *Institutions and Social Conflict*. New York: Cambridge University Press.

Lachmann, Ludwig M. (1978) *Capital and Its Structure*. Kansas City, MO: Sheed Andrews & McNeel.

Laitos, Robby, et al. (1986) 'Rapid Appraisal of Nepal Irrigation Systems', Water Management Synthesis Report No. 43, Colorado State University, Fort Collins.

Lam, Wai Fung (1994) 'A Comparative Study of Farmer-managed and Agency-managed Irrigation Systems in Nepal: An Institutional Analysis', PhD diss., Indiana University, Bloomington.

Lam, Wai Fung, Myungsuk Lee and Elinor Ostrom (1994) 'The Institutional Analysis and Development Framework: Application to Irrigation in Nepal', in Derick W. Brinkerhoff (ed.) *Policy Analysis Concepts and Methods: An Institutional and Implementation Focus*. Greenwich, CT: JAI Press, forthcoming.

Lewis, D. K. (1969) *Convention: A Philosophical Study*. Cambridge, MA: Harvard University Press.

Libecap, Gary D. (1989) *Contracting for Property Rights*. Cambridge: Cambridge University Press.

Martin, Edward G. and Robert Yoder (1983) 'The Chherlung Thulo Kulo: A Case Study of a Farmer-managed Irrigation System', in *Water Management in Nepal: Proceedings of the*

Seminar on Water Management Issues, July 31-August 2, Appendix I, 203-17. Kathmandu, Nepal: Ministry of Agriculture, Agricultural Projects Services Centre and the Agricultural Development Council.

Martin, Fenton (1989/1992) *Common-pool Resources and Collective Action: A Bibliography*, Vols. 1 and 2. Bloomington: Indiana University, Workshop in Political Theory and Policy Analysis.

McGinnis, Michael and Elinor Ostrom (1993) 'Design Principles for Local and Global Commons', in Robert Keohane, Michael McGinnis and Elinor Ostrom (eds) *Proceedings of a Conference on Linking Local and Global Commons*, pp. 16-65. Bloomington: Indiana University, Workshop in Political Theory and Policy Analysis.

McKean, Margaret (1992) 'Success on the Commons: A Comparative Examination of Institutions for Common Property Resource Management', *Journal of Theoretical Politics* 4(3) (July): 247-81.

North, Douglass C. (1990) *Institutions, Institutional Change and Economic Performance*. New York: Cambridge University Press.

Olson, Mancur (1965) *The Logic of Collective Action: Public Goods and the Theory of Groups*. Cambridge, MA: Harvard University Press.

Ostrom, Elinor (1990) *Governing the Commons: The Evolution of Institutions for Collective Action*. New York: Cambridge University Press.

Ostrom, Elinor (1992) *Crafting Institutions for Self-governing Irrigation Systems*. San Francisco, CA: Institute for Contemporary Studies Press.

Ostrom, Elinor, Paul Benjamin and Ganesh Shivakoti (1992) *Institutions, Incentives, and Irrigation in Nepal*, Vol. 1. Bloomington: Indiana University, Workshop in Political Theory and Policy Analysis.

Ostrom, Elinor and Roy Gardner (1993) 'Coping with Asymmetries in the Commons: Self-governing Irrigation Systems Can Work', *Journal of Economic Perspectives* 7(4) (Fall): 93-112.

Ostrom, Elinor, Roy Gardner and James Walker (1994) *Rules, Games, and Common-pool Resources*. Ann Arbor: University of Michigan Press.

Ostrom, Elinor, Larry Schroeder and Susan Wynne (1993) *Institutional Incentives and Sustainable Development: Infrastructure Policies in Perspective*. Boulder, CO: Westview Press.

Ostrom, Elinor, James Walker and Roy Gardner (1992) 'Covenants With and Without a Sword: Self-governance is Possible', *American Political Science Review* 86(2) (June): 404-17.

Ostrom, Vincent, David Feeny, and Hartmut Picht, eds (1993) *Rethinking Institutional Analysis and Development: Issues, Alternatives, and Choices*, 2nd edn. San Francisco, CA: Institute for Contemporary Studies Press.

Putnam, Robert D. (1993a) 'The Prosperous Community: Social Capital and Public Life', *The American Prospect* 13 (Spring): 35-42.

Putnam, Robert D. (with Robert Leonardi and Raffaella Y. Nanetti) (1993b) *Making Democracy Work: Civic Traditions in Modern Italy*. Princeton, NJ: Princeton University Press.

Rasmusen, Eric (1989) *Games and Information: An Introduction to Game Theory*. Oxford: Basil Blackwell.

Repetto, Robert (1996) *Skimming the Water: Rent-seeking and the Performance of Public Irrigation Systems*, Research Report No. 4. Washington, DC: World Resources Institute.

Schelling, Thomas C. (1960) *The Strategy of Conflict*. Oxford: Oxford University Press.

Selten, Reinhard (1978) 'The Equity Principle in Economic Behavior', in H. W. Gottinger and W. Leinfellner (eds) *Decision Theory and Social Ethics*, pp. 289-301. Dordrecht, Netherlands: D. Reidel.

Singh, Katar and Vishwa Ballabh (1993) 'Cooperatives in Natural Resource Management', Workshop Report No. 10. Anand, India: Institute of Rural Management.

Small, Leslie, Marietta Adriano and Edward D. Martin (1986) *Regional Study on Irrigation Service Fees: Final Report*. Colombo, Sri Lanka: International Irrigation Management Institute.

Snidal, Duncan (1985) 'Coordination Versus Prisoners' Dilemma: Implications for International Cooperation and Regimes', *American Political Science Review* 79: 923–42.

Sugden, Richard (1996) *The Economics of Rights, Co-operation, and Welfare*. Oxford: Basil Blackwell.

Tang, Shui Yan (1992) *Institutions and Collective Action: Self-governance in Irrigation*. San Francisco, CA: Institute for Contemporary Studies Press.

Taylor, Michael (1989) 'Structure, Culture, and Action in the Explanation of Social Change', *Politics and Society* 17: 115–62.

Telser, L. G. (1980) 'A Theory of Self-enforcing Agreements', *Journal of Business* 53(1): 27–44.

Wade, Robert (1987) *Village Republics: Economic Conditions for Collective Action in South India*. New York: Cambridge University Press.

Weissing, Franz and Elinor Ostrom (1991) 'Irrigation Institutions and the Games Irrigators Play: Rule Enforcement without Guards', in Reinhard Selten (ed.) *Game Equilibrium Models II: Methods, Morals, and Markets*, pp. 188–262. Berlin: Springer-Verlag.

Weissing, Franz and Elinor Ostrom (1993) 'Irrigation Institutions and the Games Irrigators Play: Rule Enforcement on Government- and Farmer-managed Systems', in Fritz W. Scharpf (ed.) *Games in Hierarchies and Networks: Analytical and Empirical Approaches to the Study of Governance Institutions*, pp. 387–428. Frankfurt: Campus Verlag; Boulder, CO: Westview Press.

World Bank, The (1988) *Rural Development: World Bank Experience, 1965–86*, Operations Evaluation Study. Washington, DC: The World Bank.

Yoder, Robert D. (1986) 'The Performance of Farmer-managed Irrigation Systems in the Hills of Nepal', PhD diss., Cornell University.

Yoder, Robert D. (1991) 'Peer Training as a Way to Motivate Institutional Change in Farmer-managed Irrigation Systems', in *Proceedings of the Workshop on Democracy and Governance*, Decentralization: Finance and Management Project Report, 53–67. Burlington, VT: Associates in Rural Development.

Young, Oran (1982) *Resource Regimes: Natural Resources and Social Institutions*. Berkeley: University of California Press.

7. THE CONDITIONS FOR SUCCESSFUL COLLECTIVE ACTION

Gary D. Libecap

Introduction

In some cases, the losses associated with the uses made of a common-pool resource, or CPR, lead to timely and successful private cooperation or to agreements between private parties and government officials for beneficial institutional change. In other cases, common-pool problems are not successfully resolved, either privately or with state intervention. Empirical research has identified a number of factors that characterize collective action regarding common-pool resources that critically affect the outcome. Although institutional change affecting the common pool typically involves local issues and a comparatively small number of parties, the patterns of behavior and the conditions for successful resolution of conflicts seem likely to have implications for more global issues of international relations. Indeed, some commons problems, such as the management of ocean fisheries, explicitly involve parties across countries and cultures. The purpose of this paper is to summarize some of the bargaining issues involved in collective action to address local common-pool problems and to illustrate them in

The author benefitted from comments by Robert Keohane and Elinor Ostrom. Grants from the National Science Foundation (SES-8207826 and SES-8920965) financed parts of the analysis reported in the paper.

three empirical cases. The importance of timing or the sequence of coalition building and the heterogeneity of the participants' preferences and capabilities (assets, skills, knowledge, information and past performance) are emphasized.

In the paper two of the empirical cases involve traditional CPR problems and efforts to resolve them in fisheries and oil fields. The third involves collective action by private firms to obtain government assistance to control orange shipments so as to fix prices. Although the cases are quite different, with one involving a non-renewable resource, another a renewable resource and a third addressing cooperation for provision of an industry public good, the bargaining problems encountered among heterogeneous parties are very similar. This condition allows for generalizations to be drawn about the conditions for successful collective action. As described below, collective action to resolve rent dissipation from technological externalities in common-pool resources is similar to that required for reducing the losses from pecuniary externalities among competing parties within an industry. In the first case, rent dissipation occurs from overexploitation of the resource and in the second case, rent dissipation occurs from overproduction by firms in the industry. In each case, successful collective action to mitigate rent dissipation requires the bargaining parties to reduce production. Output quotas must be devised and adhered to. Yet, as is well known in the cartel literature, the problems of negotiating and policing total production levels and individual firm quotas within them are formidable ones. Similarly, the research on regulation of the exploitation of fisheries and oil fields also reveals conflicts over total output limits and individual quotas. The ways in which these issues have been addressed in the three cases have determined the nature of the regulatory policies adopted and their success in limiting rent dissipation.[1]

The Common-pool Problem

There is confusion in the literature on the terms, common property and open access. Technically, open access occurs when there are no controls on the access to and use of a valuable resource. It is the most extreme case. A

---

1. Although technological externalities are stressed in most CPR problems, there can be important pecuniary externalities from common-pool production as well. In the case of oil the rapid production from a single large field in the 1920s and 1930s in the US caused oil prices to fall. Indeed, falling prices, more than concerns over maintaining the resource, motivated firms to attempt to limit output through cooperative action.

common-property condition can mean open access; that is, the resource is common to all parties and open to competitive, unrestricted entry and production. Too-rapid exploitation and resource rent dissipation are the outcomes. This description is how common property generally is viewed in the economics literature. But among many social scientists, common property describes a less extreme case, where a well-defined group has access to a resource (holds it in common) and non-group members are denied use. Hence, there are restrictions on entry and use by non-members, and among members, rules are devised to control exploitation. Many of these CPR management regimes historically have been very successful. They involve local management by the very parties who are familiar with the resource and depend upon its maintenance for their wellbeing.[2] These groups tend to be quite homogeneous and stable.

If these conditions break down, however, the CPR management regime may no longer be effective. One possibility is new entry by outsiders who are attracted by higher resource prices. This, for example, is occurring in many fisheries. The new entrants, by definition, will not be group members or part of past management arrangements. They have no stake in an institution that is designed to exclude them from the resource and they typically will have different harvest time horizons. Modification of existing CPR institutions to incorporate large numbers of new, heterogeneous entrants will be very difficult. Another possibility is intervention by higher levels of government, when there are overlapping jurisdictions over the resource. These governments can be responsive to the very constituents who are excluded by the CPR regime. Local harvest rules that deny access to influential external constituent groups may be overturned by higher authorities. An example is anti-trust prosecution by the US Department of Justice in the 1950s against local fishery unions along the US coasts to limit entry and harvests.[3] These arrangements appear to have been reasonably successful in controlling fishing effort by members and in excluding non-members, but were disbanded after being found in violation of the Sherman Act.[4] Accordingly, even CPR regimes that have been successful in mitigated open-access conditions can lose their effectiveness and traditional common-pool losses can emerge.

---

2. See Ostrom (1990) for discussion of successful cases.

3. Higgs (1982) provides another telling example, where state governments in Oregon and Washington repeatedly intervened in the early 20th century to dismantle local salmon conservation arrangements at the bellest of influential fishery groups who were disadvantaged by the local institutions.

4. See Johnson and Libecap (1982) for discussion. It is unlikely that any local harvest restrictions could have had serious impact on fish prices. There were many close substitutes and fish were internationally traded. Justice Department action appears to have been in response to the complaints of those whose fishing was restricted by local union rules.

The classic articles on the potential losses or rent dissipation from an open-access resource are those by Gordon (1954) and Cheung (1970).[5] Capturing a portion of rents saved by mitigating open-access conditions provides the individual motivation for collective action. Complete open access occurs when property rights to a valuable resource are absent. If property rights are poorly defined, open-access losses will occur along unregulated or unconstrained margins. Under these circumstances, net private and social costs diverge, since individuals who use the resource do not have to consider the full social costs of their activities. Except in unusual circumstances, their production lowers the productivity of others who are also using the resource.

Because private costs are less than the social costs for each party, total output by all exceeds the social wealth-maximizing level, where social marginal costs equal social marginal returns. By equating only their relevant private marginal benefits and costs, individuals exploit the resource too rapidly, relative to what interest rate and price projections would suggest. Further, competitive pressures under conditions of poorly defined property rights encourage short time horizons in production, leading user costs and other long-term investment possibilities to be ignored. Moreover, the absence of secure property rights will limit market exchanges and the associated emergence of prices to direct the resource to its highest valued use.[6] This condition can be a particular problem in the allocation of resources over time, since there will be little information available or incentives for economic agents to postpone resource use to the future, even if it is socially desirable to do so. Finally, resource values will be reduced as productive inputs are diverted from socially valued production to predatory and defensive activities. Hence, where open-access conditions are prevalent, the value of the resource will be reduced and the economy will be less responsive to current and future opportunities.

These open-access losses define the potential gains from collective action: to assign more exclusive property rights within groups, or to individuals for controlling resource access and use. Capturing a portion of the aggregate resource rents that are saved motivates individuals to bargain for institutional change. The bargaining stands taken by the various interested parties depend upon their private expected gains from institutional change as compared to the status quo. Hence, allocation rules are critical. Each party will attempt to mold the resulting agreement in ways that maximize its share of the aggregate returns. This maneuvering affects both the nature of the property rights that are ultimately adopted and the aggregate benefits that can be obtained.

---

5. The discussion here is taken from Libecap (1989: 12–28).
6. For discussion, see Demsetz (1967).

In considering whether or not to support proposed changes in property rights at any time, the bargaining parties implicitly compare their expected income stream under the status quo with that offered by the new arrangement. The benefits of the status quo are determined by the current property-rights allocation and any expected adjustments in future shares achieved by delaying institutional change. Interest groups may choose to delay agreement on a proposed adjustment in property rights if they anticipate that new information will be forthcoming to bolster their claims for a larger share of rents in the new arrangement or if they expect favorable changes in political conditions to strengthen their bargaining power. Delay, however, has costs since it means the continuation of open-access conditions. Hence, the bargaining parties must trade off the expected private gains from delaying agreement with the expected losses from maintaining the status quo.

Heterogeneities of Capabilities and Collective Action

In the absence of serious disputes over the aggregate gains or benefits of assigning or modifying property rights to an open-access resource, the problem of collective action is one of distribution, achieving agreement on the individual shares of resource rents that are implicit in the assignment of property rights. Generally, the magnitude of the losses associated with open-access conditions will not be controversial. The losses are observable by most parties and can be documented with publicly available information. For example, a general decline in fishing harvests and incomes or a fall in oil field production can be understood and linked to the problem of uncontrolled access and too rapid production. Accordingly, there will be agreement on the need for institutional change regarding the creation or refinement of controls on resource use. The problems, however, are with how much production should be restricted and how those cut-backs should be distributed among the bargaining parties. Hence, the center of dispute will be over the allocation rule – how the resulting benefits and costs of collective action to address the common pool are to be distributed. In this sense, the collective-action problem in addressing local CPRs centers more on coordination or distributional dilemmas as described by Lisa Martin (paper 4 in this collection) for international bargaining, than on the collaboration dilemmas she outlines.

The intensity of debate over distribution and the likelihood of collective action are influenced by (a) the size of the aggregate expected gains, (b) the number and heterogeneity of the bargaining parties and (c) information problems. The role of the size of the aggregate expected gains is discussed below because of its impact on the sequence of agreements. In general, however, the larger the expected aggregate gains, the more likely an acceptable share arrangement can be devised. With large expected gains, enough influential parties will see themselves made better off, relative to the status quo, so that collective action for institutional change can proceed. Indeed, with regard to renewable versus non-renewable resources, the expected gains of agreement may be greater for the latter, if the parties generally agree that resource rents will be permanently lost if collective action is not forthcoming. In the case of renewable resources, there may be disagreements as to whether exogenous factors may lead to a rebound of the resource without action. More abundant rainfall on common grazing lands or a change in ocean current temperatures in fisheries are examples of external factors that can influence the size of the aggregate gains of agreement.

The number of bargaining parties involved can make it more difficult to reach agreement for the usual bargaining reasons (Olson, 1965). The greater the number of competing interests with a stake in the new definition of property rights, the more claims that must be addressed in building a consensus on institutional change. An important related problem is heterogeneity in capabilities across the parties in information regarding resource values, in production costs, in output history and in organizational size, wealth and political experience. These differences affect share negotiations and the ability to engage in collective action.

In many common-pool settings where the parties are heterogeneous, changes in property institutions involve risks for some groups. Those parties who have had informal claims or have been unusually productive under the status quo may be made worse off by institutional change unless their claims or past productivity are recognized. Their particular concerns must be addressed to gain their agreement on the new assignment of property rights. In negotiations, prior possession or prior production can be used to document past use and be the basis for quota definition or shares in the resource under the new arrangement. If these criteria can be documented with public information, quotas based on prior possession or prior production are popular because they recognize those parties who have a significant stake in the resource and in any adjustments in property rights to it.

Even so, conflicts may still arise over the division of future rents and delay or block collective action. Prior possession and prior production, as bases for more formal property rights, reward those who have adapted well to open-access conditions. Locking past success into future allocations, however, may be considered inequitable by those who seek to do proportionately better under the proposed arrangement. New entrants particularly will resist grandfathering past production as a formula for allocating future property rights. Further, there may be information problems in documenting past production or use. Such information is often private and the bargaining parties have incentives to overstate their past successes to increase the size of their quota allocations. Since this will be understood by all parties, private documentation of past harvests may be discounted unless it can be verified by neutral sources, which may not exist.

A simple allocation rule that avoids these problems, but one that harms those who have been successful under open access, is a uniform allocation of future rents, whereby all parties with past production receive an equal share. If very productive parties expect the redistribution of wealth to be large relative to their share of the losses of continuing open-access conditions, they will oppose collective action. Side payments are a way of adjusting shares or property rights to mitigate the opposition of influential groups. The range of feasible exchanges for building an accord, however, may be quite limited when the parties are very heterogeneous with regard to past production costs and output. Side payments require agreement on who should pay the compensation, who should receive the wealth transfers and the form the payment should take. Equity issues can arise if those who are to receive compensation are viewed as having had an unjustifiably large share under the status quo.

Information problems can also complicate an accord on the amount of the side payments, even when there is agreement that they are necessary. Compensating payments require agreement on the value of past and current harvests and of any losses that some parties expect as a result of a new definition of property rights. Agreement on the valuation of individual wealth under current and proposed property rights, however, can be difficult in the presence of serious information asymmetries among the parties regarding individual holdings. Valuation disputes will occur quite aside from any strategic bargaining efforts if private estimates of the value of an individual's current share of the resource and of potential losses from the new arrangement, due to reductions in harvest, cannot be conveyed easily or credibly among the other bargaining parties. In such cases, acceptable future shares in the resource will be hard to define and collective action will be delayed.

In addition to honest disagreements on the value of individual claims, the information problems encountered in devising side payments will be intensified if the parties engage in deception to increase their compensation or share in future rents. Deception occurs through willful distortions of the information released to the various parties to inflate the value of current claims and the losses institutional change might impose. Widespread deception by competing interests can make collective action even more difficult by reducing any trust that might otherwise promote the more rapid evaluation and consideration of claims in side payment and share negotiations.

The Sequence of Agreements and Collective Action

As described previously, collective action to address open-access conditions will be particularly difficult to organize when the bargaining parties are heterogeneous. As a result, any agreements that are reached typically will be delayed and collective action (both private and involving the state) will occur late. It is more likely to occur at that time, because as losses mount, the bargaining parties become more homogeneous. With serious dissipation of resource rents, the value of individual shares under the status quo declines so that more and more, all of the parties see themselves made better off by collective action. The expected aggregate gains from reaching agreement to limit further rent dissipation at that point become so large that they dwarf individual distributional concerns and the conflicts over shares that had bedeviled action before can now be resolved. A contributing factor for eventually reaching agreement is a decline in the number of bargaining parties. As individual harvests and incomes fall from open-access conditions, some parties exit.

The problem, however, with this pattern of events is that by the time collective-action agreements to address CPR issues can be reached, many of the resource rents have been dissipated permanently. This result is revealed repeatedly in the empirical cases described below and in other settings, and it is an unfortunate outcome of the difficulties of reaching agreement when the bargaining parties are heterogeneous.

The sequence of bargaining over potential rental losses begins with discussion of the aggregate gains of new institutional arrangements. As noted previously, these generally are not controversial and are recognized for some time before collective action is taken. The problem is reaching agreement on the distribution of the benefits and costs of collective action. Resolving distributional conflicts becomes the next round of negotiations. This round takes the most time and is the most contentious when the parties differ with respect to their individual expected gains from institutional change. If the negotiations are lengthy, many resource rents can be lost before collective action is initiated. Finally, after conditions have become so severe regarding the state of the resource and the ability of the parties to obtain income from its use, agreement on closing some of the margins for rent dissipation becomes possible through collective action.

An exception to this pattern of late agreement occurs when newly discovered resources are to be divided among the competing parties. If no production has occurred, the parties will be reasonably homogeneous, with all having a more-or-less equal stake in saving resource rents through collective action. Moreover, the information asymmetries that plague the valuation of individual shares under current and proposed arrangements are absent because none of the parties have established production histories. None have a vested interest in at least the temporary maintenance of the common pool. Hence, under conditions of new production and mutual ignorance regarding the distribution of future resource rents, agreement on closing potential open-access losses is possible. The circumstances for such early agreements, unfortunately, are quite limited, at least for common-pool natural resources. Nevertheless, they have been encountered in bargaining over mineral rights in the 19th-century American west and in bargaining over the allocation of exploration and production rights to very new oil fields and new fisheries (see Libecap, 1978).

Oil Field Unitization

The Common-pool Problem

Since the first discovery of petroleum in the United States in 1859, oil production has been plagued by serious common-pool losses.[7] These losses arise as numerous firms compete for migratory oil lodged in subsurface reservoirs. Under the common-law rule of capture, private property rights to oil are assigned only upon extraction. Oil reservoirs are commonly found below numerous independently owned surface tracts. The surface landowners initially hold the mineral rights, but transfer them to firms through mineral leases. By this process, many firms gain access to the pool and the lease, rather than the field, becomes the unit of production. In the United States, with fragmented surface land ownership and tiny leases, many firms are very small, with only a few leases on a single reservoir. Typically, oil reservoirs are compressed between an upper layer of natural gas and a lower layer of water. The pressure of these two layers, as well as of the gas dissolved in the oil, drives the oil to the surface when the surrounding formation is punctured by a well. Oil migrates to the well, draining neighboring areas. The extent of migration depends upon subsurface pressures, oil viscosity and the porosity of the surrounding rock. Reservoirs are not uniform. These characteristics differ across the field, generating inherent variation in well productivity. As a firm drills additional wells, oil migrates more rapidly into the created low-pressure zone, raising the firm's share of field output. For each of the firms on a reservoir, a strategy of dense well drilling and rapid production allows it to drain oil from its neighbors and to take advantage of the low extraction costs that exist early in field development. In new, flush oil fields, subsurface pressures are sufficient to expel the oil without costly pumping or injection of water or natural gas into the

---

7. Discussion of oil field unitization is drawn from Libecap (1989: 93–114), Libecap and Wiggins (1984, 1985) and Wiggins and Libecap (1985).

reservoir to drive oil to the surface. Under these conditions, when there are multiple firms on a reservoir, each firm has an incentive to drill competitively and drain to increase its share of oil field rents, even though these individual actions lead to aggregate common-pool losses.

Oil field rents are dissipated in a number of ways. First, increases in the rate of production by any one firm reduce ultimate aggregate oil recovery. With high withdrawal rates associated with competitive common-pool production, the ratio of natural gas to water to oil production increases, leading to a greater loss of subsurface reservoir pressure. With the loss of pressure and dissolved gas, oil becomes more viscous, closing pore spaces in the reservoir and requiring more pressure to move it. Pockets of oil become trapped and are retrievable only at high extraction costs, including the premature need for artificial pumping or reinjection of water or gas to drive the oil to the surface. Second, capital costs are driven up with the drilling of excessive numbers of wells (more than geologic conditions require or price and interest-rate projections warrant) and with the construction of surface storage, where the oil can be held safe from drainage by other firms. These storage practices are costly. Third, rapid extraction also increases production costs as subsurface pressures are vented prematurely, forcing the early adoption of pumps and injection wells. Finally, rents are dissipated as production patterns diverge from those that maximize the value of output over time.

Problems of Collective Action: Information Asymmetries and the Sequence of Agreements

There never has been much disagreement over either the nature of the common-pool problem or the general solution to it. Early discussions of unrestrained oil production in the United States emphasized extraordinary wastes. In 1910 oil losses from fire and evaporation from surface storage in California (wooden tanks or behind earthen dams) ranged from 5 to 11 percent of state production. In 1914 the Director of the Bureau of Mines estimated losses from excessive drilling at $50 million, when the value of US production was $214 million. In 1926 the Federal Oil Conservation Board estimated oil recovery rates of only 20 to 25 percent with competitive extraction, whereas recovery rates of 95 to 90 percent were thought possible with controlled withdrawal. In 1937 the American Petroleum Institute estimated that unnecessary wells on the East Texas field cost over $200 million. In 1980 intensive drilling under prevailing ownership and regulatory practices in the United States left the United States with 88 percent of the world's oil wells and only 14 percent of the world's production.[8]

---

8. Referenced in Libecap (1989: 94–6).

Although the common-pool problem and its costs have been long recognized in the industry, so has been the most complete solution to it – field-wide unitization. Both the Federal Oil Conservation Board and the American Institute of Mining and Metallurgical Engineers issued various reports in the 1920s and early 1930s on the merits of unitization. Under unitization, production rights are delegated through negotiation to a single firm, the unit operator, with net revenues apportioned among all parties on the field (including those that would otherwise be producing). Shares are based on estimates of the value of each firm's leases and their potential contribution to the unit. As the only producer on the field and a residual profit claimant, the unit operator has incentive to maximize field rents. Accordingly, unitization results in important economic gains: a time stream of output that more closely approximates the rent-maximizing pattern, increased oil recovery, fewer wells and other reduced capital costs. For instance, *Oil Weekly* (13 April 1942; 3 May 1943) estimated that early unitization of oil fields would increase recovery from two to five times that of unconstrained production. Similarly, on the Fairway field in Texas estimates were that unitization would increase oil recovery by 130 million barrels (Libecap, 1989: 95).

Despite these attractions for mitigating the substantial losses involved in common-pool crude oil production, complete field-wide unitization has not been widespread. In his study of the oil industry in the 1940s, Joe Bain noted: 'It is difficult to understand why in the United States even admitting all obstacles of law and tradition, not more than a dozen pools are 100 percent unitized (out of some 3,000) and only 185 have even partial unitization' (1947: 29). Similarly, Libecap and Wiggins (1985) reported that as late as 1975 only 38 percent of Oklahoma and 20 percent of Texas production came from field-wide units.

The key issue in blocking agreement on the voluntary unitization of oil fields is conflict over a share formula to divide the net proceeds of unit production among the various parties. In share negotiations two serious problems arise. First, unitization contracts must assign once-and-for-all shares at the time the contract is completed. This is because changes in reservoir dynamics after unitization make it impossible to link unit production to particular leases, which would be necessary for adjusting shares. A second problem is general uncertainty and asymmetrical information regarding relative preunitization lease values, which determine unit shares. These problems block agreement on lease-value estimates and proposed unit shares in unit rents.

The level of information available to the contracting parties depends upon the stage of production in which contracting occurs. In exploration, little is known regarding the location of oil and its commercial extraction possibilities. At that time, all leases are relatively homogeneous and unitization

agreements are comparatively easy to reach, using simple allocation for-
mulas, often based on surface acreage. Since no party knows whether the
formula is to its advantage or disadvantage, negotiations can focus on the
aggregate gains from unitization. Information problems and distributional
concerns, however, arise with development, as oil reserves are proved and
expanded. With the initial discovery well and the drilling of subsequent
wells, lease production heterogeneities emerge. Because reservoirs are not
uniform, the information released from a well is descriptive of only the
immediate vicinity. Hence, through drilling their individual leases, firms
gain knowledge of their portion of the reservoir but the full extent of the
deposit and the productive potential of other areas of the reservoir will be
revealed only through the drilling activities of other firms.

The production potential and commercial value of a lease are functions of
both public and private data. Public data include objectively measured and
non-controversial variables, such as the number of wells on the lease, its surface acreage, the record of current and past production. These data are
available to all of the contracting parties. Private data on lease parameters
involve geological variables, which tend to be subjectively assessed and
valued by individual company engineers. These variables include bottom
hole pressure, gross acre feet of pay (volume of the producing formation),
net acre feet of pay (non-porous and non-oil-bearing rock is subtracted from
the gross measure) and remaining reserves (original oil in place less
cumulative production). These variables describe the condition of the oil
reservoir under each lease and data on them are obtained from well logs and
production histories and require interpretation by geologists and engineers
to be translated into production potential. The assessments and their
implications for lease values and unit shares are often controversial and subject to dispute, because the estimating procedures and interpretations vary
across firms, even when examining the same data. There are no uniform
standards for what is often an ad hoc or 'seat-of-the-pants' guess by engineers who are familiar with individual well performance. These judgements,
however, are not easily verified by other parties, and accordingly are difficult to incorporate into the unit allocation formula.

For instance, in unit negotiations on the Prentice field in West Texas, there
were differences in rock porosity estimates of 60 to 100 percent (Libecap,
1989: 99). The estimation of dynamic reservoir characteristics, such as
remaining oil reserves, involves even greater complications. Companies
often have differing opinions about the correct estimation procedure, when
choices can reallocate millions of dollars. Remaining primary reserves are
estimated using simple ordinary least square regressions on specific functional forms that are often inaccurate. In the case of unsuccessful unit
negotiations on the Wasson field of Texas in 1971, there were disputes over
the amount of ultimate primary oil recovery (cumulative production plus

remaining primary reserves) under certain leases. In 1978 negotiations were re-opened after 2 million additional barrels (6 percent of total cumulative output) had been produced from the field, releasing new information on ultimate primary recovery for those leases. This 6 percent change in total output, however, led to a revision of remaining lease reserves estimates by approximately 50 percent (Wiggins and Libecap, 1985: 370). The problems of asymmetric, private information are particularly important for long-lived, highly productive leases. These are the leases that require the greatest projections into the future to estimate value and hence, the ones where differences in estimating techniques and disputes between the private estimations of the owners and the other bargaining parties are most likely. Owners of these leases are most likely to hold out in unit negotiations.[9]

As a result of different interpretations of private information and of differences in procedures, unit negotiating parties generally cannot reach early agreement on lease values or unit shares. To avoid conflict over subsurface parameters, negotiations often turn to a small set of objectively measurable variables, such as cumulative output or wells per acre. These objective measures, however, may be poor indicators of lease value. The resulting asymmetry in lease value calculations, based on differential information and interpretation among firms, is the primary cause of breakdown in unit share negotiations.

These conflicts over lease values and unit shares among heterogeneous producers continue until late in the life of a reservoir. With the accumulation of information released through development and production, public and private lease value estimates converge and primary production (production based on natural subsurface pressure) approaches zero. At that point, a consensus on shares and the formation of the unit is possible. Lease values become much more homogeneous, since without unitization and the artificial injection of natural gas or other substances to supplement underground pressure (secondary recovery), all leases will approach zero values. Unfortunately, by the time that at least partial field unitization is essential to maintain production, most of the common-pool losses will have already occurred.

The information in Table 1 indicates just how long unit negotiations can take. The data were compiled by Libecap and Wiggins (1985) and Wiggins and Libecap (1985) and they involve seven oil fields in Texas and New Mexico where unit negotiations took place: North Cowden, Goldsmith/ Landreth, Prentice Northeast, Western RKM, Slaughter Estate, Empire Abo and Goldsmith San Andres.

The table reveals that negotiations to address common-pool problems

---

9. This hypothesis is confirmed in Wiggins and Libecap (1985).

Table 1. Unit Negotiations

Oil field	Negotiation time (years)	Final acreage as a share of initial acreage
North Cowden	8	.57
Goldsmith/Landreth	4	.84
Prentice Northeast	9	.80
Western RKM	4	.30
Slaughter Estate	5	1.00
Empire Abo	6	1.00
Goldsmith/San Andres	4	.85

Source: Adapted from Libecap (1989: 103).

through unitization took a long time, ranging from four to nine years. Moreover, in five of the seven cases, the acreage in the final unit was less than that involved in the early negotiations. As unitization negotiations were drawn out over share conflicts, some firms decided to create partial field units, or sub-units, which are less effective than field-wide cooperation. On small sub-units, secondary recovery methods work less well and overall recovery declines. Further, partial unitization leads to increased capital costs. For instance, after the unsuccessful efforts to completely unitize the 71,000-acre Slaughter field in West Texas, 28 separate sub-units were established, ranging in size from 80 to 4,918 acres. To prevent migration of oil across sub-unit boundaries, some 427 off-setting, water injection wells were sunk along each sub-unit boundary at a per well cost of $360,000 for a total of $156 million. These wells and related expenses were not needed for production and could have been avoided with a field-wide unit. Such practices have been routine, particularly in Texas where multiple units are common.

Fisheries

The Common-pool Problem

Fisheries are the classic common-pool resources. In most cases in the US and in many throughout the world, there are no restrictions on entry. In part, this is due to the migratory nature of many species. The area necessary to effectively manage the stock is large and policing property rights to it is costly. This is a particular problem for offshore fisheries, where the areas involved are extensive and government jurisdictions overlap. Another constraint, particularly in the US, is the legal prohibition of private property rights or even communal rights to natural fish stocks. For inshore fisheries where migratory distances are less, exclusive rights institutions would be an option for collective action if they were allowable by law, but they are not. For off-shore fisheries where 200-mile territorial limits are in place, exclusion applies to foreign fishers, while access is available to native fishers. In these fisheries, arrangements must be devised to limit access and harvest by local fishers and these arrangements typically have not been very successful.

Hence, many (if not most) of the world's fisheries are characterized by limited or no effective restrictions on entry and harvest and the severe dissipation of fishery rents. Individual harvests and incomes are down and fishery communities are economically depressed. Lacking ownership in the stock, individual fishers do not consider the total costs of their private harvests. Aggregate catch is too great because fishing occurs until the average private cost of harvest equals the market price, rather than where marginal social costs and benefits are equated. Each fisher imposes costs on others by dispersing fish and lowering the size of the stock. Further, competitive pressures lead to excessive amounts of labor and capital inputs in the fishery. As entry continues and the stock declines over time, average catch and income falls.

The losses of the common pool in fisheries have a long history and unfortunately, little record of success in collective action. Historical examples of fisheries that have disappeared or have very diminished commercial viability include the California sardine fishery and the Pacific Northwest salmon fishery. Currently, few of the world's fisheries escape problems of overfishing, falling yields and rising costs.[10]

Collective-action Problems: Heterogeneities and the Sequence of Agreements

The losses of common-pool fisheries provide important incentives for fishers to engage in collective action to devise restrictions on entry and harvest, both among themselves and with politicians for regulatory policy (given the general absence of private or communal property rights for most migratory species in US waters). The pattern, however, is one of little successful collective action until the fishery is severely overfished. At that time, both fishers and regulatory agencies are more able to agree to and implement transferable quota schemes. The limited exception to this pattern is in a few very new fisheries where quotas have been adopted early to limit catch. As noted previously, at that time the parties are comparatively homogeneous and better able to agree to restrictions on fishing harvests. Additionally, unions in inshore fisheries along the US coasts appear to have been able to devise local arrangements in the 1940s and 1950s to conserve fish stocks. Fish prices were

---

10. The discussion follows from Libecap (1989: 73–92) and Johnson and Libecap (1982).

comparatively lower and entry pressure may have been limited, at least with respect to current conditions. Nevertheless, such union restrictions were ruled violations of anti-trust laws and are no longer options.

Differences among fishers according to skill, capital and size create conflicting interests and incentives for regulating fishing. These differences limit the informal agreements that might be reached among fishers to reduce fishing effort. They also diminish the effectiveness of fishers as cohesive lobbyists for influencing the more formal regulatory controls on access and harvest in open-access fisheries that now are required by law. As fish stocks, yields and incomes have fallen, regulatory policies have been adopted, but these generally have been costly and relatively ineffective.

Differential abilities among fishers exist according to fishing skills, which include ability to set nets correctly and regulate their spread, ability to determine effective trawling speed and ability to locate fish quickly before they are dispersed by the trawling of other fishers. The effects of variation in skills are observable in persistent catch differences per unit of effort across fishers. Because those skills are unlikely to be readily transferable assets, economic rents will be earned by better fishers, even under open-access conditions. With the differential rents that exist among heterogeneous fishers, some fishers may have a stake in maintaining current conditions in the fishery and in opposing collective action if proposed changes seriously upset status quo rankings and redistribute income. Further, because of the costs of designing regulations that respect skill and catch differences, skilled fishers have reason to be wary of regulatory change.

Accordingly, the nature of individual benefits or rental shares under the status quo, relative to that under a new arrangement achieved through collective action, is a critical issue. Understandably, existing fishers are concerned about how they will fare with restrictions on entry and catch. Those fishers who have adapted well to existing conditions are under risk that their shares of fishery rents with any new program to control fishing will be less than they currently receive. This hazard can exist at least until the fishery is depleted. At that point, when individual catch and incomes are very low and many fishers have left the fishery, those that remain are more homogeneous with regard to expected future prospects and are more likely to see themselves as becoming better off with more restrictive controls on harvest. Agreement on new regulatory initiatives is then more probable. As with the case of oil fields, by that time common-pool conditions will already have inflicted serious and perhaps permanent damage on the fishery stock.[11]

---

11. The extent of recovery of fish stocks in response to regulatory policies is also a source of dispute, since it depends upon the condition of the stock at the time that the regulations are imposed and upon exogenous factors, such as availability of food, ocean temperatures and water pollution. If there are outside parties who are not regulated, as may be the case in offshore fisheries, then those who are regulated have little reason to expect a major rebound in the stock.

Redistribution concerns not only affect the stands taken by fishers in bargaining over proposed regulations but they also affect the positions of regulatory officials who will have a stake in how the proposals affect their authority and jurisdiction. Politicians who must enact legislation regarding fishery regulation will seek policies that maximize their political support. The political influence of fishers in this process will depend upon their numbers and cohesion as lobbyists. Differences among fishers, as well as their traditional independence, limit their effectiveness as a political force for enacting restrictions on their own fishing practices. The likelihood of successful collective activity is greater when fishers are seeking restrictions on their rivals or when they are attempting to obtain programs that will raise total catch or wealth without placing tight controls on individual fishing effort. In political negotiations among fishers, politicians and bureaucrats for regulatory policies, those programs that recognize existing share allocations or rankings of fishers, while increasing total catch or yields, generally will have broad support. If yields can be increased through the adoption of season closures or through the construction of fish hatcheries, existing fishers can be made better off and no divisive redistribution of catch or fishing effort need be involved.

Where restrictions on individual catch or effort are necessary as part of setting a total allowable catch for a species, which may be necessary in more depleted fisheries, incumbent, skilled fishers will prefer a quota scheme that maintains status quo rankings. Individual quotas assigned on the basis of historical catch will therefore be popular with those fishers because they recognize past performance and minimize redistribution. On the other hand, new entrants and young fishers have incentive to oppose any quota schemes that recognize historical catch patterns or place restrictions on new entry. The regulations adopted will depend in part on the relative political power of the competing fishing groups and established fishers may have important advantages in the political process.

Another source of concern among fishers in collective action to mitigate rent dissipation in the fishery is limited information on what the ultimate impact of regulation will be on the fish stock and on the returns to individual fishers. In many fisheries knowledge is extremely limited regarding the nature and size of the stock, its relationship to the environment, the impact of harvest and the reaction of the stock to proposed regulatory efforts. These information problems make it more difficult for fishers to determine whether their welfare will be improved by the adoption of new regulations relative to the status quo.

The general preferences of fishers to favor visible, yield-enhancing policies where the costs are spread among taxpayers and where more conventional distributional restrictions are avoided, frequently coincide with the interests of politicians and bureaucrats. The latter have an incentive to respond to organized interest-group pressures regarding common-pool losses in fisheries, while avoiding as much as possible the disruptive distributional conflicts that may be part of more binding restrictions on harvest and access. Accordingly, at least in early regulations, politicians and bureaucrats will also favor those policies that raise total yields and that minimize interference with the activities of more influential groups of fishers. Such policies, though, may leave many margins for fishery rent dissipation uncontrolled.

Policies that are likely to be supported early in fishery regulation include hatcheries; direct government subsidies and tax relief; season closures and gear restrictions to protect adolescent, lower-valued fish; minimum fish size requirements; and access denials to foreigners through 200-mile coastal zones or to other less-influential fishers. Procedures that enhance the value of total catch forestall the application of more restrictive and controversial controls on access and catch. Increases in the total value of the catch will invite greater fishing by incumbent fishers and further entry by new fishers, intensifying competitive pressures on incomes and the stock of fish and continuing the losses of the common pool. Eventually, when conditions have so deteriorated in the fishery, more restrictive regulations will be adopted, such as total closures or the adoption of individual transferable quotas.

To illustrate the problems of heterogeneity and sequencing in fishery regulation, consider the Gulf Coast shrimp fishery (Johnson and Libecap, 1982). As previously discussed, fishers have not been able to agree on individual quota schemes and other constraints on entry and harvest, even though average catch has fallen in the fishery from its peak in 1963. Unlimited numbers of licenses have been available for both the bay and Gulf shrimp fisheries with the payment of minimal fees. The fishery has remained virtually an open-access one. Regulations exist to increase the value of aggregate catch by protecting immature shrimp through season closures, gear restrictions and minimum-size limits for harvesting shrimp. Shrimpers have agreed to season closures, which are designed to expand the aggregate stock and do not discriminate in access during the open season. Conflicts, however, have developed over access to particular kinds of immature shrimp.

Beginning in the 1950s, two separate shrimp fisheries developed in Texas, based on the kinds of shrimp of commercial importance to each – the bay fishery that focused on white shrimp that remained as adults in the bays and the Gulf fishery that focused on adult brown shrimp that developed in the bays in the spring, but migrated as juveniles to the Gulf. Bay shrimpers have an incentive to agree to seasons that protect immature white shrimp because they have access to them as adults. But they do not have the same incentive to protect immature brown shrimp, which migrate to the deep waters of the Gulf and are harvested by Gulf shrimpers.

Since brown and white shrimp tend to be in different areas in the bays, bay shrimpers can harvest them while minimizing the catch of young white shrimp. Gulf shrimpers naturally oppose this practice because it reduces the number of shrimp that make it to the Gulf. In 1959 Gulf shrimpers lobbied the Texas legislature to close the bay fishery from 1 March to 15 July to allow brown shrimp to develop and to close the Gulf from 1 June to 15 July for the same reason. Bay shrimpers opposed the spring closing of the bays and they succeeded in amending the law to allow for a limited spring season from 15 May to 15 July. Nevertheless, political conflict has continued between the two groups.

Although shrimpers generally have not agreed to internal effort controls, bay shrimpers have accepted gear restrictions on minimum net mesh size. These regulations reinforce the effect of season closures by allowing small shrimp to escape the pull of nets. Bay shrimpers also have supported other limits on the number and size of nets that can be used in the bays. During the fall white shrimp season, only one net, 25 feet in width, can be pulled by any vessel. This restriction is not designed to limit the harvest of bay shrimpers but to reduce the incentive of larger Gulf vessels to enter the bays during the fall season. By limiting the size and number of nets the larger Gulf vessels can pull, the restrictions reduce their competitive advantage over inshore boats. There are no restrictions on the number or size of trawl nets used in the Gulf. The conflict between Gulf and bay shrimpers over the harvest of immature shrimp has also led to the imposition of individual catch limits on bay shrimpers during the spring brown shrimp season. Daily limits of 300 pounds per vessel have been assigned in the bays in the spring, but no catch restrictions are imposed for the fall bay white shrimp season or for the fall and winter brown shrimp season in the Gulf. Various possible controls on individual fishing effort have received little support and hence, historically, there has been no collective action to seriously limit harvests in the shrimp fishery. More recently, however, as shrimp harvests have fallen even more, interest among shrimpers in individual quotas and limits on entry has grown. This mirrors practices in other fisheries, where quotas and access controls have not been adopted until stocks have been very depleted, fishers have left the industry and conditions have become desperate for those who remain.

The collective-action problem faced by Gulf and bay shrimpers is similar to the one described by Elinor Ostrom in coordinating use of irrigation water between head-end and tail-end farmers in Nepal. In that case, farmers often have been able to devise rules for labor input in the maintenance of irrigation canals that also serve to allocate water successfully. Unlike the Texas shrimp fishery, however, the farm communities in Nepal seem to have been quite stable with little outside entry and the parties generally have relied upon locally generated rules to govern water access and the maintenance of canals. These conditions have given rise to a comparatively more homogeneous group in terms of preferences and capabilities than have those along the Gulf of Mexico, where outside entry is frequent and there is little sense of community. Further, in the case of Texas shrimpers, both Gulf and bay shrimpers have resorted to external government organizations to impose restrictive rules on one another. This practice has changed the nature of the relationship between the two groups and the bargaining conditions they face in ways that reduce the opportunities for successful private collective action. In any case, the range of private agreements to foster cooperation within the groups for limiting entry and harvest is likely to be quite limited, given past intervention by the Justice Department to block such arrangements as violations of the Sherman Act.[12]

Orange Marketing Orders

The Common-pool Problem

In the case of orange marketing orders, the common-pool problem is not a technological one. That is, entry into the industry and the growing and harvest of oranges does not cause serious external effects on other growers, as is the case in oil extraction or fisheries. Instead, the external effects are pecuniary. Each firm's output, made to maximize firm profits, contributes to additional market supplies and potentially, to a decline in industry prices. Agriculture has been particularly sensitive to this because of fluctuating growing conditions that contribute to market gluts and shortages, easy entry and large numbers of producers. For products like citrus, storage of fresh fruit has been limited, making the stockpiling of commodities difficult. Hence, farmers have attempted collective action to control production and the amounts of the product placed on the market at any point in time. Although this problem of industry-wide pecuniary losses from individual production decisions does not involve efficiency issues, as are found in classic common-pool cases, the collective action to limit total output through the assignment of firm quotas reveals many similarities to behavior found in collective action regarding fisheries and oil fields.

Although agriculture has always encountered price fluctuations, the problem was an especially severe one in the 1930s. Between 1919 and 1933 wholesale farm prices had fallen by 67 percent, whereas over the same period non-agricultural wholesale prices had fallen by 45 percent.[13] Moreover, the fall in agricultural prices was particularly severe after 1929 (US Department of Commerce, 1975: 199–200). For oranges, nominal prices fell by 75 percent

---

12. Ostrom (paper 6 in this collection) points out how outside intervention can lead to the breakdown of local rules for irrigation systems.

13. The discussion is drawn from Hoffman and Libecap (1994).

between 1930 and 1933, and the industry, led by the California Fruit Growers Exchange (CFGE), lobbied for provisions in the Agricultural Adjustment Act (AAA) for marketing agreements to secure government control of the shipment of commodities in order to raise prices. Marketing agreements for oranges were implemented on 18 December 1933 and were among the first marketing agreements put into place.

Among agricultural products, specialty crops, such as oranges, offered the greatest potential for a successful cartelization policy. There were relatively fewer growers than existed for general commodities; production was concentrated in a few isolated regions; there was a consensus among orange growers that government cartelization was necessary (established, formal cooperatives, such as the California Fruit Growers Exchange, existed to implement the marketing agreements); and oranges were a perishable crop that limited the build up of inventories that could depress prices.

Under AAA, the Secretary of Agriculture could issue a marketing agreement if 50 percent of the shippers and two-thirds of the growers in the state agreed to the provisions. The marketing agreements authorized the Secretary to limit interstate orange shipments through weekly allotments to shippers that were enforced through revokable shipping licenses and fines of $1,000 for violation. Violators were to be prosecuted by the Justice Department and the agreements were exempted from antitrust regulations. The weekly shipping quotas were to be determined by industry boards in California and Florida, based on estimates of supply and demand consistent with targeted prices. There were provisions in the law for national prorationing of total orange shipments by region. With national prorationing, a national control commission was to be established to assign state quotas and prorate shipments among the states throughout the growing season. Excess production was to be diverted to other uses, such as by-products (livestock feed) or foreign markets.

Despite this framework, an orange cartel was not established as envisioned by the Agricultural Adjustment Act. National prorationing among the producing regions was never adopted. Further, there were sharp differences between California and Florida in the industry response to the marketing agreements proposed by the Secretaries of Agriculture. California growers and shippers accepted their 1933 marketing agreement with weekly prorationing of interstate orange shipments and although some modifications were made, the basic thrust of these regulations remained intact through December 1992. Growers and shippers in Florida, however, rejected a 1933 marketing agreement that was virtually identical to that implemented in California. It was terminated in 1934. Between 1934 and 1937 two other marketing agreements were executed by the Secretary of Agriculture for Florida, but terminated before an acceptable arrangement could be devised in 1939. The final Florida marketing order did not involve prorationing of orange shipments. Instead, it relied on temporary shipping holidays and adjustable size and quality controls to limit interstate shipments. Florida never adopted weekly prorationing of orange shipments as practiced in California. Under these circumstances, orange prices did not rise to target parity levels.

Collective-action Problems: Heterogeneities and the Sequence of Agreements

Throughout the summer of 1933 orange producers and shippers from California/Arizona, Florida and Texas met with Agricultural Adjustment Administration personnel in Washington, DC, to draft marketing agreements for their respective states and to conclude a national prorationing agreement. The representatives of the CFGE lobbied hard for national prorationing with fixed state quotas and a national price stabilization plan (national cartelization). They offered their draft marketing agreement for adoption by the Agricultural Adjustment Administration.

At the Washington meetings on 20 July 1933 California had nine delegates, Texas had nine, Arizona one, but Florida had 37 because of differences in opinion within the state as to the nature of the regulations that should be adopted.[14] Indeed, this reflected disagreement in Florida as to just what arrangement to support. The Agricultural Adjustment Administration recognized that this would be a problem for successful collective action and regulation and to remedy it, the agency worked closely with the Florida Citrus Exchange (FCE) to adopt regulations that would *force* membership in the cooperative.

The Florida industry presented at least two competing draft marketing agreements, one supported by the FCE and similar to that proposed by the CFGE and one backed by the Florida Citrus Growers Clearing House Association (FCHA). Many of the independent growers and shippers in Florida were organized under the FCHA, but they did not enter into long-term sales contracts to pool fruit as practiced by the cooperatives. The Department of Agriculture supported and ultimately adopted the draft marketing agreements proposed by the CFGE and FCE that called for the weekly prorationing of orange shipments among shippers whose quotas would be based upon season-long contracts for fruit.[15] These long-term contracts were an integral part of the pooling agreements of the CFGE and FCE.

Importantly, independent shippers, who did not pool fruit and belong to cooperatives, would not have been able to get shipping quotas under the

14. *Citrus Leaves*, August 1933: 20; *Citrus Industry*, March 1934: 26.
15. *Citrograph*, September 1933: 301.

arrangements proposed by the CFGE and the FCE. Such shippers, who were particularly prevalent in Florida, tended to engage in spot purchases of fruit and would not have had fruit under contract at the beginning of the season, when quotas were to be assigned under the marketing agreement. We analyze the effect of the prorationing rule in more detail below, but its adoption in 1933 by the Agricultural Adjustment Administration after negotiating with representatives of the California and Florida industries was an effort to require growers and shippers in Florida to join the Florida Citrus Exchange. Officials of the Department of Agriculture argued that the success of the marketing agreement depended upon broad participation in cooperative shipping pools in Florida.

Not only did the Department of Agriculture adopt a quota rule to encourage membership in the Florida Citrus Exchange but the FCE was given a majority of the positions on the state administrative committee. Under the marketing agreement, Secretary of Agriculture Henry A. Wallace appointed the members of the Florida Control Committee that was set up to determine weekly shipping levels and to assign shipping quotas. Most of those selected were from the FCE. On the other hand, the California/ Arizona marketing agreement allowed for the election of members of the administrative committees for that region.

Independent shippers and growers within the FCHA, who attended the Washington meetings to draft the marketing agreements, understood the effect of the prorationing rule in requiring membership in pooling cooperatives. The department recommended that growers who were worried that their shippers would not have quotas under the prorationing rule link up with established shippers who did. During negotiations in the fall of 1933 the FCHA demanded that the Agricultural Adjustment Administration modify its proposed marketing agreement for Florida because it would force independents out of business.

Despite their efforts the FCHA could not block the marketing order negotiated by the Agricultural Adjustment Administration and the FCE. Since the agency basically used the California model for regulation, the marketing agreements imposed in the two states were virtually the same. Whereas there was substantial consensus in California in favour of the marketing agreements, opposition in Florida to the prorationing rule, and to the Florida Control Committee appointed by the Secretary of Agriculture, meant that additional negotiations would have to take place between the agency and the industry. These negotiations subsequently led to important modification of regulation in Florida in ways that diverged from the original aims of the Agricultural Adjustment Act and of the administrative agency. Further, negotiations between the Agricultural Adjustment Administration and the Florida industry continued for the rest of the decade before a satisfactory arrangement could be devised.

Table 2. Federal Orange Marketing Agreements

Marketing agreement	Time in operation	Shipping proration	Grade and size regulation	Shipping holiday	National proration
Florida					
First	18 Dec. 1933–13 Aug. 1934	Yes	Yes	No	Yes
Second	18 Dec. 1934–15 July 1935	Yes	Yes	No	Yes
Third	8 May 1936–31 July 1937	Yes	Yes	No	N/A
Fourth	22 February 1939–1955	No	Yes	Yes	N/A
California					
First	18 Dec. 1933–17 May 1947	Yes	No	No	Yes

Source: Adapted from Hoffman and Libecap (1994).

Table 2 summarizes the pattern of regulation of orange shipments under the AAA and subsequent federal legislation through 1941. Although the California marketing agreement remained in operation through 1947, in Florida the first marketing agreement was terminated in August 1934, a second was adopted in December 1934 and terminated in July 1935, a third was implemented in May 1936 and terminated in July 1937 and a fourth that remained in effect was adopted in February 1939. Negotiations over 6 years led ultimately to a marketing agreement without the prorationing of shipments because of disagreement over quotas. In the final agreement shipping controls were limited to shipping holidays and adjustable grade and size restrictions. Neither of these regulations required individual quotas or membership in agricultural cooperatives.

The original marketing agreements in both California and Florida called for weekly prorationing of interstate orange shipments as set by the industry administrative committee. In Florida, there was one committee, appointed by the Secretary of Agriculture, while in California there were two committees, both elected. Quotas to individual shippers within the weekly prorate were to be set by the administrative committee. The allocation was determined by a 'prorate base' assigned to each shipper on the basis of the amount of fruit held under contract with growers at the beginning of the season. The prorate base was the shipper's fraction of total seasonal orange shipments from the state, and multiplying it by the authorized weekly total determined each shipper's weekly quota.

This prorationing rule emphasized long-term, seasonal contracts between growers and shippers as to when fruit would be picked and shipped and the division of returns. It posed an immediate threat to independent Florida growers and shippers who relied upon short-term, spot, cash exchanges for fruit whenever market conditions warranted. As designed by the marketing agreement, however, these transactions did not qualify for determining the shipper's prorate base. A shipper with no seasonal contracts would have a zero prorate base and hence receive no weekly quota. Typically, only growers and shippers who were part of seasonal pools engaged in such contracts, since pooling cooperatives like the Florida Citrus Exchange relied on long-term arrangements to manage the flow of shipments throughout the season.

The independent shippers and growers in Florida strongly objected to this prorationing rule that was designed to force them into pooling arrangements. They also objected to the assignment of quotas by the Florida Control Committee, appointed by the Secretary of Agriculture and dominated by the Florida Citrus Exchange. Additionally, independent growers were concerned that the prorationing rules would not sufficiently recognize differences in maturity dates, which were so important in Florida.[16] Instead of prorationing rules, the independents favored the use of shipping holidays and quality restrictions to regulate shipments more loosely to smooth prices. Shipping holidays could block all deliveries from the state for a specified period of time to alleviate temporary market gluts. Size and quality standards could be set to deny shipment of fruit that fell below the standard and the standard could be adjusted from time to time to provide flexible restraints. Quality standards also provided some industry-wide public goods in maintaining product reputation.[17] Enforcement for both policies would involve inspection and monitoring of all deliveries across state lines, rather than ensuring individual quota compliance, as was necessary under prorationing.

Because shipping holidays and quality standards generally applied across the board, the distributional consequences were less severe than those associated with the proposed allocation of quotas under the marketing order proposed by the Agricultural Adjustment Administration. Quality constraints did harm marginal growers with low-quality fruit, but those growers appeared not to be sufficiently influential to block their use. Shipping holidays typically were short enough not to cause serious losses. Moreover, these alternatives did not require membership in cooperatives. An example of broad-based support for shipping holidays in Florida is the call by the FCE, the FCHA and other shippers on 6 February 1933 for a 6-day shipping holiday in order to raise prices.[18]

---

16. *Citrus Leaves*, October 1933: 3, 4, 11–20; *Citrus Industry*, August 1933: 16; November 1933: 6.

17. With more heterogeneous fruit, reputation was a particular concern for Florida growers with respect to their Californian competitors. Because Florida oranges often had traces of green in their skins, unlike the more uniformly golden California Navels, fruit was often dyed in Florida. See Florida Citrus Inspection Bureau (1938: 157) for data on 'color-added' oranges.

18. *Citrus Industry*, February 1933: 5.

The 1933 marketing agreement was challenged in Federal District Court almost immediately in *Yarnell v Hillsborough Packing Co.*, 70 F.(2nd) 435. An injunction was issued against prorationing on 18 January 1934 and prorationing controls by the Florida Control Committee were temporarily halted. Although the injunction was removed on 10 February 1934 by an appellate court and the ruling was reversed by the Fifth US Circuit Court of Appeals on 14 April 1934, the injunction was applied at the height of the Florida orange season and it raised uncertainty about the future of prorationing.[19] Throughout the summer and fall of 1934 members of the FCE and the FCHA corresponded with officials of the Agricultural Adjustment Administration regarding the redrafting of the marketing agreement. Each side wanted its position considered and to be assured of adequate representation on the drafting committee. A second marketing agreement was initiated in December 1934. There were two minor modifications in the order, but the Department of Agriculture continued to maintain the basic prorationing framework.

Throughout 1934 and 1935 there were conflicts over the membership of the Control Committee and demands for access to its records in prorationing allocations. In the face of continued opposition, the second marketing agreement for Florida oranges was terminated on 15 July 1935. A third marketing agreement was not put into place until May 1936, 10 months after the termination of the second agreement and after the 1935–36 shipping season had passed. As before, the Department of Agriculture maintained prorationing of orange shipments as the primary method of regulation and conflicts continued over the assignment of quotas and Department efforts to force membership in cooperative pools. Court challenges of the prorationing quotas continued. The third marketing agreement for Florida oranges was terminated on 31 July 1937.

Over a year of negotiations between the Agricultural Adjustment Administration and the Florida industry was necessary before a final and successful marketing agreement was implemented on 22 February 1939. Pooling remained relatively limited in Florida and the new marketing order contained no quota rules or prorationing provisions. Regulation, instead, focused upon uniform grade and size restrictions and shipping holidays, the framework originally demanded by independents.

The differences between the reactions of the Florida and California industries with regard to federal marketing agreements were due to important heterogeneities in Florida production. California and Florida were by far the dominant producers of oranges, with California accounting for 67

---

19. The constitutional issues raised by Judge Akerman and the hostility to the Agricultural Adjustment Act are discussed in Irons (1982: 142–9).

percent of US output in 1930–1 and Florida 32 percent (Hoffman and Libecap, 1994). Oranges from both regions competed as close substitutes in the fresh fruit market. Until the late 1940s there was no frozen concentrate or significant use of oranges in juice. California produced two kinds of oranges: winter navels with a season of October to June and summer Valencias with a season from May through October. Florida produced at least five varieties, all during the winter season: Parson Brown and Hamlin (October–December), Homosassa and Pineapple (January–March) and Valencia (April–June). Florida growers tended to specialize in a certain variety, which was often determined by growing conditions. Storage possibilities at this time were limited, especially for Florida fruit. Because of climate conditions, Florida oranges did not store well on the tree and had to be harvested quickly in order to avoid fruit drop. In California, because of relatively cool nights, oranges could be stored on the tree for up to two or three months.

Because of important differences in growing conditions and crops, most Florida growers and shippers were independents, with only about 25 percent of the state's production pooled and marketed through the Florida Citrus Exchange. In California, with more homogeneous growing conditions and output, 90 percent of the state's output was handled through the California Fruit Growers Exchange and the Mutual Orange Distributors. These differences in pooling practices were due to much more heterogeneous fruit in Florida, which raised the costs of pooling, and sharply different subseasons and corresponding price expectations among Florida growers, which reduced the incentive to engage in seasonal pools. Nevertheless, the Department of Agriculture attempted to force membership in the cooperatives through the marketing agreements. A final agreement was not reached until 1939. By that time there were reasons for concluding an agreement. Prices had not rebounded to their targeted levels and the future of the marketing agreement effort looked bleak for the agency. Moreover, Florida growers and shippers were concerned that federal regulation would be withdrawn altogether. Finally, the Department of Agriculture agreed to change the allocation rule within the regulation to reduce potential redistribution.

Concluding Remarks

Traditional CPR problems, involving technological externalities, and competitive conditions within an industry, involving pecuniary losses, provide incentives for collective action among the affected parties to regulate total output through the assignment of individual production quotas. Yet, as the empirical cases summarized in this paper reveal, the collective response is often late and quite limited. Heterogeneities in capabilities among the parties, including differences in information, past production, costs and size, provide obstacles to reaching agreement on the allocation rules for sharing the net benefits that result. Unless influential parties are able to see their private welfare improved by collective action, they will not participate, even though there may be important social gains (in the case of CPR problems). Hence, in local and likely in global commons, collective action is not apt to take place in a smooth or timely fashion when there are important heterogeneities among the bargaining parties.

Conflicts over quotas or shares in the benefits of collective action tend to diminish as the magnitude of the rental losses grows and becomes widespread among all parties. At that time, the parties become relatively more homogeneous in future production capabilities, with fewer information asymmetries about the value of their claims to resource rents, and have a greater stake in reaching agreement on production limits. Moreover, there are likely to be fewer bargaining parties, since some will have exited in the face of declining individual revenues.

These empirical results suggest that sequential bargaining is a characteristic of collective action in CPR and industry public goods. In the cases examined in this paper sequencing is the result of an inability of heterogeneous parties to reach early agreement on the distribution of the net gains of collective action. When the parties are more homogeneous, either very early, before different production capabilities and patterns are established, or very late, when all parties expect future revenues to be uniformly small, then agreement is more likely. In the more general interim situation, where the parties have differential views as to the private benefits of collective action, each round of bargaining involves the consideration of new information (especially for CPRs) on both the aggregate and individual net benefits of agreement. As described here, the process continues until public and private information about the value of individual shares converge and the bargaining parties become more homogeneous in their stake in the new regime.

For non-renewable CPRs collective action may occur more quickly, since the parties may see the rental loss from competitive exploitation as permanent. For renewable CPRs rebounds in the stock are possible due to exogenous factors, so that the parties may disagree on whether strict group restrictions on exploitation are required. Further, they may disagree as to how the resource will respond to conservation practices, especially in cases where information about the stock and its reaction to reductions in harvest pressure is limited. Uncertainties about future regulatory policies, which are compounded when there are competing government jurisdictions, are an additional problem for those who are trying to estimate their individual net benefits from collective action. In either case, for many local and global CPR situations, effective collective action will not occur until many of the losses have already been absorbed. In the case of cartel negotiations, where pecuniary externalities are the concern, firm heterogeneities will impede agreement on production limits and there are incentives for each party to cheat. Since a resource stock is not at risk from violation of production rules, cartel agreements may be more prone to cheating and breakdown than are CPR arrangements where the fragility of the resource is widely recognized.

The conclusion drawn from these empirical case studies for successful collective action is more pessimistic than that suggested by Elinor Ostrom's findings for Nepal and by the laboratory results presented by Hackett et al. (papers 5 and 6 in this collection). There appear to be critical differences between the Nepal case and those described here that may account for the differential contracting success. In fisheries, oil fields and orange production, the number of bargaining parties has been comparatively large; the parties have been heterogeneous in their capabilities, including access to information, and because of easy entry by outsiders there has been little sense of community or shared preferences for collective action until late in resource use. These factors are likely to make it more difficult for the parties to reach a consensus on the aggregate gains of addressing commons problems and rules for the distribution of those benefits. Similarly, although the experiments also focus on problems of heterogeneity and asymmetric information, it seems likely that in these three empirical cases, it is much more difficult than in the laboratory to assemble sufficient information across the parties to reach agreement on the benefits and sharing rules for collective action to mitigate CPR problems.[20]

REFERENCES

Bain, Joe (1947) *The Economics of the Pacific Coast Petroleum Industry*, Part III. Berkeley: University of California Press.

Cheung, Steven N. S. (1970) 'The Structure of a Contract and the Theory of a Non-exclusive Resource', *Journal of Law and Economics* 13: 49–70.

Citrograph, (1933), September.

Citrus Industry, (1933), August, November; (1934), March.

Citrus Leaves, (1933), August, October.

Demsetz, Harold (1967) 'Towards a Theory of Property Rights', *American Economic Review* 57: 347–59.

Florida Citrus Inspection Bureau (1938) *Annual Report*, Lakeland, Florida.

Gordon, H. Scott (1954) 'The Economic Theory of a Common Property Resource: The Fishery', *Journal of Political Economy* 62: 124–42.

---

20. This conjecture is supported by Hackett et al.'s experimental findings (paper 6 in this collection) that rent dissipation is greater in settings where the parties cannot engage in face-to-face communication. When such communication is allowed the private information problem is resolved. In the empirical cases examined here, with important differences in private assessments of individual production capabilities, in oil fields and fisheries especially, even though direct communication was possible, the asymmetry problem has persisted, confounding efforts to devise quotas or other sharing rules.

Higgs, Robert (1982) 'Legally Induced Technical Regress in the Washington Salmon Fishery', *Research in Economic History* 7: 55–86.

Hoffman, Elizabeth and Gary D. Libecap (1994) 'Political Bargaining and Cartelization in the New Deal: Orange Marketing Orders', in Claudia Goldin and Gary D. Libecap (eds), *The Political Economy of Regulation: An Historical Analysis of Government and the Economy*, pp. 189–221. Chicago: University of Chicago Press.

Irons, Peter H. (1982) *The New Deal Lawyers*. Princeton, NJ: Princeton University Press.

Johnson, Ronald N. and Gary D. Libecap (1982) 'Contracting Problems and Regulation: The Case of the Fishery', *American Economic Review* 72: 1005–22.

Libecap, Gary D. (1978) 'Economic Variables and the Development of the Law: The Case of Mineral Rights', *Journal of Economic History* 38: 338–62.

Libecap, Gary D. (1989) *Contracting for Property Rights*. New York: Cambridge University Press.

Libecap, Gary D. and Steven N. Wiggins (1984) 'Contractual Responses to the Common Pool: Prorationing of Crude Oil', *American Economic Review* 74: 87–98.

Libecap, Gary D. and Steven N. Wiggins (1985) 'The Influence of Private Contractual Failure on Regulation: The Case of Oil Field Unitization', *Journal of Political Economy* 93: 690–714.

Oil Weekly, (1942), 13 April; (1943), 3 May.

Olson, Mancur (1965) *The Logic of Collective Action*. Cambridge: Harvard University Press.

Ostrom, Elinor (1990) *Governing the Commons: The Evolution of Institutions for Collective Action*. New York: Cambridge University Press.

US Department of Commerce (1975) *Historical Statistics of the United States*. Washington, DC: Government Printing Office.

Wiggins, Steven N. and Gary D. Libecap (1985) 'Oil Field Unitization: Contractual Failure in the Presence of Imperfect Information', *American Economic Review* 75: 368–85.

8. SELF-INTEREST AND ENVIRONMENTAL MANAGEMENT

Kenneth A. Oye and James H. Maxwell

Introduction

This paper offers a moderately optimistic view on the management of environmental problems. We argue that a central problem of environmental management is to establish systems of regulation and compensation that bring about a convergence of narrow self-interest and the common good. Our optimism derives from the perverse observation that general environmental concerns are often advanced through the particularistic pursuit of rents and subsidies. We are especially interested in situations where regulations have heterogenous effects, with costs and benefits falling upon different groups.

Funding for research was drawn from the Kann Rasmussan Foundation, the Robert Wilhelm Innovation Fund, the Norwegian Ministry of Environment and the MIT International Motor Vehicle Program. The authors acknowledge with gratitude the comments of Lawrence Bacow, Mark Levy, Michael Lynch, Dale Murphy, Vicki Norberg-Bohm, Jerome Rothenberg, Inger Weibust and the editors and contributors to this collection as well as the research assistance of Tamar Gutner and Byoung-Joo Kim. We would especially like to thank Sanford Weiner for his important contributions to the work on DuPont, ICI and the Montreal Protocol.

In what could be termed 'Stiglerian' situations, this convergence of self-interest and the general interest is a natural by-product of cartelization by regulation. In these cases regulations confer rents upon the few while simultaneously advancing general interests in management of environmental problems, albeit at the expense of would-be rivals and/or consumers. In our Stiglerian cases environmental regulations constrain competition in a variety of ways, most commonly by limiting entry by potential producers and by encouraging use of monopolistic products. Because those who are regulated benefit from and lobby for regulation, these situations are usually characterized by regulatory stability.

In what could be termed 'Olsonian' situations, regulatory benefits are diffused across the many, while regulatory costs are concentrated on the few. In these cases the relatively few clear losers will tend to mobilize and organize against regulation with greater effectiveness than the many weakly motivated beneficiaries. Because those regulated seek to undercut or reverse regulation, these situations are marked by a high degree of regulatory instability. However, Olsonian regulatory instability can be mitigated, though not eliminated, through compensation from the many to the few. Narrow self-interest and the common interest can be brought together, however crudely, by grafting compensation payments on to what would otherwise be unstable systems of regulation.

Our empirical cases suggest strongly that environmental regulations may work most effectively when, whether by chance or by design, they confer palpable benefits upon the regulated. Many of the most important regulations affecting air, water and waste fit the Olsonian pattern where the costs are concentrated (often on industry) and the benefits are widely dispersed. Often overlooked are the Stiglerian situations where the benefits are concentrated and the costs are widely dispersed. Compensation can be used in Olsonian situations to create incentives that approximate those that occur naturally in Stiglerian situations. Yet compensation schemes are difficult to design and implement in these Olsonian situations. We are optimistic, however, that the reconciliation of private self-interests and environmental interests can yield stable environmentally sensitive regulations in both Stiglerian and Olsonian situations.

Stiglerian Cases: Concentrated Benefits and Diffuse Costs

In Stiglerian cases regulatory benefits are concentrated on the few, while regulatory costs are diffused across the many (Stigler, 1971). More precisely, producers will fight for regulations that provide: (1) direct monetary subsidies, (2) constraints or subsidies on substitutes or complements of commodities produced, (3) price fixing and (4) control over entry by new rivals. Environmental justifications for regulation may foster Stiglerian rent seeking by offering legitimating principles for regulation and by adding environmentalists to regulatory coalitions. Of course, regulations that advance the particularistic interests of existing producers and a general interest in effective management of environmental problems may also harm potential entrants and consumers. In Stiglerian situations the central institutional design problem is to define and achieve an appropriate balance between managing the environmental problems and minimizing the unfairness and welfare losses associated with rent-providing regulations.

Our review of the Montreal Protocol case stresses the economic consequences of the second and fourth of Stigler's benefits of regulation, the creation of markets for substitutes and the creation of barriers to entry by potential rivals. Specifically, long-term economic interests in creating the market for CFC (chlorofluorocarbon) substitutes were one of the primary reasons that DuPont sought and ICI (Imperial Chemical Industries) accepted international regulation. In this case narrow material interests interacted with broader environmental and political concerns. The international community successfully adopted the Montreal Protocol because of the concordance of political values, scientific knowledge and economic incentives. Regulation and restriction would not have been possible if there were not a plausible and substantive connection to very real environmental concerns.

Our review of the efforts of a small farming community in Kansas to manage local water resources has important similarities to the Stiglerian regulation that characterizes the CFC case. The irrigators of Fowler, Kansas, managed their common groundwater supplies in their local artesian valley first by excluding potential entrants and then by limiting their own drawing rights. In the Fowler case, local stakeholders developed a solution to a local common-pool resource (CPR) problem, albeit by appealing to the water resource board of the state of Kansas. By contrast, interstate efforts to address the depletion of the Ogallala Aquifer proved to be far less effective. The physical scale of the problem and the large number of jurisdictions with governing responsibilities cut against successful decentralized management. This example suggests that pessimism may be in order as one moves from local and regional CPR problems toward global CPR problems.

Product Substitution: DuPont, ICI and the Montreal Protocol

The DuPont and ICI experience with restrictions on CFCs represents a classic Stiglerian illustration of producers benefitting from regulations that mandated product substitution.[1] From the 1930s when they were invented, until the early 1970s, CFCs were considered to be one of the great success stories of the chemical industry. Because they did not react with other substances, the chemicals were non-toxic in either industrial or environmental settings. They were relatively easy and inexpensive to produce and widely used in applications such as refrigeration, air conditioning and aerosols. The 1974 *Nature* paper by Molina and Rowland caught both the manufacturers and scientists by surprise (Molina and Rowland, 1974). They argued that CFCs might prove a significant source of chlorine in the stratosphere following decomposition by ultraviolet radiation and that, over a long period of time, this free chlorine could lead to serious reductions in the stratospheric ozone layer.

Both US and British government responses to Rowland and Molina's hypothesis were swift. The National Academy of Sciences (NAS) reported in 1976 that the non-essential uses of CFCs would have to be drastically reduced if the science was borne out (National Academy of Sciences, 1976). A far more cautious response came from the British Department of the Environment (DoE), which emphasized the uncertainties contained in the scientific analysis and dismissed the need for immediate regulatory action (Department of the Environment, 1976).

In 1977 American regulatory authorities proposed banning the use of CFCs in aerosols. But this use had already fallen due to shifts to alternatives by consumer-products companies. Confronting state bans and rising consumer concerns driven by environmental groups, Johnson Wax had announced in June 1975 its intention to phase out CFCs; other consumer-products companies in the US had followed its example (Dotto and Schiff, 1978). Implementation of the proposed ban had thus been greatly facilitated by market forces acting in anticipation of regulation.

Despite strong American encouragement to eliminate an unnecessary 'luxury', the British rejected the American approach, arguing that automobile air-conditioning systems in the US were also luxuries. The weak scientific case, as they perceived it, discouraged the British from regulating its CFC industry, especially ICI, the nation's largest manufacturing company and one of the world's largest CFC producers. In 1974 UK consumption of CFCs remained heavily concentrated in aerosols (80 percent versus 50 percent in the US) (Department of the Environment, 1976). A ban on the use of CFCs as aerosol propellants would have imposed markedly different economic consequences for the United Kingdom than the United States. Thus DuPont,

1. The material for this case is based upon Maxwell and Weiner (1993a, b) and Weiner and Maxwell (1993).

the largest American producer, lost half its CFC market because of domestic policies while ICI was unaffected.

In 1979 the National Academy of Sciences estimated that a 16 percent ozone depletion would result eventually in several thousand more cases of melanoma per year (many fatal), several thousand more cases of non-melanoma skin cancers, and a likely reduction in crop yields (National Academy of Sciences, 1979). Following the publication of the NAS report, the Carter administration launched new regulatory initiatives. While seeking to further limit US production, the Environmental Protection Agency (EPA) pressed European governments to ban CFCs in aerosols and other non-essential uses (Rivkin, 1983). The European Community (EC) responded with a compromise CFC regulation that was essentially symbolic. The regulation required a 30 percent reduction in CFCs for aerosols by 1981 (from 1976) and limited overall production capacity (Council of the European Communities 1980). But even in Europe CFC use in aerosols had declined and the total production limit was set too high to constrain.

As Figure 1 shows, the weak European regulation and the American ban on aerosols led to a long-term shift in worldwide production of CFCs. From the mid-1970s, US production for CFC 11 and 12 fell rapidly in response to market pressures on aerosols, while it continued to expand in Britain and the EC. The fall in US demand led to manufacturing overcapacity and under-mined the ability of producers to raise prices and improve profit margins. As Figure 2 demonstrates, prices in real terms for both CFC 11 and 12 remained constant for more than a decade. The British industry successfully overcame these adverse market conditions by expanding its production, an option that was unavailable to its US rivals because of the weakness of demand.

Political and scientific developments in the early 1980s reduced concerns over the ozone depletion issue.[2] The new Reagan administration was opposed to further environmental regulations. At the same time scientific assessments seemed to confirm earlier British skepticism by lowering the estimates of the long-term ozone depletion to be expected; the NAS estimates dropped from 16 percent (1979) to 2–4 percent (1984) (National Academy of Sciences, 1984). Nevertheless, international negotiations began at low diplomatic levels, given that the stakes involved were perceived to be small. The Vienna Convention for the Protection of the Ozone Layer, signed in 1985, committed the international community to the eventual control of ozone-depleting substances, but lacked any specific control measures.

The CFC industry felt reassured by these events. Research started in the mid-1970s had identified about a dozen possible new replacement chemicals for applications in aerosols, refrigeration and foam blowing, but in the early 1980s the entire ICI and DuPont CFC alternative research programs

---

2. For an analysis stressing the importance of ideas and institutions see Parson (1993).

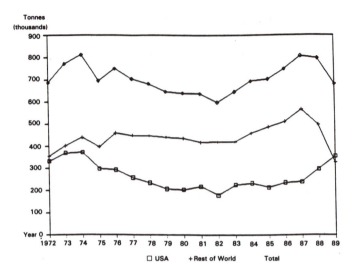

Notes: Data for world production are taken from the Chemical Manufacturers'
Association Fluorocarbon Program Panel, December 1990. 1989 Production and sales
of fluorocarbons 11 and 12 US data were taken from the US International Trade
Commission (ITC) report *Synthetic Organic Chemicals*. Data for the rest of the world were
estimated by subtracting the US data from the world total.
    Source: CMA, AFEAS and US ITC.

Figure 1. Production of CFCs 11 and 12.

were discontinued because of the lack of a market for the higher-priced
alternatives.

    The policy stalemate was broken in 1985 when the science of ozone
depletion was thrown into disarray by Farman's discovery of the destruction
of stratospheric ozone in the Antarctic polar vortex, the infamous ozone
hole (Farman et al., 1985). Farman's observations caused turmoil in the
scientific community because its members did not have a theory to explain
the unexpectedly large depletion discovered over Antarctica. The discovery
of the ozone hole dramatically transformed the politics of the international
negotiations as well as the science. The image of a hole in the sky that was
allowing dangerous levels of ultraviolet radiation to reach the earth's surface
captured the public's imagination (Warr, 1990). No longer did there seem to
be uncertainty about prospects for an international agreement; the major
question concerned the content. The United States position leading into the
international negotiations was that substantial cuts should be enacted in
CFC production with a total phase-out within 10 years. Even if the link
between chlorine and ozone depletion had not been definitively demon-

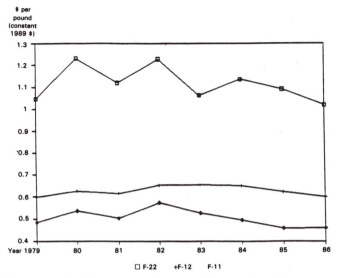

Notes: The data are for US sales, taken from the US International Trade Commission publication *Synthetic Organic Chemicals*. The figures are the average unit values calculated from rounded figures. Prices have been deflated using the yearly average Producer Price Index.
    Source: US ITC.

Figure 2. Average value of CFCs.

strated, the EPA was concerned about the possible risks of inaction (Thomas, 1986).

Fearful of repeating the earlier experience with strict domestic regulation that had cost it a significant share of the global market for CFCs in the 1970s, DuPont proposed in September 1986 that international regulation should limit worldwide production to the then existing levels (Environmental Data Services Report, 1986; Maxwell, 1991). This was the critical moment in the more than a decade-long, ozone-depletion controversy. An agreement to cap production demonstrated a willingness to shift its capacity to the manufacture of alternative chemicals. A cap, in turn, implied an eventual phase-out of ozone-depleting chemicals. The British government rejected this in favor of freezing production *capacity*, arguing that the scientific models showed that any form of cap, including the European capacity ceiling applied globally, would be sufficient to safeguard the environment.

Divergence in the British and the US positions can be partially explained by differences in the *short-term* economic positions of their respective industries. The British showed reluctance to harm ICI's CFC business, which because of its recent expansion was more profitable than that of its US competitors. The American CFC business continued to be characterized by overcapacity, low profit margins and the impending threat of domestic regulation (Reinhardt, 1989). However, the *long-term* economic incentives facing both industries were similar. The transition to alternatives promised to expand profits even while eliminating a billion-dollar-a-year business. Favorable economics made the ozone issue different from many other environmental problems that harmed the long-term profitability of the industries involved.

The transition to alternatives was technically feasible because research in the late 1970s had identified a series of substitutes that could be used where some sort of CFC-like substance was needed. But in contrast to CFC 11 and 12, which were relatively inexpensive to produce, the substitutes required sophisticated chemical engineering processes and capital investments of hundreds of millions of dollars. This meant that the new chemicals would be inherently more expensive to produce and would demand much higher prices. Rather than being sold as commodity chemicals on a worldwide basis, they could be marketed as high-margin specialty chemicals where the leading international firms could foresee substantial competitive advantages.

Long-term economic interests were one of the primary reasons that DuPont sought and ICI would ultimately accept international regulation that helped to create the market for substitute chemicals. The new chemicals were projected to sell for 5–10 times the costs of CFC 11 and 12 so that the major users would never voluntarily shift to these chemicals without government intervention. User industry resistance to the potential price increases would, however, be reduced by the fact that CFCs actually comprised only a small percentage of the total cost of any refrigerator or air-conditioning unit (or the costs of manufacturing a circuit board). The major costs would be to adapt compressors and other technologies to the new chemicals, which again were manageable if phased in over time. So the transition would require government and industry working hand in hand. It was also to industry's advantage that the transition be staged in an orderly fashion so that existing customers could be shifted to the alternative chemicals as the new production came on line. The industry leader's incentives were clear.

The EC and the United States, the major governmental protagonists in the negotiations leading up to the Montreal Protocol, faced different incentives. Once the US government and industry publicly announced their strong positions in favor of regulation, the British and the French had strong incentives from a tactical standpoint to hold out as long as possible for an agreement reflecting their desires to delay reductions in CFC production. The EC finally accepted the goal of a 50 percent cut in CFC production by the year 2000. This could easily be met by cutbacks in aerosol use alone. The US favored reductions measured in terms of national consumption; the EC argued forcefully for limits on production. DuPont feared that the national production limits could be easily met by European producers by restricting their use in aerosols, providing an opportunity for them to expand their sales either in other applications or in other markets. For their part, the Europeans expressed concern that DuPont would use the consumption limits to rationalize its production on a global scale and export into their home markets.

A related issue concerned whether the limits would be applied to individual countries or the entire EC. US industry feared that certain European producers would rationalize production at the community level, enhancing their position vis a vis American industry. Both the US and the EC wished to prevent the other's industry from gaining a competitive advantage through the content of an international agreement that limited the usage of CFCs. So intense was the commercial jockeying that Mustafa Tolba, the executive director of the United Nations Environment Program, observed: 'The difficulties in negotiating the Montreal Protocol had nothing to do with whether the environment was damaged or not. It was all who was going to gain an edge over who [sic]; whether DuPont would have an advantage over the European companies or not' (Tolba, 1988).

In the year following the signing of the Montreal Protocol a series of events led the US and some of the European governments to renew their calls for a total CFC phase-out. This time, however, the British government and ICI, in a remarkable turnaround, accepted the proposals. During this year scientific understanding increased to the extent that it was no longer possible to justify a policy of cautious inaction towards the ozone hole. At the same time a variety of political and market factors added to the pressure on the British government and industry to revise their stand.

Two scientific reports contributed significantly to hardening public opinion against CFCs and in generating the political will required to negotiate more stringent controls. Only two weeks after the Protocol's signing the first results became available from the US-led Antarctic Airborne Ozone Experiment (AAOE), which demonstrated definitively the link between chlorine and the hole, although it was the unique characteristics of Antarctica that enabled the critical chemical reactions to take place. The second key report was that of the NASA/World Meteorological Organization (WMO) Ozone Trends Panel. Published in March 1988, it revealed unexpectedly large ozone depletion at middle/high northern latitudes during winter (Watson et al., 1989). The traditional models had predicted ozone losses in the long term, but now it was clear that depletion was already occurring. Analogous to the earlier discovery of the Antarctic ozone hole, the problem was unexplained and unbounded at this time.

Within ten days of the study's release DuPont announced its plans to curtail production of CFCs and to speed the transition to alternative chemicals, underlining the technical feasibility of a shift within the decade (*ENDS Report*, 1988a; *DuPont Corporate News*, 1988). Referring to DuPont's announcement, Lee Thomas, the EPA administrator, stated that it 'sends an unmistakable signal that alternatives and substitutes can be made readily available in the near future' (Thomas, 1988).

At the same time ICI and DuPont both realized, even more strongly than before, the potential commercial opportunities as well as risks involved in shifting to substitute chemicals. Products and market share would accrue to the companies that developed process technology for making substitutes in the most cost effective and rapid manner possible. In August 1988 ICI announced its intention to join DuPont in an orderly phase-out of existing CFCs and in a rapid commercialization of substitutes.

A series of crises also began to focus British public attention on environmental issues. The death of seals in the North Atlantic, fears about the quality of drinking water, and concerns about global warming all fostered growth among environmental advocacy groups. In the light of these mounting interests and pressures the Conservative Party began to reassess its positions and to raise the priority of environment issues on the policy agenda. Mrs Thatcher's speech to the Royal Society in September 1988 argued that the health of the economy and the environment were totally dependent on each other (*Financial Times*, 1988; *ENDS Report*, 1988b). Only a few years before she had referred to environmental groups as subversives, calling them the enemy within. This marked the official 'greening' of Mrs Thatcher. Ozone depletion and global warming were the two primary issues through which she demonstrated her new environmental commitment.

The roots of the transformation in British CFC policy can be found in these shifting commercial and political sands. At an EC meeting in March 1989 British officials expected to take the lead in pressing for an 85 percent cut in CFC production before 1999. Instead, according to the London *Times*: 'The British delegation . . . were upstaged by their more enthusiastic European counterparts, whose demands, first for 95% but then for the complete withdrawal of the chemicals, took them by surprise' (*The Times*, 1989).

The resulting agreement marked the UK and the EC's official commitment to the eventual total phase-out of CFCs. The remaining obstacles to an international agreement on the total phase-out were predominantly issues of assistance to developing nations and the control of non-CFC ozone-depleting substances. Two of the major obstacles to an international agreement on the total phase-out were access to technology and financial aid for developing countries. Why did these issues arise in London and not Montreal? Under the Montreal agreement signatories could have obtained the moderate 50 percent reductions in emissions through advanced industrial country actions alone. However, the global bans at the heart of the London discussions required the cooperation of developing countries. The developing countries argued that the ozone-depletion problem was not of their own making because industrialized countries consumed more than 80 percent of CFCs. Yet consumption was growing rapidly among the developing countries so that the Montreal treaty would be in jeopardy if these countries refused to ratify it. Compensation was then a necessity for reducing the CFC build-up in the atmosphere. The industrialized countries agreed to establish a multilateral fund to provide financial assistance to developing countries' phase-out efforts. In response to strong demands for mandatory technology transfer, the industrialized countries promised to facilitate access to technology to developing countries and promote exchange of information and technical assistance. But the agreements lacked specificity as to how this technology transfer and licensing were to be accomplished. Nevertheless, the resolution of these difficulties enabled the London revisions to the Protocol to be signed in June 1990, establishing a timetable leading to total phase-out of CFC production by the year 2000.

Our review of the US and British experiences suggests that the international community successfully adopted the Montreal Protocol because of the concordance of political values, scientific knowledge and economic incentives. All were necessary to create international change. By the mid-1980s the production of CFC 11 and 12 was no longer as profitable a business as it once was. Renewed domestic environmental pressures created by the discovery of the ozone hole threatened to weaken an industry already characterized by overcapacity. International regulation mandating a switch to CFC substitutes offered major producers the Stiglerian solution of new and more profitable markets in the long term. The heterogeneity of technological capabilities and access to major markets gave DuPont and ICI potential competitive advantages over smaller producers and those in developing countries. Many consumer industries showed reluctance to give up CFCs, but the costs of transferring to alternatives were widely dispersed, diminishing potential resistance. Despite the concordance of political and economic interests for phasing out CFCs, the industrialized countries had to agree to compensation for developing countries so that the treaty was not thwarted by politically influential nations, such as India and China.

Groundwater Management: An Artesian Valley and the Ogallala Aquifer

Environmental regulation may confer concrete benefits on small farmers as well as large chemical companies. Fowler is a farming town of 500 residents in arid south-west Kansas. Until recently the farmers of Fowler grappled unsuccessfully with a classic common-pool resources problem. The farms of Fowler rest above a local artesian valley that sits in turn above the Ogallala

Aquifer Formation. Before irrigation the water table in the local artesian valley was high and the farmers of Fowler enjoyed an advantage over those farming neighboring areas. Natural springs had filled the banks of Crooked Creek and spilled over into marshes (Buchanan, 1987). The high local water table provided easy irrigation, as groundwater and a system of shunts moistened the soil of low-lying fields. To irrigate higher fields Fowler's farmers drilled shallow wells and relied on natural water pressure. As the water table fell the farmers drilled deeper and deeper wells and installed natural gas-powered pumps to bring the water to the surface. The development of the center pivot in the late 1950s and early 1960s greatly expanded irrigation acreage. In the short term each farmer benefitted directly from these measures. Over the long term the pumping gradually depleted the local artesian valley on which they relied. By 1990 Crooked Creek was reduced to a trickle, the marshes were dry and the water table in the artesian valley was dropping slowly toward the level of the underlying Ogallala Formation.

The failure of farmers in the small village of Fowler to address this obvious environmental problem is surprising. The geology of the local artesian valley placed clear limits on the number of individuals whose cooperation would have been required to reach an effective agreement on water usage. The farmers recognized that unregulated drilling and pumping was destroying the local artesian valley. Furthermore, Fowler is a tightly knit community with strong civic and religious institutions and long-standing patterns of association that should be conducive to cooperation; yet local efforts to restrict shunts and to limit drilling and pumping failed. The poor farmers could not make their mortgage payments if they switched from wet to dry crops and the rich farmers would not subsidize the poor. Although virtually all members of the community could see where unrestricted pumping was leading, the farmers of Fowler did not limit their use of water from the local artesian valley. The water table continued to drop.[3]

In 1991 effective new restraints on drilling and pumping came into force. The farmers of Fowler turned to two institutions of the state to manage their local artesian valley. In the Fowler area groundwater is regulated by the local Garden City Water District and by the Kansas State Division of Water Resources. The governing board of the local water district consisted of farmers with wells and pumps in place – the irrigators who were pumping the artesian valley dry and were alarmed at the falling water table that was a consequence of their individual actions. Potential drillers and irrigators were not well represented at these agencies. The governing board of the

3. On changes in Crooked Creek and local responses, interviews with Don Hildebrand, Ed Hildebrand, Chris Hildebrand and John Hildebrand, Fowler, Kansas, August 1991.

Garden City Water District asked the Chief Engineer of the State Division of Water Resources to adopt a strict interpretation of regulations governing groundwater use in their local district. Under Kansas law the state can prohibit new appropriations of groundwater where (a) there is a 40 percent drawdown in groundwater reserves over 25 years; or (b) the depth of an aquifer is 40 feet or less; or (c) where the depth of an aquifer is depleted by 20 percent or more since 1940. The state can refuse to grant permits for new well drilling if any of these conditions are not met. Under the old interpretation of these regulations the State Office would draw a circle with a two-mile radius around the site of a prospective well and determine whether these conditions were satisfied within it. The board of the Garden City Water District observed that wells within one circle affected groundwater supplies for wells in other circles. The board of the local water district asked the Chief Engineer to reject permits for new drilling if conditions were not satisfied within a two-mile circle around a prospective well or for the whole township containing the prospective well. This seemingly minor adjustment in interpretation of regulations – the addition of a new township-wide criterion to the preexisting two-mile radius criterion – had major consequences. In 1991 the new regulations closed the Fowler area to all new well drilling.

The freeze on new drilling did not stop depletion of the aquifer. The large number of existing wells with natural gas pumps was draining the local artesian valley. The board of the local Garden City Water District worked together with the state to tighten the regulations. The district and the state set up a schedule to phase in metering on existing wells, proceeding from quarter to quarter within each section. To spread costs over time the plan began with wells in south-east quarters in January of 1993 and ended with all wells in all quarters metered by July of 1996. Under the new plan the state and the local district established depletion rates for south-west Kansas and for the Garden City Water District. These depletion rates are less than the rates that had prevailed under the old unregulated system but are more than the rate that can be sustained indefinitely. The planned depletion rates will determine the total amount of groundwater that can be used by Fowler farmers, with the total amount of water to be drawn distributed evenly across existing wells. The new meters will permit effective monitoring and enforcement of the new plan.

What factors account for this tilt towards management of the common-pool resource? One Fowler farmer offered an explanation along the following lines. Who are the winners and losers in this story? The winners are farmers with preexisting wells and irrigated land. The losers are those without preexisting wells and no prospect for irrigation. Under Western water law prior use establishes property rights. As new wells were installed the number of farmers that would benefit from a drilling freeze expanded and the number of farmers that would be adversely affected by a drilling freeze contracted. The critical factor in his explanation is coalition size, with coalition size driven by exploitation of the common-pool resource. As the farmer explained: 'When enough folks had drilled, we just got together and created a barrier to entry against the young and the poor.'[4] Only after potential entrants had been frozen out did the stakeholders in Fowler ration the use of water at levels that were sustainable in the long term. Without limits on entry the rationing of water use would only have attracted new users.

The tale of the local artesian valley in Fowler appears to be paralleled by the emerging story of management of the Ogallala Formation that sits in Nebraska, western Kansas, the Texas and Oklahoma panhandles and bits of Colorado, Wyoming, New Mexico and South Dakota. The Kansas Ogallala Task Force Committee Report and the recommendations of the local Garden City Water District Board have similar content and rest on similar motivations. The use of natural gas-fueled pumps to feed center pivot irrigation systems increased demands on the Ogallala Aquifer in all eight states. In the late 1940s 4 million acre-feet of water were pumped to irrigate 2 million acres. By 1980 18 million acre-feet of water were being pumped to 13 million acres. Annual pumpage is exceeding recharge and water levels have declined more than 10 feet in 29 percent of the area of the aquifer. The Kansas State Task Force's non-binding recommendations include creation of barriers to entry, establishment of limitations on use by stakeholders and compensation payments to stakeholders who reduce their reliance on irrigation. In areas where groundwater mining is taking place owners of existing wells used for irrigation may irrigate. Furthermore, owners of active irrigation wells taken off-line under the conservation program would be protected from abandonment by the Division of Water resources. Finally, the task force suggested that owners of wells used for irrigation receive United States Department of Agriculture (USDA) deficiency payments if they take their wells off-line to meet limits on exploitation of the Ogallala under a to-be-investigated multi-year allocation system. In short, as in the Fowler case, stakeholders drew a line against entrants and then moved for limitations on their use of the resource (Kansas State Board of Agriculture, 1993). However, unlike the Fowler case with its local artesian valley, the boundaries of the Ogallala Formation extend well beyond Kansas. No effective plan for management of the Ogallala common-pool resource makes sense unless virtually all of the states establish limits on entry and limits on use.

---

4. Telephone interview with John Hildebrand, Fowler, Kansas, August 1992.

Extensions and Implications: Doing Well by Doing Good

In Stiglerian situations, local and global environmental regulations serve the interests of the regulated. New coalitions of the green and the greedy often result in management of environmental problems in a sustainable manner. The managers of DuPont and ICI benefitted from a phase-out of CFCs that preserved atmospheric ozone while requiring a shift to substitutes that DuPont and ICI dominated even more than traditional CFCs. Those taking a possible short-term hit had the capacity to identify and recognize their long-term interests. The large farmers in Fowler obtained substantial benefits from restrictions on new drilling. The decision makers at DuPont and the large farmers in Fowler could advance their particularistic interests through regulation by framing the issue in terms of the public good.[5]

These examples of Stiglerian management of environmental problems provide a modest basis for optimism. In these cases producers seeking to force substitution and/or to create barriers to entry contributed directly to the adoption of regulations that fostered management of environmental problems – though regulations were sometimes unfair and may have decreased the general welfare. But how common are these Stiglerian situations?

The Montreal Protocol case represents but one of many examples of 'regulation of a substitute or complement'. DuPont and ICI profited from regulations that forced consumers to switch from one set of products that they produced to another set of products that they had the potential to dominate. Other examples of Stiglerian 'profiting from product substitution' include the following:

1. Regulations barring leaded gasoline created a market for unleaded gasoline. These regulations reduced emissions of lead into the air, water and soil, while serving the interests of refiners by forcing a shift toward higher-profit unleaded gasoline.

2. Regulations restricting the sale of DDT promoted the market for a variety of higher-priced pesticides. The banning of DDT eliminated an unusually persistent, biocumulative and toxic substance that presented

---

5. Why did compensation play a significant role in the London revisions to the Montreal Protocol? China and India demanded and received compensation and special provisions for technology transfer to offset the costs that they would bear in shifting to substitutes for CFCs. Their objections to the unfairness of Stiglerian regulation threatened to unravel the original Montreal Protocol. These sovereign nations received compensation for giving up their presumptive right to produce anything, including CFCs. However, the most fundamental point follows from the basic observation that those bearing diffuse costs must transcend dilemmas of collective action if they are to prevail against those that benefit from regulation. As a generalization, Stiglerian regulation is not packaged with compensation because opposition from those adversely affected by regulation does not represent a substantial threat to the fruits of regulation.

substantial health risks to humans and that was clearly threatening many animals that were high on the food chain. The ban on DDT also forced a move from a cheap, easy-to-produce commodity chemical toward specialized substitutes that were far more difficult to produce. These major chemical producers enjoyed a substantial advantage in the market for DDT substitutes relative to the market for DDT.

Many examples of environmental regulations exist that have the effect of benefitting existing producers at the expense of potential entrants by creating de facto or de jure barriers to entry. The Fowler case is but one example.

1. Restrictions on development, ranging from strict zoning through difficult percolation tests to stringent environmental impact assessment, advance a public interest in preserving the quality of the local environment. These restrictions also raise the rents that accrue to owners of previously developed properties at the expense of would-be developers and owners.

2. Regulations limiting new salmon farming in Norway and requiring the installation of advanced equipment for managing wastes from aquaculture preserve water quality in the fiords. These restrictions also raise the rents that accrue to owners of existing salmon farms at the expense of would-be developers and owners.

3. Germany's regulations requiring packaging that permits ready recycling advance a common interest in reducing use of non-renewable resources. At the same time they create a barrier to entry by non-German firms interested in exporting to the German market. Canadian beer-bottle recycling requirements operate similarly by excluding American beer-producing companies and others interested in exporting to the Canadian market.

4. American regulations barring the sale of lobsters under one pound within the United States prevent the unsustainable taking of lobsters by prohibiting the sale of immature American lobsters. Because lobsters in colder Canadian waters attain sexual maturity at a smaller size, the American-size regulations have the effect of creating a barrier to entry by excluding mature Canadian lobsters.

5. American regulations governing medical waste require special procedures for its handling and disposal. Large waste-disposal firms could promote the public interest in safer disposal techniques while obtaining larger revenues and profits from stricter environmental regulations governing the disposal of medical wastes.

Olsonian Cases: Diffuse Benefits and Concentrated Costs

In Olsonian situations regulatory benefits are diffused while regulatory costs are concentrated (Olson, 1965). Regulation commonly engenders opposition that blocks reforms or the expectation of opposition commonly results in anticipatory weakening of reforms. The benefits of cleaner air, biodiversity or cleaner water are spread across large numbers of people over long periods of time. The costs of regulating emissions, limiting habitat destruction, or siting sewage treatment facilities are concentrated on smaller numbers of people over shorter periods of time. This sets up a classic collective-action problem in which long-term diffuse benefits are under-represented relative to short-term concentrated costs. Unlike our Stiglerian cases, no natural coincidence of particularistic and general interests exists or is likely to arise. In the absence of compensation those adversely affected by regulation will organize and mobilize to overturn or modify systems of regulation. Oil refiners and automobile producers oppose emission control regulations, loggers resist endangered species acts and homeowners fight sewage treatment facilities located upwind.

In Olsonian cases compensation payments from the many who benefit from regulation to the few who bear the concentrated costs of regulation may reduce the instability of regulations. The core argument here is straightforward. Compensation payments reduce incentives to lobby against regulation by neutralizing in whole or in part the distributional consequences of regulation. Those who bear the costs of regulation confront a tradeoff between the costs of organizing against regulation and the benefits of deregulation. They must balance investments of time, energy and money in organizing countervailing antiregulatory activity against the benefits of blocking or reversing regulations. How then do compensation payments increase regulatory stability? *General compensation* payments to *all* of those who bear the costs of regulation reduce the costs of regulation and thereby diminish incentives to lobby against regulation. However, such general compensation can be costly. *Selective compensation* payments to *some* of those who bear the costs of regulation may reduce countervailing activity by driving wedges into antiregulatory coalitions. Although such selective payments to the most strategically significant members of potential antiregulatory coalitions may be less costly than payments to all, the effectiveness of selective payments may be reduced by their manifest unfairness. Both general compensation to all and selective payments to the few operate by neutralizing all or some of the costs associated with what would otherwise be unstable Olsonian systems of regulation.

The American and Japanese air quality cases presented below suggest that Olsonian regulation without compensation can be highly unstable. In the United States those bearing the concentrated costs of air quality regulation have consistently forced revisions in the regulatory timetables. On numerous occasions regulatory agencies or Congress backed off from scheduled reductions in emissions under industry pressure. In Japan regulation has been controversial but far more stable than in the United States. Japan adopted emissions standards that resembled those in the US, but implemented them without substantial mid-course modifications in the standards or in the timetables. One reason for the greater stability is Japan's reliance on compensation payments that partially offset the costs of regulation. Our extended discussion of compensation in this section suggests that these differences in air quality cases are typical of Japanese and American practices.

American and Japanese Air Quality Regulations

The regulation of automobile emissions is a classic example of Olsonian regulation where the costs are concentrated on a small number of industry participants and the benefits are widely dispersed among consumers. The first major emissions control initiative occurred in the state of California in 1960 with the passage of the California Motor Vehicle Pollution Control Act. The California program, which regulated CO, HC (hydrocarbon) and NO_x, in new vehicles, has since served as a prototype and testing ground for later federal initiatives. The history of federal involvement in the regulation of automobile emissions began with the passage of the 1965 Motor Vehicle Pollution Control Act. This Act required the Secretary of Health, Education and Welfare to promulgate standards for any level of pollution found to endanger human health and welfare and specifically mandated that the automobile industry meet the 1967 California standards in the 1968 model year. Since the first federal standards were both technically feasible and very modest in cost, they aroused little controversy.

The next major step in the regulation of emissions was the passage of the 1970 Clean Air Act amendments, a watershed in US environmental policy. This act was adopted amid the then rich political fervor and activism of a growing environmental movement. The political debate over the Clean Air Act Amendments took place in a unique context in which the proposed versions of the Act became increasingly protective of public health during the course of the legislative process. Typically, decision makers had refined existing policy by determining what was technically and administratively feasible, as well as what was acceptable to those being regulated (Jones, 1975). The political atmosphere in 1970, however, demanded stronger action and resulted in a law that may have been beyond then existing technical capabilities. The act that finally emerged mandated a 90 percent reduction in three primary pollutants by 1975-6.

The Clean Air Act amendments represented a radical departure from past

Table 1. Comparison of Japanese and US Motor Vehicle Emission Standards (grams per mile)

Year	CO US	CO Japan	HC US	HC Japan	NO$_x$ US	NO$_x$ Japan
1975	15.0	3.4	1.5	0.4	3.1	1.9
1976	15.0	3.4	1.5	0.4	3.1	1.4
1977	15.0	3.4	1.5	0.4	2.0	1.4
1978	15.0	3.4	1.5	0.4	2.0	0.4
1979	15.0	3.4	1.5	0.4	2.0	0.4
1980	7.0	3.4	0.4	0.4	2.0	0.4
1981	3.4	3.4	0.4	0.4	1.0	0.4
1982	3.4	3.4	0.4	0.4	1.0	0.4
1983	3.4	3.4	0.4	0.4	1.0	0.4
1984	3.4	3.4	0.4	0.4	1.0	0.4
1985	3.4	3.4	0.4	0.4	1.0	0.4
1986	3.4	3.4	0.4	0.4	1.0	0.4
1987	3.4	3.4	0.4	0.4	1.0	0.4
1988	3.4	3.4	0.4	0.4	1.0	0.4
1989	3.4	3.4	0.4	0.4	1.0	0.4
1990	3.4	3.4	0.4	0.4	1.0	0.4
1991	3.4	3.4	0.4	0.4	1.0	0.4
1992	3.4	3.4	0.4	0.4	1.0	0.4
1993	3.4	3.4	0.4	0.4	1.0	0.4
1994	3.4	3.4	0.4	0.3	0.4	0.4

Note: Table 1 presents Japanese and American timetables for reducing motor vehicle emissions. The Congress and EPA modified US timetables substantially in response to industry objections. The original timetable in the Clean Air Act contained even more rapid reductions in the permissible levels of pollutants than those in the Table. By contrast, the Japanese did not substantially modify their original timetables. Because Japanese and American test procedures differ, care should be taken when making direct comparisons between Japanese and US emissions standards.

Source: Automotive Emissions Management Group, CONCAWE, 1992 and Japanese Environmental Agency, *Quality of Environment in Japan*, 1990.

approaches to environmental policy (Krier and Ursim, 1977). First, the Clean Air Act was an experiment in technology-forcing that established goals admittedly unachievable with existing technology. The underlying belief among members of Congress was that industry would not develop the requisite control technology unless it was forced to do so. Nevertheless, Congress did provide an escape hatch, allowing for a one-year delay in the standards if the industry could prove to the EPA Administrator that they were technically infeasible. Passage of the Clean Air Act Amendments marked a significant shift from traditional regulatory approaches, which had been based upon economic feasibility, to a health-based standards approach. Congress designed emissions standards for automobiles to protect those most susceptible to the health effects of air pollution in the most highly polluted areas, regardless of costs. The EPA was statutorily prohibited from relying on costs and economic efficiency as primary considerations in regulatory decision making. Finally, the Clean Air Act differed from past emissions and safety statutes in that Congress had itself established specific targets and timetables for industry to meet. In prior legislation Congress had typically given administrative agencies greater discretion along with a less forceful legislative mandate.

The Clean Air Act amendments proved far easier to adopt than to implement. Immediately following their adoption the political atmosphere remained highly charged and polarized. The highly concentrated automobile industry, with three major domestic producers, exerted great pressure on the EPA and the Congress to modify or delay the standards. They claimed that the standards were technically infeasible and the costs of emission control were too high, potentially dampening demand for new vehicles. The big three also pressured the EPA to adopt the most flexible implementation procedures possible. On the other hand, the environmentalists lobbied to protect the original standards and timetables and prevent backsliding on this issue.

Debate over the emissions standards and timetables continued in a variety of forums. In 1972 and 1973 the National Academy of Sciences (NAS) issued two reports that examined the technical and economic feasibility of the US emissions standards and timetables. Broadly construed, the NAS reports concluded that the technology was not then available in adequate production volumes to meet the 1975 standards and that the benefits of the amendments were most likely exceeded by their costs.

Pressure on EPA Administrator William Ruckelshaus to delay the standards increased with publication of the NAS reports. At first, he rejected industry's application for a suspension, ruling that the 1975 standards could be achieved with existing engine technology (Grad, 1975). The domestic industry promptly challenged the Administrator's decision and in a celebrated 1972 case the Court of Appeals for the District of Columbia refused to uphold it. The court balanced the potential costs to the nation's economy against the risks posed by a suspension, implicitly defining limits on the costs industry should bear by suggesting that the adverse consequences of delaying the standards were less severe than the economic disruption that would be caused through their implementation. Ruckelshaus subsequently granted a one-year delay despite evidence from Honda and several other foreign producers that they would be able to meet the standards (Grad, 1975).

Initial postponement in implementing the Clean Air amendments was just the first in a long series of delays. The 1973 energy crisis, with its resulting economic havoc, further undercut Congress's and the President's commitment to reducing automobile pollution (*Environment Reporter*, 1974). The automobile industry used the energy crisis and the need to make improvements in automobile fuel economy as a new basis from which to attack the emissions standards and timetables. In a political and media blitz the domestic automobile industry contended that the available emissions control technology in the early 1970s had seriously hampered the fuel economy performance of automobiles. Congress acquiesced in the industry's position and authorized two additional extensions to the timetables for the HC and CO standards and one for the NO_x standard, delaying the deadlines for meeting all three standards until September 1978 (Altshuler et al., 1979).

The 1977 Clean Air Act amendments represented an additional step toward the abandonment of the health-based and technology-forcing approach contained in the 1970 statute. By 1977 the issues of energy, unemployment and inflation proved to be more politically salient than that of air pollution. When faced with the choice between a tough environmental policy and significant economic consequences for the big three domestic producers, Congress continually compromised its health-related regulatory objectives. Given the altered political climate that was less favorable to environmental regulation, Congress relaxed the NO_x standard from .4 to 1.0 grams per mile, delayed the timetables for the NO_x standard for three additional years, permitted the EPA to delay the CO standard for an additional five years and delayed the HC standard for two additional years (Altshuler et al., 1979).

For more than a decade following the passage of the 1977 amendments the control of emissions from motor vehicles remained a source of political controversy. In 1981 the Reagan administration, as part of a sweeping regulatory reform initiative, promoted legislation that would have dramatically relaxed emissions standards for motor vehicles. The bill was resisted effectively by environmental groups and key congressmen. Two years later with William Ruckelshaus back at the helm of the EPA, the momentum had shifted toward greater regulation. Proposals to reduce NO_x emissions and hazardous air pollutants were subsequently introduced in Congress.

In 1989, Congress outlined an aggressive program to control motor vehicle emissions, which caused industry to respond that it was too costly and 'simply not feasible' (Waxman et al., 1991). Industry feared the proposed controls would add hundreds of dollars to the costs of new vehicles, once again threatening to undermine sales. Reminiscent of the 1970 Clean Air Act, the 1990 amendments went considerably beyond earlier proposals, enacting controls that were not even on the table in earlier Congresses. Among other things, the 1990 amendments tightened tailpipe emissions standards for NO_x and hydrocarbons, extended durability requirements so that equipment would have to last 10 years and required the smoggiest cities to use reformulated gasoline (*Congressional Quarterly Weekly Report*, 1990). Despite substantial costs imposed on the automobile industry, the 1990 amendments were embraced by Congress and signed by Republican

President George Bush. Yet the most aggressive provisions of the Act once again had an escape hatch, allowing EPA to delay the implementation of the tailpipe standards if they were economically or technically infeasible.

A month before the enactment of the 1990 Clean Air Act amendments, the California Air Resources Board adopted even more stringent standards to regulate emissions from motor vehicles (Nowell, 1991). The Air Resources Board increasingly established technology — forcing standards for emissions reduction that would be phased in during the 1990s. The most ambitious and controversial part of the regulatory package involved standards requiring the development and sale of electric vehicles that would not emit any pollutants to the environment. Beginning in 1998, automobile manufacturers will be required to sell a specific percentage of electric vehicles. The standards for low emissions and zero emissions vehicles cannot be met by existing technologies, necessitating large research and development expenditures by the automobile and petroleum industries. Because of the technology-forcing nature of the California standards, they were bitterly resisted by industrial interests. Political opposition, when combined with the magnitude of the costs and technological challenges, may lead the California Air Resources Board to back off from its most ambitious standards.

The history of motor vehicle emissions control reveals the instability and inefficiency of US policymaking under Olsonian conditions. The US has followed a pattern of adopting strict Clean Air legislation and timetables, only to back off from the standards during implementation. Table 1 presents scheduled emission reductions that Congress and the EPA imposed on industry. This timetable reflects substantial midcourse modifications in implementation of US emissions standards. Over the last two decades, a bitter debate has raged among environmentalists, key congressmen and major automobile companies about the costs and benefits of clean air. In the early 1970s and the early 1990s Congress (led by California) adopted very specific standards and timetables that mandated significant reductions in motor vehicle pollution that went beyond existing technical capabilities. Yet the domestic industry marshaled its political resources in a variety of forms – courts, regulatory agencies and Congress – to modify or delay the scheduled implementation of the 1970 Clean Air amendments. This enduring political struggle has led to less pollution reduction and at higher cost than might otherwise have been the case. Unlike the ozone case, there was no feasible way that one of the major domestic producers could have obtained a competitive advantage by promoting more stringent emissions regulations, as the major domestic producers had homogeneous interests.

In Japan the regulation of emissions from automobiles has been highly controversial but more stable than in the United States. The Japanese adopted strict emissions reductions modeled on the US but implemented them without all the mid-course modifications that characterized US environmental policy (see Table 1). Japanese policy toward emissions in the early 1970s was characterized by a high degree of partisan political activity, public activism and media attention. The strong degree of public concern, coupled with a high level of political participation, led to the adoption of stringent emissions control standards and timetables. Unlike the US the Japanese implemented the strict standards contained in the 1970 Clean Air Act with only one significant delay. Several factors combined to explain the Japanese pattern of policy formulation: first, public opinion was aroused by a series of severe pollution episodes that the press covered widely; second, a well-organized environmental movement exerted pressure on the Japanese parliament, bureaucracy and media; third, policymaking was strongly influenced by events abroad, particularly the passage of the 1970 Clean Air Act amendments; and fourth, compensation was used effectively to offset regulatory costs.

While the first steps in regulating emissions occurred in 1966, the major progress in emissions regulation occurred in the period 1970–8. In 1972 the Central Council on Environmental Pollution Control, an advisory body to the Japanese Environment Agency, proposed the adoption of the standard contained in the 1970 US Clean Air Act amendments (Porges, 1980). The Council also proposed applying the same timetable contained in the US act (standards to be met by 1975–6). Following vitriolic debate between environmentalists and the automobile industry the Environment Agency adopted the standards proposed by the Central Council for 1975. Nevertheless, under mounting pressure from the automobile industry and its political allies in the bureaucracy, the Environment Agency postponed the .25 NO_x standard until 1978, adopting a less stringent interim standard for 1976.[6] This was the only postponement in meeting the Japanese emissions standards. Japanese emissions standards for automobiles have remained unchanged since 1978.

What is remarkable about the Japanese bureaucracy, particularly in contrast to the US, was its ability to adopt and implement stringent regulations in a highly unfavorable economic climate. The Japanese implemented emissions requirements in the middle of the 1973 Arab oil embargo, which increased the costs of energy to the automobile industry by nearly 60 percent. In spite of the increased costs of energy and pollution control the position of the Japanese industry in international commerce remained unscathed.

The Japanese government undertook a number of actions to soften the economic consequences for industry, particularly in international markets. In this, as in other areas, compensation was a central element of Japanese regulatory policy. For example, the Ministry of Finance used tax incentives to ease the transition to less-polluting vehicles, reducing the high commodity and motor vehicle acquisition tax for passenger cars meeting the 1975, 1976

---

6. The discussion of emissions regulation in Japan draws heavily on Gresser et al. (1981: 268–75) and Maxwell et al. (1980).

and 1978 emissions standards and making further reductions in ownership taxes for passenger cars meeting the emissions standards (Porges, 1980). In addition, the Ministry of Transport (MOT) practiced a flexible implementation policy and viewed emissions standards as targets, not as inflexible legal requirements. Instead of applying its standards uniformly across the industry, MOT modeled its implementation procedures to an individual assessment of company capacity. Another example of Japanese implementation flexibility is shown in the MOT's adoption of its own test procedures. Less demanding than those in the US, the Japanese tests also apply to model averages, not to every vehicle. These features provide Japanese companies with greater flexibility in certifying vehicles. The Japanese government use of compensation helped foster the development of less-polluting vehicles and helped avoid the costly and politically divisive struggles that characterized US policy. The contrast between Japanese and American traditions in combining compensation with regulation is striking.

In the Clean Air cases, regulation without compensation proved to be highly unstable and politically controversial. In the American case producers whose interests were compromised by regulations succeeded in delaying or modifying regulations. In Japan producers whose costs were partially offset by compensation resisted but did not receive substantial relaxation in the regulatory timetable. The air quality cases noted previously appear to be typical of differences between Japan and the United States in environmental and non-environmental cases alike.

Extensions and Implications: Compensation in Olsonian Cases

The evidence on the effectiveness of compensation in mitigating opposition in Olsonian situations is mixed. In some countries and under certain circumstances compensation seems to reduce opposition that might otherwise undermine environmental regulations. At other times compensation creates its own problems and even engenders opposition.

The Japanese government takes great care to offset costs associated with regulatory change and has been one of the most successful in using compensation to mitigate opposition. As S. Hayden Lesbirel has observed, the Japanese government has employed compensation mechanisms extensively in managing siting disputes. He found that delays in resolving conflicts were shortened when compensation and other instruments redistributed gains to losers (Lesbirel, 1993). Specifically, Lesbirel reported that the ability of Japanese energy planners to expand electricity supplies during the extraordinary growth period of the 1960s and nuclear power supplies during the energy crisis of the 1970s depended heavily on compensation agreements between power providers and local communities.

The 'Compensation Standards Governing Electric Power Development' were set up by the Ministry of Trade and Industry (MITI) in 1963 to buy out fishing and land rights that might be adversely affected by power plant construction. The 'Three Electric Power Development Laws' that were set up by MITI during the oil crisis in 1974 expanded eligibility for compensation from holders of property rights to local publics and communities near power plants. Payments were higher for large power plants than for small plants and were much greater for nuclear plants than for fossil-fueled plants. Very substantial compensation payments under these two laws have weakened opposition by offsetting the distributional consequences of plant siting. For example, in 1981 the Hokkaido Electric Company paid 300 million yen to one of four small fishing cooperatives opposed to construction of a nuclear power plant. Not surprisingly, payments of this magnitude diminished local opposition to the plant. Compensation payments are the second largest item in the Japanese nuclear power plant budget and apply to waste storage and reprocessing as well as power-generating facilities. For example, the official compensation payments for acceptance of a waste storage and reprocessing facility in Rokkasho amount to 22 billion yen (approximately $220 million) distributed to date, with 50 percent of the funds allocated to the local village and 50 percent going to neighboring areas. These sums do not include official direct payments to holders of property rights or unofficial compensation in the form of extension of the Shinkansen to Aomori prefecture in exchange for prefectoral acceptance of the project. The principle of providing substantial compensation for losers applies in trade liberalization and highway construction as well as in plant siting. Adjustments in tobacco price supports offset the effects of tariff reductions on Japanese tobacco growers. Central government payments to provincial governments offset the effects of beef liberalization on beef-producing regions of Japan.[7] Japanese highway construction entails payments to those suffering from the noise and inconvenience of highway construction in addition to those whose real property is taken for construction. In Japan, compensation is the rule rather than the exception.[8]

In contrast, the United States uses compensation less frequently and less successfully in Olsonian situations than Japan. When compensation has been used to help solve environmental siting disputes, it has often failed to break the stalemate that arises from the NIMBY ('not in my backyard')

---

7. On the interplay between domestic politics and international agricultural negotiation see Reich et al. (1986).

8. We also found that Japan offered compensation and that Japan addressed Olsonian situations with greater success than did other nations. However, it is possible that cross-national variations in factors such as culture, institutional arrangements and party structure may account for tendencies both to offer compensation and to overcome dilemmas of collective action. If these factors affect both, then the association between compensation and successful management of·collective action may be spurious.

syndrome. Offers of compensation have often prompted resistance among environmentalists who oppose its use on ideological grounds.

Compensation in the United States appears in a far more restrictive set of situations, primarily situations where compensation is provided *after* opposition has materialized. For example, the Carter administration's consumer product safety regulations required some manufacturers to discontinue whole product lines without compensation to offset the costs of these regulations. In the face of substantial opposition from manufacturers, the Reagan administration upheld the regulations but added provisions for payment of offsetting compensation to manufacturers. The Reagan administration's legislation (PL 97-395, 30 December, 1982) mandated payments to manufacturers of children's sleepwear for the stocks of Tris they held in 1977 when Tris was banned under the Federal Hazardous Substances Act. In an earlier case the Federal Insecticide, Fungicide, and Rodenticide Act of 1971 called for compensation of manufacturers for product suspensions after EPA testing showed that herbicides 2,4,5-T and Silvex were environmentally harmful (Agthe, 1986). In other areas requirements for compensation may be added through judicial rather than legislative or executive action. Coastal land use regulations greatly decrease the value of coastal property. In 1991 the US Supreme Court ruled that restrictive coastal land use regulations constituted a taking and, under the principle of eminent domain, mandated fair compensation for the taking. In these varied domestic American cases compensation is less extensive and less lucrative than in the Japanese cases (Rabe, 1992).

Under some circumstances the prospect of compensation may actually elicit opposition. In the Japanese cases handled under Compensation Standards Governing Electric Power Development of 1963, fishermen appeared to have intensified their opposition to extract greater compensation payments. By contrast, under the fixed standards of the Three Electric Power Development Laws of 1974, the intensity of opposition could not affect payments that were based on the kilowattage of plants. This point is also borne out in some Canadian fisheries cases. For example, the 1991 Canadian cod moratorium generated bitter complaints from fishermen about the loss of their livelihoods. However, lobbying by fishers did not result in the relaxation of regulatory restraints. Their complaints resulted in substantial provisions for compensation and the subsequent moderation of demands for relaxation of the moratorium. Initially, Fisheries Minister Crosbie announced a compensation package of a maximum of $225 per person per week, with the individual amount tied to prior individual earnings. One month later, after fishermen had mounted vehement protests against the package of regulation and compensation, Fisheries Minister Crosbie raised the amount to a maximum of $406 per week (Doyle, 1991).

Fishers are required to sign up for retraining courses or to opt for early retirement to qualify for compensation.[9] Furthermore, to improve enforcement, they may qualify for forgiveness of interest payments on boat loans if they take their boats out of the water. Although the costs of dislocation associated with the two-year moratorium remain severe, the package of compensation has softened opposition to the moratorium.[10]

Although the illustrations provided here suggest that Olsonian regulation without compensation is unstable and that compensation can mitigate regulatory instability, it is difficult to assess with rigor the effectiveness of compensation. Offsetting inferential problems complicate analysis of compensation and resistance within particular countries. On the one hand, positive correlations between compensation and resistance at the national level may be spurious because compensation payments do not appear to be randomly distributed across cases. Rather, compensation is likely to be awarded in cases where resistance is substantial enough to threaten a regulation or a project, as in the American product liability example previously mentioned. If so, selection effects may account for positive correlations between resistance and compensation within any given regulatory jurisdiction. To infer the ineffectiveness of compensation on the basis of simple positive correlations at the national level is akin to suggesting that fire trucks are of limited usefulness in fighting fires after observing a simple positive correlation between the number of fire trucks and the severity of fires.

On the other hand, positive correlations between compensation and resistance at the national level may not be spurious. Simply put, compensation payments may foster resistance, as in the Canadian and Japanese fishing examples above. A perverse version of Say's Law may apply here – the supply of compensation may generate its own demand. The practice of buying off resistance by providing compensation often encourages resistance by those hoping to extract compensation. Perhaps the intense opposition of rice farmers to Japanese acceptance of rice imports is

---

9. The retraining requirement for fishers centered on preparation for the construction trades. The prospects for fishers securing employment in the construction trades seem very limited. At the time that the retraining program was announced only 17 percent of Newfoundland Construction Trades Council Union Members were employed. Not surprisingly, the retraining program was opposed by the Provincial Construction Trades Councils (see 'No Room at Sites for Fishermen', *Newfoundland Telegram*, 17 July 1992).

10. Telephone interview with Ryan Cleary, conducted by Tamar Gutner, *Newfoundland Evening Telegram*, March 1993.

directed at acquiring more substantial compensation from the Japanese government.[11]

Perceived unfairness and arbitrariness can undercut the effectiveness of compensation and these standards may vary across nations. The idea of providing compensation from the many to the few may be derived from a principled belief in fairness or a pragmatic interest in buying off resistance. If society is to derive (plausible) net benefits in both NIMBY and environmental cases, then compensation is both desirable and necessary. However, it is difficult to devise standards for determining fair and appropriate levels of compensation for those adversely affected by regulations (Craig, 1992; O'Hare and Sanderson, 1993).

Conclusions

The principal finding of this paper is straightforward. Environmental regulations work most effectively when systems of regulations, whether by chance or by design, confer tangible benefits upon the regulated. We find that the relationship between particularistic self-interest and general environmental awareness is not antagonistic. But this general conclusion does require some qualification.

In Stiglerian cases coalitions of rent seekers and environmentalists provide stronger support for rent-providing environmental regulations than either rent seekers or environmentalists could secure alone. The primary problem in the Stiglerian situations is not regulatory instability. Instead, policymakers must be wary of equity issues and the potential for erosion of general economic welfare. For example, in both the CFC and Fowler cases, small, relatively less-advanced producers were disadvantaged by the introduction of environmental restraints.

In Olsonian cases regulations without compensation tended to be unstable. However, coalitions of subsidy seekers and environmentalists provide stronger support for regulation with compensation than either could

---

11. To explore these problems with greater rigor, systematic cross-national studies on compensation and resistance are needed. For example, comparisons of Japanese, American, French and Canadian compensation practices and levels of resistance to Olsonian regulations may provide one route to assessing the effectiveness of compensation. The issues of agency and representation problems, as well as definitions of fairness, could be central to comparative national studies on this subject. However, the inferential problems complicate comparisons of compensation and effectiveness across nations. Our American cases are marked by extraordinary penetration of the American state by groups with veto power over regulations. The instability of regulations in the American case and the relative paucity of compensation may both be affected by the extraordinary degree of penetration; simply put, why bother to compensate if it is hopeless?

secure alone. Our Japanese and American illustrations suggest that regulatory instability is to be expected in Olsonian situations and that compensation can mitigate instability in Olsonian cases, at least to some degree. The problem here is that the effectiveness of compensation appears highly variable. At times, offers of compensation reduce the level and intensity of opposition. In other cases, the expectation of compensation actually elicited opposition to regulation. We suggest that further research may be needed here to address methodological problems associated with simple correlational studies.

We end this essay with a conclusion, a caveat and a look ahead. First, we offer a general conclusion. In both Stiglerian and Olsonian situations the reconciliation of private self-interests and public environmental interests may be a requisite of stable, environmentally sensitive regulations. This general point has both explanatory and prescriptive implications. To *explain* the stability or instability of systems of environmental regulation, analysts should search for the presence or absence of coalitions of the self-interested and the environmentally interested. To *promote* stable systems of environmental regulation, policymakers should take care to design regulations and systems of compensation that foster formation of coalitions of the self-interested and the environmentally committed. Second, we present a caveat and a look ahead. Stable systems of regulation are *not* necessarily welfare enhancing or fair. Coalitions of the self-interested and the environmentally interested can produce robust but inefficient and/or inequitable systems of regulation. We direct readers to the other essays in this collection for explicit discussion of the management of tradeoffs across equity, efficiency and stability under conditions of heterogeneity. The insights to be found in the essays in this collection may be of particular value to those who are seeking to design fair, welfare enhancing as well as stable systems of environmental regulation.

REFERENCES

Agthe, Donald E. (1986) 'Indemnity for Companies Adversely Affected by Environmental Regulation Changes', *Policy Studies Review* (6 August): 11–12.

Altshuler, Alan, James Womack and John R. Pucher (1979) *The Urban Transportation System*. Cambridge, MA: MIT Press.

Buchanan, Rex (1987) *Roadside Kansas: A Traveler's Guide to Its Geology and Landmarks*. Lawrence: University Press of Kansas.

Congressional Quarterly Weekly Report (1990) 'A Decade's Acrimony Lifted in the Glow of Clean Air' (27 Oct.): 3587–92.

Council of the European Communities, Decision 80/372/EEC (1980) *Official Journal of the European Communities* L90, 3 April.

Craig, Paul (1992) 'Siting a Liquid Hazardous Waste Incinerator: Experience with California's Tanner Act', *Environmental Impact Assessment Review* 12: 363–86.

Department of the Environment, Central Unit on Environmental Pollution (1976) *Pollution Paper No. 5. Chlorofluorocarbons and Their Effect on Stratospheric Ozone*, p. 16. London: HMSO.

Dotto, L. and H. Schiff (1978) *The Ozone War*. Garden City, NY: Doubleday.

Doyle, Pat (1991) 'Fishermen Receive Emergency Help', *Newfoundland Evening, Telegram* (5 October).

DuPont Corporate News, External Affairs (1988) DuPont Policy Statement: CFCs, 24 March.

Environment Reporter (1974) Vol. 4, No. 40 (1 Feb.): 1607.

Environmental Data Services Report (ENDS Report) (1986) DuPont Leads Industry Shift on CFCs (Oct.): 6.

ENDS Report (1988a) 'DuPont Again Breaks Ranks on CFCs, Announces Phase-out Goal', 158 (March): 6.

ENDS Report (1988b) 'Prime Minister's Discovery of Environment to Speed Greening of Political Landscape', 64 (Sept.): 21.

Farman, J. C., B. G. Gardiner and J. D. Shanklin (1985) 'Large Losses of Total Ozone in Antarctica Reveal Seasonal ClO_x/NO_x Interaction', *Nature* 315: 207–10.

Financial Times (1988) 'Thatcher's Green Mantle Seems an Ill Fit' (29 Sept.): 7.

Grad, Frank (1975) *The Automobile and the Regulation of its Impact on the Environment*. Norman: University of Oklahoma Press.

Gresser, Julian, Koichina Fujikura and Akio Morishima (1981) *Environmental Law in Japan*. Cambridge, MA: MIT Press.

Jones, Charles O. (1975) *The Policies and Politics of Pollution Control*. Pittsburgh: University of Pittsburgh Press.

Kansas State Board of Agriculture (1993) '*Report of the Kansas Agriculture Ogallala Task Force*' (Sept.).

Krier, James and Edmund Ursim (1977) *Pollution and Policy*. Berkeley: University of California Press.

Lesbirel, Hayden (1993) 'Externalities, Bargaining and Compensation: Managing Environmental Conflict in Japan', mimeo, Department of Japanese Studies, National University of Singapore.

Maxwell, James (1991) Interviews with DuPont Officials, October.

Maxwell, James and S. Weiner (1993a) 'Green Consciousness or Dollar Diplomacy: The British Response to Ozone Depletion', *International Environmental Affairs* 5: 19–41.

Maxwell, James and S. Weiner (1993b) 'Industry's Role in the Development of the Regulatory Regime for Ozone Depleting Substances', paper presented to the 1993 meeting of the Association of Public Policy Analysis and Management.

Maxwell, James, George Heaton and Janet McCleary Jones (1980) *Environmental Regulation of the Automobile*, pp. 48–72. Cambridge, MA. MIT Center for Policy Administration.

Molina, M. and F. S. Rowland (1974) 'Stratospheric Sink for Chlorofluoromethanes: Chlorine Atom Catalyzed Destruction of Ozone', *Nature* 249: 10–12.

National Academy of Sciences Committee on Impacts of Stratospheric Change (1976) *Halocarbons, Environmental Effects of Chlorofluoromethane Release*. Washington, DC: National Academy of Sciences.

National Academy of Sciences (1979) *Protection Against Depletion of Stratospheric Ozone by Chlorofluorocarbons*, p. 5. Washington, DC: National Academy of Sciences.

National Academy of Sciences (1984) *Causes and Effects of Stratospheric Ozone Reduction: An Update*. Washington, DC: National Academy Press.

Nowell, Gregory P. (1991) 'California Initiatives on Air Quality and Alternative Fuels', Working Paper. Cambridge, MA: MIT, Center for Technology Policy and Industrial Development.

O'Hare, Michael and Debra Sanderson (1993) 'Facility Siting and Compensation: Lessons from the Massachusetts Experience', *Journal of Policy Analysis and Management* 12: 364–76.

Olson, Mancur (1965) *The Logic of Collective Action: Public Goods and the Theory of Groups*. Cambridge, MA: Harvard University Press.

Parson, Edward A. (1993) 'Protecting the Ozone Layer', in Peter M. Haas, Robert O. Keohane and Marc Levy (eds) *Institutions for the Earth*. Cambridge, MA: MIT Press.

Porges, Amelia (1980) *Car Wars: Automobile Regulation, Policy, Strategy in Japan*. Cambridge, MA: MIT, Center for Policy Alternatives.

Rabe, Barry G. (1992) 'When Siting Works, Canada Style', *Journal of Health Politics, Policy and Law* 17: 119–42.

Reich, Michael R., Yasui Endo and C. Peter Timmer (1986) 'Agriculture: The Political Economy of Structural Change', in Thomas K. McCraw (ed.) *America Versus Japan*, pp. 151–92. Boston, MA: Harvard Business School Press.

Reinhardt, Forest (1989) *DuPont Freon Products Division (B)*, Harvard Business School case prepared for the National Wildlife Federation, Washington, DC.

Rivkin, Kenneth A. (1983) *Decision-making Under Uncertainty: The International Response to Protect Stratospheric Ozone*, Thesis for Master of Science in Management, Massachusetts Institute of Technology.

Stigler, George (1971) 'The Economic Theory of Regulation', *Bell Journal of Economics* 2: 3–21.

Thomas, Lee (1986) Cited in Paul Brodeur, 'Annals of Chemistry in the Face of Doubt', *New Yorker* (9 June): 86.

Thomas, Lee (1988) Cited in 'How Long a Farewell to CFC Production?', *Chemical Week* (6 April): 7.

The Times, London (1989) 'Total Ban on CFCs to Save Ozone Layer' (3 March): 1.

Tolba, Mustafa (1988) Cited in MacKenzie, Deborah, 'Now it Makes Business Sense to Save the Ozone Layer', *New Scientist* (29 Oct. 1988): 25.

Warr, K. (1990) 'Ozone: The Burden of Proof', *New Scientist* (27 Oct.): 39.

Watson, R. T., M. Prather and M. J. Kurylo (1988) *Present State of Knowledge of the Upper Atmosphere 1988: An Assessment Report*, 15 March.

Waxman, Henry A., Gregory S. Wetstone and Phillip S. Barnett (1991) 'Cars, Fuels, and Clean Air: A Review of Title II of the Clean Air Act Amendments of 1990', *Environmental Law Journal* 21: 1947–2019.

Weiner, S. and James Maxwell (1993) 'The Political Economy of the CFC Phaseout: Learning the Right Lessons', in *Dimensions of Managing Chlorine in the Environment*, Report of the MIT/Norwegian Chlorine Study, March.

9. HETEROGENEITIES AT TWO LEVELS: STATES, NON-STATE ACTORS AND INTENTIONAL OIL POLLUTION

Ronald B. Mitchell

Heterogeneities among states, among non-state actors and between state and non-state actors explain the timing, process, form and effectiveness of international regulation of intentional oil pollution. General claims regarding the impact of heterogeneity on cooperation in this issue-area provide little useful insight. Rather, understanding the progressive movement toward rules that reduced intentional oil discharges depends on identifying different varieties of heterogeneity and their unique influences on the process and outcomes of cooperation. Success at reducing discharges by tanker operators, who had few incentives to provide the public good of a cleaner ocean, depended on rules that took advantage of existing heterogeneities in preferences and capacities to build a regulatory structure that coerced compliance by preventing most violations and deterring the rest.

Although the process is less dramatic, the traditional practice by tankers of discharging waste oil overboard has regularly accounted for far more of the oil that enters the ocean than have accidents. Analysts estimated in the 1970s that a million tons of oil entered the ocean each year from intentional

I would like to thank Robert O. Keohane, Elinor Ostrom, Margaret McKean and other participants at the conference on Heterogeneity and Collective Action for comments on earlier drafts of this article. This article draws heavily on Mitchell (1993, 1994).

discharges, while only one-third as much came from accidents (National Academy of Sciences, 1975; National Academy of Sciences and National Research Council, 1985). Since the 1920s international diplomats have sought to reduce the environmental impact of the oil transportation process. After a tanker delivers its cargo, a small fraction adheres to the tank walls. This clingage becomes mixed with water through two shipboard operations. First, the clingage mixes with the sea water that tankers place in their cargo tanks to ballast themselves on the return voyage. Second, tankers clean their tanks with sea water en route to prepare for their next cargo. For an average tanker these processes generate some 300 tons of oil/water mixtures per voyage.[1] The easiest, cheapest and customary method of disposal was to discharge these mixtures while at sea. With thousands of tanker voyages per year, however, this disposal method soon became more than a minor problem. While scientific uncertainty remains regarding the extent of damage to marine life caused by the low-concentration, chronic oiling from discharges, their visible impact as well as that of accidents on seabirds and resort beaches have provided the impetus for regular efforts at international regulation (National Academy of Sciences and National Research Council, 1985; GESAMP, 1990: 2; Hawkes and M'Gonigle, 1992: 178).

This paper begins by describing the dynamic history of attempts to control intentional oil pollution from tankers. It then argues that this history reflects a pattern of progressive cooperation from initial rules that had no hope of achieving the desired goal of reducing intentional oil pollution to rules with which actors were more likely to comply and compliance with which was more likely to produce real pollution reductions. The analysis then successively evaluates how four types of heterogeneity – of preferences and capabilities in producing the public good, among states, among non-state actors and between state and non-state actors – and learning account for particular elements of this process.

History

The 1954 International Convention for the Prevention of Pollution of the Sea by Oil[2]

Regulation of intentional oil pollution has been on the international agenda since the US convened an intergovernmental conference in 1926. The UK

---

1. For comparison, the *Exxon Valdez* spilt 35,000 tons into Prince William Sound in 1989 and the *Braer* spilt 85,000 tons off the Shetland Islands in 1993.
2. This section relies heavily on Pritchard (1987) and M'Gonigle and Zacher (1979).

prompted a similar effort in 1935 under the auspices of a League of Nations Committee of Experts. Both conferences produced draft conventions. While major oil companies agreed to 'voluntarily comply' with the limits these agreements put on discharges near shore, neither convention ever took legal effect. After World War II, growing demand in Western countries for Middle East crude oil produced growing complaints of spoiled beach resorts and large numbers of dead sea birds in the UK and in Europe (Ministry of Transport, 1953: 1). In the UK, bird protection societies, hotel and tourist organizations and local governments formed the Advisory Committee on Oil Pollution of the Sea (ACOPS) and pressed for international action.

In response to such pressures, the British government set up a committee to study oil pollution. The Faulkner Committee recommended a unilateral ban for all British ships of discharges over 100 parts per million (ppm) 'within a wide zone around the United Kingdom' until an international ban on such discharges could be established (Ministry of Transport, 1953: 1, 33). The British – believing that even a large prohibition zone around the UK was inadequate, facing pressures from ACOPS and not wanting to encumber their domestic shipping and oil interests – hosted an intergovernmental conference in London in 1954. They proposed an ocean-wide ban on discharges, rather than merely discharging farther from shore as required by the prewar agreements (M'Gonigle and Zacher, 1979: 90). Tankers, it was contended, could eliminate oil pollution if they 'refrained from cleaning their cargo tanks and mixed oily ballast residues with new cargo oil' or retained slops on board for discharge in port (Pritchard, 1987: 95).

At the time the US viewed its pollution problems as having been solved by its own national legislation and voluntary restraints by industry and had lost interest in international regulation (International Conference, 1954a: 4). Denmark, France, Japan, Norway, Sweden and most developing states – lacking domestic concern over coastal pollution, believing oil evaporated and biodegraded if discharged far from shore, or seeking to protect their maritime interests – saw any regulation as unnecessary (United Nations Secretariat, 1956; Pritchard, 1987: 98–9).[3] Oil and shipping companies objected to an ocean-wide ban because discharging slops in port, rather than at sea, involved lengthy delays. Governments resisted the complementary requirement to provide reception facilities for these slops as too expensive.

The final 1954 International Convention for the Prevention of Pollution

---

3. For example, the British commission found no evidence that fish or shellfish beds were harmed by oil pollution (Ministry of Transport, 1953: 2–3). The French argued that their research had 'produced no proof that its effects upon marine life were harmful' (International Conference, 1954b: 5).

of the Sea by Oil (OILPOL) failed to limit discharges throughout the ocean, reflecting 'the fact that most governments were still not willing to accept any important control costs themselves or even to impose such costs on their industries' (M'Gonigle and Zacher, 1979: 89). Instead, the British garnered Commonwealth and Soviet bloc support to adopt a convention that prohibited discharges above 100 ppm within 50 miles from shore.[4] Discharge rates outside these zones and total oil discharged were unrestricted, relying on redistribution of discharges to mitigate coastal pollution. The final agreement required states to 'ensure provision' of reception facilities but only to meet the needs of non-tankers, leaving tankers with few real alternatives to discharging at sea (Pritchard, 1987: 108). However, even these weak reception facility clauses led several countries, including the US, to lodge objections.

Enforcement was based on requiring ship masters to record all ballasting, cleaning and discharge operations in an oil record book. Port states could inspect these books but, in most cases, had to turn over evidence to flag states for prosecution (Pritchard, 1987: 112). All states had to report to the Secretariat on reception facilities installed and flag states had to report on actions taken on violations referred for prosecution, although the Convention established no schedule or format for these reports. The Convention entered into force in 1958.

This initial deterrence-based regulatory system did not look promising. Existing monitoring devices could not reliably measure the 100 ppm standard, so even conscientious captains could assure compliance only by making all discharges outside the zones. Many captains could have done this with little additional cost in time or fuel, since those plying the main Europe – Middle East route could deballast and clean their tanks in the still-legal discharge area in the central Mediterranean (Kirby, 1968: 203). Yet few incentives existed to incur even minimal costs of compliance, since successful detection of violations was highly unlikely. Likewise, the evidentiary and incentive-related obstacles posed by exclusive flag state jurisdiction made prosecution, let alone penalization, even less likely.[5]

The 1962 Amendments

As tankers transported more oil by sea, increases in discharges prompted increased concern over pollution. Dissatisfied with OILPOL's results, ACOPS sponsored a conference in 1959 that recommended a global

---

4. It established wider zones near Australia, the North Sea states and in the Atlantic off the European and UK coasts.
5. These problems had been noted as early as the 1926 Conference (Pritchard, 1987: 23).

discharge ban (Pritchard, 1987: 119). The Intergovernmental Maritime Consultative Organization (IMCO) itself prepared a conference in 1962 to amend the 1954 Convention. By then, French and German studies had prompted a new scientific consensus that crude oil persisted so long that zones would not prove environmentally effective (Pritchard, 1987: 130–1).

The British sought to reduce the immediate costs of, and hence resistance to, their proposal for an ocean-wide discharge ban by applying it only to *new* tankers over 20,000 tons. New tankers would need to retain slops on board and monitor all discharges, although oil content monitors and oily water separators were not explicitly required. The US opposed this proposal for reducing, rather than redistributing, discharges because reliable devices for a tanker to monitor its own compliance did not exist (Pritchard, 1987: 138). Japan, Norway and the Netherlands also opposed the proposal as expensive in itself and imposing competitive disadvantages for compliant states (M'Gonigle and Zacher, 1979: 95–6). The provision was adopted, however, with the support of the Commonwealth and Soviet bloc states that had supported Britain in 1954 (Pritchard, 1987: 139). Discharges below 100 ppm remained legal within somewhat expanded zones and all discharges by existing tankers remained legal outside them. Industry raised few objections: whether the zones were 50 or 100 miles, experience had shown that enforcement never extended beyond a country's 3-mile limit. Since compliance with the rules for new tankers required discharging slops into reception facilities, the parties replaced the 1954 language with broader but weaker requirements for governments to 'promote provision' of facilities in all ports, including tanker ports. The clear implication was that the oil industry should shoulder this burden (M'Gonigle and Zacher, 1979: 93–4).

Changes in enforcement and reporting were also considered. Parties adopted a clause that penalties be severe enough to discourage violations. They rejected proposals to increase the enforcement powers of coastal and port states. The Conference recommended, but did not require, that IMCO 'produce reports for which the Contracting Governments should contribute information' on oil pollution, Convention effectiveness, reception facilities, enforcement and violations (IMCO, 1962: Resolution 15). The 1962 Amendments entered into force in 1967, but only for those parties explicitly ratifying them. Future amendments could be made within the IMCO structure rather than requiring a conference (OILPOL, 1954/62: Article XVI). IMCO established the Subcommittee on Oil Pollution (SCOP) to evaluate existing rules, recommending amendments to governments through the Maritime Safety Committee, the IMCO Council and the IMCO Assembly.

Evidence soon showed enforcement of the 1954 and 1962 rules was exceedingly hard even for the two countries – the UK and Germany – seriously attempting it. Violations were commonplace (IMCO, 1964; Mitchell, 1994: ch. 7). As late as 1975 a British oil pollution expert did not think 'there was a tanker over 20,000 [tons] in the world complying with the 1962 Amendments' (M'Gonigle and Zacher, 1979: 99). Few new reception facilities were built.

The 1962 Amendments did prompt considerable research into alternative oil control technologies: the US developed segregated ballast tanks and the Soviets developed chemical washing techniques (Pritchard, 1987: 145). Likewise, oil companies, which had been 'strangely silent' previously, recognized that explicit requirements for equipment were just around the corner (M'Gonigle and Zacher, 1979: 95). These pressures and a request from the British government led Shell researchers to develop and promote a technique called Load-on-Top (LOT). LOT involved reducing tank cleaning, consolidating all oil/water mixtures in a single tank, decanting the separated-out water from beneath the oil and loading subsequent cargo on top of these slops, allowing slops to be discharged with the next load of cargo. Oil companies liked LOT because it eliminated equipment requirements and reception facility discharge time while increasing 'outturn,' i.e. the amount of oil delivered compared to oil originally loaded, by several hundred tons per voyage.[6] Governments liked LOT because it reduced the amount of oil discharged at sea without requiring them to build expensive reception facilities.

Yet, to make LOT work without equipment required tanker operators to determine by sight when to stop discharging water from beneath oil slops. Oil companies admitted that this would frequently violate the existing discharge limit of 100 ppm by large amounts. Nonetheless, by 1964 Shell and Exxon had allegedly encouraged 60 percent of tankers to adopt LOT (Kirby, 1968; M'Gonigle and Zacher, 1979: 97).

The 1969 Amendments

In a context in which it had become 'axiomatic that the less oil discharged into the sea, the better', the 1967 *Torrey Canyon* accident provided a major new impetus to oil pollution control (Sutton, 1964: 9; Kirby, 1968: 210). The accident raised public concern in many European countries, prompting negotiation of several agreements on tanker accidents and, coupled with growing environmental pressure, on all ocean pollution.

Conflicting pressures to modify the OILPOL Convention came to a head in IMCO's SCOP in the late 1960s. On one side Shell proposed scrapping OILPOL's zonal system altogether in favor of voluntary adoption of LOT (Kirby, 1968). The British government, now working more closely with its

6. On the development of LOT, see Kirby (1965: 26; 1968), Ministry of Transport (1953), and Moss (1963: 42).

oil companies and supported by Norway, the Netherlands and France, more modestly proposed that governments promote LOT and revise OILPOL to legitimize its use while retracting the 1962 amendments' equipment costs (M'Gonigle and Zacher, 1979: 99). This required replacing discharge limits defined in oil content (ppm) terms with an equivalent rate metric, i.e. volume discharged over a given distance that tankers could monitor using existing on-board machinery.

On the other side, newly pro-environmental states were seeking to strengthen the discharge regulations. The American environmental movement had influenced the US government to take increasingly strong positions advocating international environmental protection, bringing with this stronger concern a greater capacity to influence international rules (M'Gonigle and Zacher, 1979: 100). The Americans wanted to tighten the 1962 regulations and, after much oil industry lobbying, they and other opponents of LOT agreed to legitimize LOT and eliminate the 1962 requirements on new tankers in exchange for more stringent standards. The final amendments constituted a compromise. The 50-mile zones were retained. Within the zones discharges could only involve 'clean ballast' – those leaving no visible trace. Therefore 'any sighting of a discharge from a tanker . . . would be much more likely to be evidence of a contravention' (IMCO, 1977: Annex, par. 5). Outside the zones, all tankers would need to keep discharges below the new rate limit of 60 liters per mile (60 l/m).[7] Finally, the US seized on the oil industry's claim that LOT could make the convention 'automatically enforced worldwide', forcing through a limit on total discharges of 1/15,000th of a tanker's cargo capacity. Under these rules port authorities in oil loading states could assume that any tanker with clean tanks had blatantly violated the agreement (Kirby, 1968: 200, 209; Burke et al., 1975: 129).[8]

The clean ballast, the rate metric and the total discharge limits all increased the ability, if not the incentives, of tanker operators to monitor their own compliance. The total discharge limits also made independent detection of violations possible in oil loading ports. However, international law still barred port states from the intrusive inspections necessary to verify compliance with the total discharge standards and no changes were made to exclusive flag state enforcement rights. The IMCO Assembly adopted these

---

7. The 60 l/m rate posed few problems for tankers since it was 'a figure within which any responsibly run ship, no matter how big, could operate' (Kirby, 1968: 208).

8. A new tanker that loaded 150,000 tons of oil in Kuwait would deliver 149,400 tons in Rotterdam, 600 tons remaining as clingage. If it arrived in Kuwait with less than 590 tons of oil residues ('slops'), it would clearly have discharged more than 1/15,000th of its 150,000 tons. The more likely scenario would involve arrival in Kuwait with completely clean tanks or negligible slops.

amendments in October 1969, replacing the earlier principle of redistribution of discharges with one of reduction. Unfortunately, it would take nine years for these amendments to enter into force.

The 1973 International Convention for the Prevention of Pollution from Ships

Environmental interest continued to grow and led in the early 1970s to the UN Conference on the Human Environment. Concern over oil pollution also increased as sea-borne oil trade went from 264 million tons in 1954 to 1,695 million tons in 1973. Even if each tanker had discharged significantly less cargo than previously, total discharges would have increased. Countries previously opposing strict rules, including Greece and Italy, became supportive as they experienced more pollution and greater calls for environmentalism at home (M'Gonigle and Zacher, 1979: 118).

The US continued to push for stricter regulations. While oil companies had been promoting LOT's advantages since 1964, the US contended that history showed it to be far less effective than oil companies alleged. The US noted how easily tanker crews could violate the 1969 amendments and the massive resources and diligence needed to detect violations (M'Gonigle and Zacher, 1979: 108). Domestic pressures led Congress to pass the Ports and Waterways Safety Act of 1972. It required the Coast Guard to unilaterally adopt strict equipment standards by 1976 unless other countries agreed to international equipment requirements (United States Congress, 1972: Sec. 201[13]). In response, IMCO hosted a conference in 1973, which produced the International Convention for the Prevention of Pollution from Ships (MARPOL). At this conference the US proposed supplementing more stringent discharge standards with more enforceable requirements for new tankers over 70,000 tons to install segregated ballast tanks (SBT) and double bottoms. While double bottoms strictly addressed accidental pollution, SBT reduced the amount of slops generated by levels comparable to that required by the 1969 discharge standards by designating certain tanks exclusively for ballast, not cargo. Both proposals were very expensive and correspondingly controversial.

Developed states with long coastlines and small shipping industries supported the US SBT proposal. Motivated by both environmental and territorial concerns, Australia, Canada and New Zealand persuaded developing states to attend the 1973 Conference to lobby for coastal state environmental rights (Grolin, 1988: 32). Italy, lacking strong shipping interests but traditionally opposed to stringent requirements, joined the environmental ranks as coastal pollution increased. Developing states – such as Argentina, Egypt and India – supported SBT to reduce growing pollution from developed countries' ships without imposing large direct costs on their own small tanker fleets. SBT tankers also generated fewer slops, which reduced pressures on them to build expensive reception facilities. In an era of detente Soviet bloc countries saw support as having low economic costs and both political and environmental benefits.[9] This diverse coalition was large enough to pass the SBT requirement.

Two factors converted initially strong oil company opposition into support for the SBT requirement. First, a recent construction boom and the proposal's definition of new tankers as those delivered after 1980 put costs far out in the future. Second, 'with the American submission, the handwriting was on the wall', and the major oil companies – five of which were American-based – realized that support for SBT requirements on all nations' tankers would avert the competitive disadvantages of US unilateralism while derailing pressures for the even more expensive double bottoms (M'Gonigle and Zacher, 1979: 109).

Opposition to mandatory SBT remained strong from countries with large independent shipowning interests – Denmark, Germany, Greece, Norway and Sweden – less able than oil company fleets to pass on the costs involved, and those with shipbuilding interests – France and Japan – concerned that new requirements would cause deferrals in ship orders (M'Gonigle and Zacher, 1979: 114). Independent shippers opposed SBT to the end, contending that entry into force and enforcement of the less costly and more economically efficient 1969 amendments would 'effectively eliminate oil pollution arising from operational discharge' (International Chamber of Shipping, 1972: 2, 1973).

Despite US pressures for wider prohibition zones and stricter discharge limits, the final agreement maintained the 1969 standards with the exception of limiting new tankers to total discharges below 1/30,000th of cargo capacity (M'Gonigle and Zacher, 1979: 113). The rules did seek to improve implementation, enforcement and compliance. The Conference agreed, for the first time, to require annual reporting on penalties and enforcement 'in a form standardized by the Organization' (MARPOL 1973/78: Article 11[f]). Continuing ratification delays were addressed through a tacit acceptance procedure that automatically brought amendments into effect in 16 months for all parties unless more than one-third explicitly objected. Construction standards applied to ships built after set dates, regardless of the number of ratifications. Within special areas states were to 'ensure provision' of reception facilities on a schedule independent of the treaty's date of entry into force.

Compliance with equipment standards relied on initial surveys by national

---

9. For an insightful argument on the impact of détente on Soviet bloc positions in negotiations on acid rain, see Levy (1993).

governments and ship classification societies documented in an International Oil Pollution Prevention (IOPP) Certificate. Port states were given expanded rights to inspect this certificate and to verify that required equipment was on board and operating properly. To improve compliance the generally more-environmentalist port states were obligated to detain a ship caught violating until it no longer posed 'an unreasonable threat of harm to the marine environment' (MARPOL 1973/78: Article 5[2]). More drastic increases in port and coastal state enforcement were discussed but defeated by powerful flag states and the desire of many states to make these jurisdictional decisions in the Law of the Sea context (M'Gonigle and Zacher, 1979: 231–4). MARPOL did attack a wider range of issues than had OILPOL, addressing oil platforms as well as ships, including refined as well as crude oil and using five annexes (including Annex I for oil) to address liquid chemicals, harmful packaged substances, sewage and garbage discharged by ships. IMCO affirmed this broader perspective on pollution by establishing the Marine Environment Protection Committee as a full committee answering directly to the IMCO Assembly.

The 1973 Conference significantly changed the compliance system. The US interpreted enforcement difficulties and low compliance rates as evidence of inherent obstacles to an effective compliance system for discharge standards. SBT requirements created a fundamentally different regulatory structure, based on a coerced-compliance model that prevented, rather than deterred, violations (Reiss, 1994). Responsibility for compliance shifted from tanker captains to tanker owners. The site of potential violation shifted from the open ocean to the shipyard. Inspection provisions 'piggybacked' on the existing information infrastructures of classification societies and government inspections of tanker certificates and tankers' actual conditions. The greater ease of identifying violations and the international authority to detain tankers caught in violation did provide a strong deterrent. However, the equipment rules would prove especially successful because tankers would find it difficult to violate them in the first place. While a tanker captain faced no constraints in discharging illegally, a tanker buyer would have found it difficult to get cooperation from a builder, a classification society and an insurer in having a tanker built without the required equipment. While the inability to trade with an illegal tanker posed a credible threat if one could have bought a non-SBT tanker after 1980, MARPOL's regulatory system relied heavily on preventing the purchase of such ships.

The 1978 Protocol to the 1973 Convention

By 1978 only three states had ratified the 1973 MARPOL Convention. Besides the usual delays in ratification, resistance stemmed from the linkage of Annex I addressing oil pollution to the even more stringent and costlier

Annex II on chemical pollution. Then, just as the *Torrey Canyon* incident had motivated earlier agreements, a series of accidents in December 1976 and January 1977 combined with activist pressures to produce unilateral US action that put oil pollution back on the international agenda.

The 1977 Carter Initiatives expanded on the 1973 proposals, calling again for double bottoms to address accidental spills and SBT on all tankers to address intentional discharges. Under direct threats that 'if IMCO tailors its moves to suit and protect the US, we will accept; if not, we reserve the right to impose our own rules', IMCO called the Tanker Safety and Pollution Prevention Conference in 1978 (M'Gonigle and Zacher, 1979: 130). This Conference produced a Protocol that became integral to the 1973 MARPOL agreement, together known as MARPOL 1973/78.

At the Conference the US proposed to apply the 1973 SBT rule to new *and existing* tankers over *20,000* tons. A few states with heavy pollution supported the SBT retrofit proposal. Support also came from states with large independent fleets – Greece, Norway and Sweden – which had many tankers laid up during the tanker glut caused by the decreased demand for oil at post-1973 prices. For these states SBT retrofits promised to reduce the carrying capacity of all trading tankers, allowing their laid-up tankers to reenter the world market (M'Gonigle and Zacher, 1979: 123, 135). Most states, however, including Soviet bloc and developing ones, saw SBT as too costly even as they recognized the need to compromise, given US power and determination (M'Gonigle and Zacher, 1979: 138). Proposals to revert to performance standards only or to voluntary compliance were clearly non-starters, reflecting a fundamental shift from the debates of the late 1960s. As with the 1962 Amendments and LOT earlier, the 1973 rules had led the oil industry to reevaluate its technological options. Crude oil washing (COW), available since the late 1960s, became far more attractive in light of rising oil prices and US pressures for retrofitting SBT. COW reduced slops by spraying tanks with oil during cargo delivery rather than with water during the ballast voyage. Especially for those who owned the cargo, as oil companies did, COW was far more attractive than SBT because it had lower capital and operational costs. From an environmental perspective COW reduced discharges almost as much as SBT, but from an economic perspective COW was far superior since it recovered oil that was wasted under traditional transportation procedures. The oil industry and the UK proposed, as an alternative to retrofitting tankers with SBT, requiring existing tankers over 70,000 tons to install COW.

The 1978 Conference had to resolve three distinct issues in the conflict between SBT and COW. The first two involved whether to broaden the scope of MARPOL 1973's equipment rules that had applied only to large new tankers: would equipment requirements apply to small tankers and would they apply to existing tankers? Equipment rules for tankers above 20,000 (rather than 70,000) tons meant far more transporters would incur equipment costs. Equipment rules for existing tankers entailed far more immediate costs for existing oil transporters than rules that applied only to new tankers. The third issue was what equipment to require of tanker owners. While the Americans had proposed requiring double hulls, the real debate was between SBT and COW.[10] Most states opposed SBT requirements on all tankers as too costly; 40 states preferred COW while 11 favored SBT retrofits (M'Gonigle and Zacher, 1979: 136–7). Most states clearly had limits to the costs they would impose on their industries to achieve a cleaner marine environment. Yet the American threat of unilateralism could not be ignored. The final compromise greatly expanded the scope of the requirements to meet the American objective of essentially all ships having to install some form of pollution control equipment in the near future, while allowing existing tankers the industry-desired flexibility to fulfill these requirements in the cheaper manner: existing tankers could choose between SBT and COW while new tankers had to install both (MARPOL 1973/78: Annex I, Regulation 1). Existing tankers were sure to choose the cheaper COW option.

The requirements for COW and SBT have proved remarkably effective. Ninety-eight percent of all tankers have installed COW, SBT or both as required by the Convention (Mitchell, 1994; Clarkson Research Studies, 1991). This is especially remarkable in light of the significant costs involved in the case of SBT. Not surprisingly, of existing tankers that can legally install either of the technologies, 9 out of 10 installed the more economic COW while only one-third installed SBT. Along with states that supported equipment requirements, Japan and many European states that opposed equipment requirements in 1973 and 1978 have established extensive programs, including regional cooperation, to inspect equipment on board tankers entering their ports (Kasoulides, 1989; IMO, 1991, 1993: 24; Secretariat of the Memorandum of Understanding, 1992). Through these programs governments can directly sanction violating tankers, including those that are nationals of states whose governments have been reluctant to impose such sanctions themselves. Likewise, classification societies appear to issue accurate equipment certificates and conduct thorough and regular inspections as required by MARPOL.

The negotiators also took steps to reduce potential delays in the legal entry into force of the rules. First, the ratification of oil pollution requirements was delinked from that of the more controversial chemical pollution rules. Second, following the 1973 approach, the equipment requirements applied

---

10. The American concern regarding protection against accidents was addressed by requiring new tankers to install SBT in 'protective locations'.

to new ships delivered after June 1982 regardless of whether enough ratifications had led to legal entry into force. This proved prescient, since the slowness of ratifications meant that MARPOL 1973/78 did not take legal effect until late 1983. MARPOL's procedures also have proved remarkably effective at promoting faster implementation of amendments. Seven sets of amendments adopted by the Marine Environment Protection Committee since 1983, including requirements for costly accident-prevention equipment in the wake of the *Exxon Valdez* accident, have entered into force automatically in 16 months under MARPOL's tacit acceptance procedure, vastly improving on previous experience in which new rules had never entered into force in less than 4 years.

Heterogeneity and the Provision of Public Goods

International regulation of intentional oil pollution has produced rules progressively more capable of producing the public good that had been the nominal goal of cooperation since the outset. Requirements in OILPOL and MARPOL have been consistently more stringent than many states desired, often being adopted over the dissenting votes of states wielding considerable power in oil transportation markets. This success at putting in place rules that can remedy this environmental problem raises two questions in the context of this collection of papers. First, what factors explain why, in this case, the obstacles that generally inhibit creation of a public good in international affairs were successfully overcome? Second, did heterogeneity, in any of its various forms, contribute to this success?

The 1954 Convention sought 'to take action by common agreement to prevent pollution of the sea by oil discharged from ships' (OILPOL, 1954). That goal has not changed: MARPOL 1973/78 calls for 'the complete elimination of intentional pollution of the marine environment by oil and other harmful substances' (MARPOL 1973/78). What has changed over time is the likelihood that the international rules governing intentional oil discharges would actually achieve these goals. Even if tanker operators had complied, the limits and zones of the 1954 rules would only have redistributed, not reduced, the amount of oil entering the ocean. Numerous obstacles to detecting and prosecuting violations prevented achievement of even this modest objective. The 1962 amendments required new tankers to reduce total discharges, but did so via requirements with which even conscientious operators could not comply because of the absence of appropriate technology and the continuing dependence on a deterrence-based strategy of regulation. The 1969 amendments were the first rules which, had they been complied with, would have achieved significantly reduced total discharges. These reductions involved greater restraint and costs than previous rules, but they averted additional capital costs and legitimized the oil companies' preferred method for reducing discharges. Improvements in enforcement that were hoped for did not materialize in practice, however, and compliance levels remained low. While none of the rules agreed to before 1973 had much prospect of producing the desired public good, progress had been made.

The 1973 MARPOL Conference retained earlier standards requiring all tankers to reduce discharges, but reinforced them with equipment requirements with which tankers were more likely to comply and which, once complied with, actually reduced the oil a tanker needed to discharge. Since the rules applied only to large new tankers, decades would have passed before enough tankers had installed SBT to produce significant reductions in discharges. Even then, all small tankers would have remained constrained only by the unenforceable operational requirements carried over from 1969. However, the equipment rules rested on a new, more sound regulatory basis of coerced compliance in which violations were minimized by prevention rather than deterrence. On this foundation the 1978 Protocol established rules that required some form of equipment on all tankers. These rules had the three virtues of applying to all potential producers of the public good, producing the public good if complied with and creating a regulatory structure likely to produce compliance.

A final element to this pattern of progressive cooperation that deserves attention is why actors who opposed adoption of increasingly stringent rules have not only remained within the regulatory regime but have actually enforced and complied with its demands. International law legally binds only those nations that consent to its constraints. Nations often opt out of international rules adopted over their opposition or withdraw from a convention altogether. The whaling treaty provides numerous examples of states opting out or withdrawing from the regime when its rules became too onerous (Mitchell, 1992). In contrast, powerful countries have opposed oil pollution regulation at every stage, but none have withdrawn or opted out. The rest of this article assesses different forms of heterogeneity and their ability to explain the difficulty, timing, direction, form and effectiveness of this consistent, if slow, pattern of progress toward production of a desired public good.

Explaining this pattern of cooperative arrangements moving progressively towards successful production of a desired public good requires evaluating (1) heterogeneities of preferences and capabilities in producing the public good, (2) heterogeneities among states, (3) heterogeneities among non-state actors, (4) heterogeneities between state and non-state actors and (5) institutional learning. All these factors help explain the fact, timing and form of the progressive convergence between means and goals.

Heterogeneities of Preferences and Capabilities in Producing the Public Good

A focus on heterogeneity first helps us understand the difficulty of resolving the collective-action problem facing the international community. Most of the other contributions to this collection focus on resolution of common-pool resource (CPR) problems. In contrast, oil pollution, or rather an ocean free from intentional oil discharges, can be more accurately characterized as a public good exacerbated by a negative economic externality. Creating a clean ocean requires resolving a problem of underprovision or free riding, but not one of overappropriation or stealing (Keohane and Ostrom, 1994). The natural system allocates the good once provided and its non-rival character prevents overappropriation by any party.

While lacking an overappropriation aspect, oil pollution's underprovision problem is exacerbated because the actors involved are sharply differentiated into heterogeneous roles, involving both different preferences and capacities for producing the public good. Analysts of CPRs and of public goods often assume relatively homogenous actors: all relevant actors are capable of contributing to *and* benefitting from the CPR in varying degrees.[11] All contributors view themselves as better off with the public good, even though fears of free riding lead to underprovision (Keohane and Ostrom, 1994). As made clear in the contributions to this collection from Ostrom, Libecap and Hackett, Dudley and Walker, numerous obstacles to cooperation arise even when the problem involves getting potential beneficiaries to jointly provide benefits that are shared among them. However, many pollution problems exhibit characteristics that further confound resolution: actors perceptually and actually are either the contributors to, or the beneficiaries of, a clean environment, *but not both*.

This heterogeneity of preferences translates into a division across, rather than within, actors. The conflict becomes externalized between those who can provide the public good but do not benefit from it and the quite separate group who benefit from it but cannot provide it. Potential beneficiaries' fears of underprovision prove especially warranted. In many CPRs the harms of overappropriation are restricted to other appropriators. In pollution cases, however, the major costs are not reduced future rents to industry but the often non-economic, non-quantifiable costs of environmental harm frequently imposed on people who contribute little to the problem. A cleaner

---

11. The Olsonian problems discussed in Oye and Maxwell's contribution to this collection highlight the obstacles to cooperation raised when potential users of a CPR will not benefit from its production, but they contend that the CPR will not be protected unless contributors receive side payments or other positive inducements. Even Olson assumes the privileged group of contributors benefits enough from the public good to provide it (Olson, 1965).

ocean does not benefit those who must provide it, but rather is only a 'good' in the social aggregate. Therefore, contributors lack the incentives to contribute that are traditionally assumed to provide the engine for solution of public good and CPR problems. In the two-level problems involving state and non-state actors that characterize many international environmental problems, resolution of such externality-plagued public goods requires an imposed order vis-a-vis the polluter, if not necessarily nation to nation (Young, 1983).

Regulation becomes more difficult if the ability to produce the public good correlates inversely with the preference for its production. When actors view themselves as either providers or beneficiaries of a public good, but not both, the public good becomes harder to provide. While it is difficult to assess whether oil pollution is 'harder' than an otherwise comparable public good with less heterogenous actors, the five decades between initial efforts and eventual regulatory success suggest it at least falls at the 'hard' end of the spectrum.

Heterogeneities Among States

Heterogeneity among states helps us understand the timing and extent of cooperative efforts to reduce intentional oil pollution. Did heterogeneity among states foster or impede the progress from initial opposition to weak controls to far more support for far stricter controls? Every proposal to deepen cooperation from 1954 to 1978 faced major opposition. Surmounting that opposition required an activist state, either the UK or US, pushing the reluctant majority of states to consider measures more likely to reduce oil pollution. Obviously, perfect homogeneity of state preferences for pollution control would have greatly eased cooperation; perfect homogeneity of state preferences against pollution control would have made it impossible. The oil pollution experience highlights that, when most states do not value a public good but some do, a heterogeneity of power must be overlayed on this heterogeneity of preferences for progress toward the public good to be made. British proposals drove other nations from no controls to zones and from zones to new tanker prohibitions; American proposals drove other nations to accept total limits on all tankers, equipment on large new tankers and then equipment on all tankers.

The higher value that the UK and then the US put on production of the public good produced progress only because these states could credibly threaten unilateral regulation if international action was not taken. Their threats prompted conferences that pressed states to consider new regulations, set the conference agenda and anchored the debate with proposals far more stringent than other countries would otherwise have considered because these states wielded power over the major oil companies. French or

Japanese proposals could not have prompted such conferences and, indeed, these powerful countries had their preferences overridden by adoption of the 1973 SBT requirements.

While the exogenous factors of tanker accidents and growing environmental consciousness in the 1960s and 1970s helped narrow the range of preferences among states, the timing and magnitude of increases in regulatory stringency owes more to proposals from powerful states that channeled concern in specific directions and on learning from existing regulatory experience, discussed below. Most other governments were not experiencing or responding to the domestic political forces prompting activism in the US and UK. Other states would not have sought international environmental regulations on their own. Only UK and US activism prevented a generally low level of environmental concern among most states from producing far slower resolution of the problem. It is not heterogeneity or homogeneity of preferences within an issue-area so much as the power of the actors valuing the public good that determines how far and how fast the international community moves toward producing that good.

Heterogeneous state preferences within the issue-area also contribute to understanding MARPOL's improved effectiveness. MARPOL did considerably better than OILPOL in mapping governments' legal authority and practical ability to enforce its rules onto the distribution of government preferences for pollution control. Violations of the 1954 and 1962 rules were hard for any state to detect and could be prosecuted and penalized almost exclusively by flag states. The 1969 total discharge limits made violations easier to detect, but only in oil loading ports. Unfortunately, the flag states and oil exporting states that could conduct inspections there had shown even less interest than most in enforcement. MARPOL's equipment requirements and detention provisions, however, expanded the practical ability and legal authority to identify and sanction violations to a group of states that included some likely to use it, namely developed port states. This matching of authority and ability to the heterogeneous interests in monitoring and enforcement proved crucial to MARPOL's effectiveness.[12]

Heterogeneous state preferences across issues help explain both the support of other governments for activist proposals and why governments chose not to opt out of rules they had opposed. Activist states consistently cobbled together support from the ranks of otherwise indifferent states that derived linked, non-environmental benefits for their support. In the sort of cross-issue linkages discussed by Martin (paper 4 in this collection), diplomatic concerns drove Commonwealth and Soviet bloc support in 1954 and 1962, jurisdictional concerns played a major role in Australian, Canadian, New

---

12. Elsewhere I have called this the strategic triangle of compliance (Mitchell, 1994).

Zealand and developing country support in 1973 and economic concerns accounted for Greek, Norwegian and Swedish support of US proposals in 1978.

States have consistently seen rules agreed to in IMCO, renamed the International Maritime Organization (IMO) in 1981, as the only legitimate forum for international regulation of shipping. Many shipping issues such as navigation, communication and safety rules require international coordination to avoid suboptimal outcomes; others, like oil pollution, are collaboration problems in which defection remains attractive (Stein, 1983). While opting out on oil pollution issues has never been explicitly linked to other issues, retaining a say on the dense network of shipping issues negotiated at IMO undoubtedly presses states to express their discontent with specific rules through loyalty and voice rather than exit (Hirschman, 1970; Martin, paper 4 in this collection).

Even without linkage as a threat against opting out, governments would have few incentives to do so. Governments opt out or withdraw from treaties to legitimately make a rule non-applicable and thereby avoid sanctions for non-compliance. Yet, in OILPOL and MARPOL, governments have never been sanctioned for failing to fulfill their commitments. For years IMO received no reports on monitoring and enforcement and even today less than a quarter of the parties regularly report (Dempsey, 1984; Peet, 1992; Mitchell, 1994: ch. 4). Government failure to rigorously detect and prosecute OILPOL and MARPOL violations has never been sanctioned and rarely even shamed. IMO has used neither inducements nor sanctions to improve the admitted lack of reception facilities. In this context governments incurred fewer costs by simply ignoring provisions they opposed than by highlighting their non-compliance through withdrawal or opting out.[13]

The oil pollution experience confirms the importance of issue-specific hegemonic power as a determinant of the type of international rules adopted. Rephrased in heterogeneity terms, given heterogeneous preferences for a public good, a heterogeneous distribution of power enhances the prospects for cooperation if those valuing the public good have greater power. Rules proved more effective that accounted for heterogeneous preferences for pollution control in designing provisions influencing the legal authority and practical ability to monitor and enforce. The recognition of heterogeneous preferences across issues explains the adoption of rules more stringent than general environmental concern would have predicted and the unwillingness of governments opposing regulations to opt out.

---

13. Such a context did not exist in the whaling case where other whaling countries would quickly have become aware of any significant illegal whaling and hence a country intent on whaling could at least maintain legal legitimacy by opting out (Mitchell, 1992).

Heterogeneities Among Non-state Actors

While international relations scholars generally focus on states in evaluating the prospects and process for cooperation, the crucial role played by non-state actors has been noted by numerous scholars (Keohane and Nye, 1972). In international environmental affairs they often prove especially important as the targets of regulation and as monitors and enforcers (Mitchell, 1994). In oil pollution heterogeneity among non-state actors as well as between non-state and state actors influences which actors make inputs to regulation, what methods of regulation are adopted and the effectiveness of regulation.

Two groups transport oil: oil companies and independent tanker owners. These groups differ in their preferences for oil conservation because the costs of recovery fall on tanker operators, the value of oil recovered accrues to cargo owners and independents generally do not own the cargo they carry. Since oil companies are tanker owner-operators as well as cargo owners, they have private economic incentives to reduce discharges (even absent environmental concerns) whenever oil prices are high enough to offset recovery costs. By contrast, the chartering arrangements under which most independents work generally involve payment for oil loaded rather than oil delivered, passing through few incentives to conserve oil. Major oil companies directly control one-third of the world's oil tankers and are based in the US or UK, while a far larger number of independents based elsewhere control the other two-thirds. Being fewer in number, oil companies have organized and influenced international rules more readily than independents. They have been more motivated to do so because UK and US unilateralism constrained their alternatives to regulation. Together, these factors explain oil companies' greater involvement in regulation, their proposed methods of regulation and their greater influence over regulation.

Three examples illustrate this. Pushed by the British government in the 1960s, Shell energetically developed and promoted LOT to derail pressures to establish international equipment requirements. Oil companies liked LOT's ability to recover most waste oil without new equipment but also wanted to avoid its mandated use. Indeed, for a period in the 1960s, oil companies promoted LOT by compensating independents for the additional expense it imposed on tanker operators (Kirby, 1968). Not surprisingly, however, data from the 1970s show that independents rarely used LOT efficiently or effectively and discharged far more oil at sea than did oil company tankers (Mitchell, 1994: ch. 7).

In 1973 MARPOL adopted SBT requirements for new tankers with the support of oil companies and over the opposition of independents. However, Stiglerian benefits from regulation do not explain oil company support (Oye and Maxwell, paper 8 in this collection). Unlike LOT, SBT involves large equipment costs, reduces tanker capacity and – because it reduces, rather than recovers, the slops a tanker generates – has no offsetting economic benefits. Oil companies had opposed SBT requirements as recently as 1971 and have since opposed SBT retrofit proposals in 1978 and 1991 (International Chamber of Shipping, OCIMF, and INTERTANKO, 1991). If requiring SBT on new tankers had raised barriers to market entry, then independents as well as oil companies should have supported it. Indeed, both should have pressed for its immediate application to all new tankers, not just those over 70,000 tons built after 1980. No such lobbying took place. Rather, oil company support stemmed from their vulnerability to even more stringent, unilateral American rules and because a recent building boom and the requirement's application to tankers built after 1980 meant costs were far in the future.

By 1978 stricter proposals and exogenous changes to the incentives of independent tanker owners created quite different positions. The US proposal to require all existing tankers to retrofit with SBT evoked the support of independent tanker owners in Greece, Norway and Sweden and the strong opposition of oil companies. The mid-1970s tanker glut reversed earlier positions vis-a-vis these more ambitious regulations. To deal with excess tanker supply oil companies chartered fewer independent tankers, retrenching to greater use of their own tankers. This concentrated laid-up tankers among independents, who now saw SBT retrofits as a means to reduce the capacity of working tankers and put their own ships back to work. Such regulations would have cost oil companies millions in the relatively short term and they developed and successfully pressed crude oil washing equipment as an alternative to, if not a replacement for, SBT requirements, over the objections of both the US and states representing independent tankers.

These incidents highlight several points. First, oil company positions consistently differed from those of independents, reflecting their divergent economic incentives as cargo owners. Their greater resources and technical expertise allowed them to develop alternatives that promoted these interests. Second, these preferences, by themselves, have not caused oil companies to support regulation; their development of the LOT and COW alternatives and their support for regulation have been direct responses to threats posed by existing or proposed regulations. Their support for regulation responded to, rather than being exogenous of, international and unilateral US pressures. Third, support or opposition to international regulation depended on the costs of proposed regulations relative to likely future alternatives rather than to the status quo ante. Over time oil company positions diverged less from those of activist governments – as evident in the absence of calls for voluntary guidelines in the 1970s – not because of a convergence of underlying preferences but because the history of regulation made earlier positions untenable. Fourth, international regulations have incorporated oil company preferences more than independents', largely because the former could more readily organize and lobby for their positions. As MARPOL's rejection of requirements in the 1972 Port and Waterways Safety Act and the 1977 Carter initiatives demonstrates, often international rules reflected oil company preferences more than domestic rules. The distribution of power and preferences at the international level let oil companies block costly rules that they failed to block at the domestic level.

MARPOL's rules also took advantage of a different heterogeneity between non-state actors, namely between the preferences of oil transporters and others involved in the oil trade. Discharge rules could be violated by any tanker operator with incentives to do so. Reducing violations depended on reducing those incentives via deterrence. MARPOL's equipment rules could only be violated by those tanker owners able to elicit cooperation from a builder, classification society and insurer in building an admittedly illegal tanker. These actors had reputational incentives not to cooperate and could effectively prevent violations. Building on heterogeneous incentives across actors, the regime delegated monitoring authority to classification societies in an example of what Martin (paper 4 in this collection) calls 'functional differentiation', thereby facilitating cooperation. The coerced-compliance regulatory strategy proved very effective and was reinforced by the deterrence stemming from the willingness of some important markets, especially the US, to link the ability to trade to compliance. A market structure involving non-state actors with divergent interests allowed creation of a regulatory strategy that prevented, rather than merely deterring, violations.[14]

Heterogeneities Between State and Non-state Actors

The fact that states, as a group, differ in capacities and incentives from non-state actors gives us further leverage in understanding the dynamics of efforts to reduce oil pollution. As Young notes (paper 3 in this collection), international environmental problems often involve a two-level implementation game that follows Putnam's two-level negotiation game (Putnam, 1988; Chayes and Chayes, 1993). While being the ultimate targets of regulation, non-state actors lack certain abilities that constrain their options relative to governments. Given rules they dislike, governments can choose to comply, violate or opt out. Non-state actors can choose only between the first two of these. While states can legitimately express their preferences by opting out, non-state actors cannot. If a government does not opt out, its corporate nationals can oppose this position only through non-compliance.

Indeed, available evidence suggests that many tanker operators chose not

---

14. On the difference between incentive-based, deterrence-based and coerced-compliance models of regulation, see Reiss (1984).

to comply with discharge standards. In contrast, even though MARPOL's SBT requirements were more widely opposed and owners had ongoing incentives to violate them, almost all have subsequently complied. This contrast is partly due to a two-level implementation problem that allowed hierarchical enforcement and coerced compliance regulatory strategies in an international context (Keohane and Ostrom, 1994). While the heterogeneity of roles and preferences described above determines the need for an imposed order, it does not determine its form. Internationally, regulatory options are assumed to include positive incentives like sidepayments (Oye and Maxwell, paper 8 in this collection), negative sanctions or their combination as linkage. Hierarchical enforcement, possible at the domestic level, is generally assumed to be unavailable to international regulators (Martin, paper 4 in this collection). However, these traditional incentive-manipulating alternatives ignore regulatory strategies that constrain actors' abilities to engage in undesirable activities, known as coerced-compliance strategies (Reiss, 1984). The oil pollution problem shows both hierarchical enforcement and coerced-compliance strategies being used at the international level.

MARPOL altered the definition of compliance and the rules regarding enforcement to provide governments with the practical ability and legal authority to easily identify and sanction violations committed by the nationals of other countries. MARPOL took advantage of the divergent preferences for enforcement among states by establishing sanctions that addressed governments' aversions to sanctioning other governments. Detaining a foreign national's tanker is far less likely to evoke retaliatory sanctions than an economic boycott or other government-to-government sanction. International authorization of transnational hierarchical enforcement, i.e. by one government against another's nationals, made sanctioning more likely by isolating intergovernmental relations from pollution enforcement. Without hierarchical enforcement, e.g. if all tankers had been government-owned, adoption of SBT would likely have been considerably less prevalent because of either opting out or unsanctioned non-compliance. Obviously, the practical possibility of such enforcement depended on international trade as part of the environmental problem's structure. While common to international regulation of endangered species, ozone protection and hazardous waste, trade is not common to many other environmental problems, limiting the use of such techniques.

While governmental enforcement can increase compliance by non-state actors, the latter lack equivalent enforcement powers to alter the behavior of governments. Ongoing non-compliance by many governments in ensuring provision of reception facilities has been a frequent complaint of tanker operators and has delayed implementation of more stringent discharge restrictions in several MARPOL special areas for over a decade (Andren and Liu, 1990; INTERTANKO, 1989, 1993). Even when tanker owners have brought the absence and inadequacy of countries' reception facilities to IMO's attention, no responses have been forthcoming (International Chamber of Shipping, 1983, 1985, 1990). Thus, differences in enforcement powers between states and non-state actors manifested themselves in different compliance levels.

MARPOL's equipment standards also enhanced effectiveness by recognizing that non-state actors may prove more able and likely than governments to monitor and enforce international regulations. While environmental non-governmental organization (NGO) involvement is frequently cited as crucial to implementation of international accords, non-environmental NGOs also can play a role. MARPOL built on the fact that classification societies, insurers and shipbuilders had abilities and incentives to monitor and enforce that exceeded those of many governments. Classification societies had greater access to information about a tanker than governments did, but had to build reputations for high standards to recruit new business. Given MARPOL's inspection and certification rules and the benefits of classifying with a reputable classification society, it became worth the costs of complying with equipment rules. Insurance depended on classification that depended, in turn, on compliance with equipment regulations. Even ordering a tanker without SBT became difficult when a prospective buyer had to identify a builder, classification society and insurer willing to cooperate in facilitating an admittedly illegal act. Tanker owners complied with MARPOL's equipment rules because private transactions prevented them from doing otherwise. While even governments found it difficult to enforce discharge standards, equipment standards gave a new role to private actors with existing capacities and incentives that were different from those of many governments, thereby facilitating provision of the public good of reduced oil pollution. The structure of the environmental problem and the heterogeneity of the capabilities, authority and incentives between state and non-state actors explain the greater effectiveness of MARPOL's equipment rules, showing up in more government enforcement, prevention of violations by non-state actors and a resultant greater overall compliance level by tankers.

Learning

Besides heterogeneity, the progressive movement toward reduction of the intentional oil pollution problem owes much to a process of learning that undercut certain positions while reinforcing others. Learning narrowed the range of positions that actors could reasonably take on alternative regulatory strategies, thus fostering cooperation. Existing strategies shown to have failed were excluded from consideration in subsequent regulation while successful strategies were built upon.

At the 1954 Conference countries unconcerned with oil pollution rebuffed British proposals for a global ban on discharges, contending that even coastal prohibition zones were unwarranted. By 1962 the increase in the amount of oil transported on and discharged into the sea, coupled with scientific findings that crude oil could persist over long distances, undercut arguments that no problem existed and allowed adoption of rules that essentially prohibited discharges for new tankers. While the 1962 requirements for new tankers had low immediate costs, they established the principle that discharges should be reduced. The 1969 amendments then expanded this principle, through total discharge limits, to all tankers, the 1962 precedent having made oil company arguments for voluntary guidelines untenable. Their arguments that effective use of LOT had already eliminated most discharges did, however, convince negotiators to legitimize LOT and not require pollution-reduction equipment. By 1973, however, evidence falsifying those claims and inherent difficulties in enforcing discharge rules removed voluntary guidelines and exclusive reliance on discharge standards from the menu of negotiable options.

The adoption of equipment standards in 1973 and their broadening in 1978 continued to build on the OILPOL experience. Similar to the 1962 events, the low immediate costs of the 1973 equipment rules allowed establishment of the principle of equipment regulations, which was then expanded to all tankers in 1978. The value attached to the enforcement benefits of equipment requirements grew directly from the obstacles to detecting and prosecuting OILPOL's discharge standards. To answer the counterfactual, without almost 20 years of history with OILPOL, MARPOL would not have adopted expensive equipment requirements as the initial approach to oil pollution reduction. Experience taught the US what regulatory strategies would better foster the environmental goal, while discrediting laggard state arguments to continue existing strategies.

The institution also prompted the more focused learning by industry reflected in the development of LOT and COW. While motivated by a desire to avoid regulatory costs, it produced information on lower cost means to achieving environmental goals. Industry promotion of these strategies signified a growing acceptance of environmental goals as the state of the world, even if it did not signify an internalization of those goals. Oil companies promoted LOT throughout the 1960s not because it conserved oil, which would not increase in value until 1973, but because it averted international equipment requirements. Oil companies supported COW retrofits in 1978 not only because they reduced oil lost during transport but because they averted the more expensive SBT retrofits. Previous regulatory decisions constrained the positions industry could expect to be acceptable to the activist state.

MARPOL's success also owes much to OILPOL's failures. OILPOL's amendments had confirmed Ostrom's view that 'the initial rules established in some systems are likely to be ill-matched to the problems they face' (paper 6 in this collection). OILPOL took four years to enter into force, the 1962 amendments took five years and by 1973 the 1969 amendments had not yet taken effect. With little opposition MARPOL incorporated decision-making procedures that shortened the delay between adoption and implementation of new rules. First, many provisions set specific dates to take effect, whether or not the agreement had entered into force. The 1973 requirements for SBT installations and for reception facilities in special areas applied after January 1980 and January 1977, respectively and the 1978 equipment requirements for new tankers applied after June 1982. Second, via tacit acceptance, amendments enter into force automatically after 16 months unless one-third of the parties object. Both tactics have succeeded. As late as 1977 oil company representatives claimed that large discharges were not illegal because the 1969 restrictions on total discharges had not yet taken effect (Gray, 1978). In contrast, tankers installed required equipment on MARPOL schedules, even though waiting for entry into force would have delayed the requirements by up to three and a half years. Likewise, while slow ratifications delayed the 1969 Amendments for nine years and plagued entry into force of MARPOL itself, all MARPOL amendments have entered into force in 16 months, including controversial 1991 requirements for expensive double hulls.

Within the context of this collection, learning can be seen as a process that promoted effective regulation of oil pollution by reducing the heterogeneity of viable positions that actors could take, even while often leaving the heterogeneity of their underlying preferences unaffected. In line with Snidal's argument (paper 3 in this collection), positions were influenced by, as much as influencing, the efforts to provide the public good of a cleaner ocean. Learning within the regime created an endogenous bias toward certain goals and means and away from others, in ways different from those that would have occurred in the regime's absence.

Conclusions and Lessons

How did heterogeneity contribute to or detract from the pattern of progressive cooperation that has characterized the international regulation of intentional oil pollution? As made clear throughout this collection, heterogeneity comes in various flavors, with corresponding variations in its impact on the ability of actors to resolve collective-action problems. This article has identified the different effects of different types of heterogeneity in a single international case. Problems in which actors have heterogeneous roles, as either producers or beneficiaries, make public goods harder to produce by introducing externalities. If the oil industry had been more homogeneously distributed among countries, then no country could have credibly threatened unilateral action. Hegemony, involving a coincidence of state heterogeneity in power and state heterogeneity in preferences, consistently provided the engine that put intentional oil pollution on the international agenda and framed the ensuing debate. The heterogeneity of preferences and of the capacity to organize between sectors in the oil transportation industry determined the content and influence of proposals made by oil companies. It was the happy coincidence, from an environmental perspective, of the concentration of oil companies in states with environmental movements capable of getting their governments to threaten unilateral action that led those companies to support international regulation of any form.

Equipment requirements proved more effective than discharge standards by creating regulations that took advantage of several types of heterogeneity. First, because oil transporters faced different legal norms from states, they could choose only to comply with or violate rules they opposed, but could not opt out. Second, certain non-state actors had greater capacities than governments to prevent, rather than merely deter, equipment violations and had interests sufficiently different from those of oil transporters to use these capacities. Third, because the problem involved international trade and two-level enforcement, MARPOL enhanced the ability for hierarchical enforcement by one government against nationals of another, greatly increasing its likelihood.

The progressive cooperation toward reducing intentional oil pollution also illustrates institutional learning. Exogenous forces have consistently influenced positions and through them the oil pollution regulations adopted. However, after adoption of initial rules, experience with and future expectations of international regulations and institutions shaped preferences and capabilities toward amendments and revisions that enhanced the likelihood of pollution control, and away from those that decreased that likelihood. By reducing the gap between opposing positions, experience with previous regulations increased the ability to move toward regulations that facilitated provision of the public good of reduced pollution.

What does this experience teach us for solving other environmental collective-action problems? First, it provides optimism that even when those required to contribute to an international public good have no exogenous incentives to do so, nations can negotiate rules that progressively and successfully lead them to provide it. Second, it suggests that rules can succeed by identifying heterogeneities in the capacities and authority needed to effectively implement a regulatory strategy and selecting that strategy which best matches the heterogeneities in preferences among states, among non-state actors and between the two groups. Different preferences and capacities can provide 'natural' monitors and enforcers whose incentives independently lead them to undertake those activities. The rules need only to give them the authority and to define compliance in ways that provide the practical ability to monitor and sanction. Third, it highlights that a strategy that alters incentives by deterring violations may prove less effective than a strategy that alters opportunities by preventing violations. For analysis of heterogeneity to improve our understanding of existing international environmental agreements and negotiation of future ones, much more research is needed to examine many more cases to identify the most important types of heterogeneity and their impact on the timing, shape and effectiveness of regulatory efforts.

REFERENCES

Andren, L. and D. Liu (1990) 'Environmentally Sensitive Areas and Special Areas Under MARPOL 73/78', in *IMAS 90: Marine Technology and the Environment*, pp. 33–43. London: Institute of Marine Engineers.

Burke, William T., Richard Legatski and William W. Woodhead (1975) *National and International Law Enforcement in the Ocean*. Seattle: University of Washington Press.

Chayes, Abram and Antonia Chayes (1993) 'On Compliance', *International Organization* 47(2) (Spring): 175–206.

Clarkson Research Studies (1991) *The Tanker Register*. London: Clarkson Research Studies, Inc.

Dempsey, Paul Stephen (1984) 'Compliance and Enforcement in International Law – Oil Pollution of the Marine Environment by Ocean Vessels', *Northwestern Journal of International Law and Business* 6(2) Summer: 459–561.

GESAMP (IMO/FAO/UNESCO/WMO/WHO/IAEA/UN/UNEP Joint Group of Experts on the Scientific Aspects of Marine Pollution) (1990) *The State of the Marine Environment*, GESAMP Reports and Studies no. 39. New York: United Nations.

Gray, William O. (1978) 'Testimony', in *Oil Tanker Pollution – Hearings*, 18 and 19 July, H401-8. United States Congress, House of Representatives, Committee on Government Operations, Government Activities and Transportation Subcommittee (95: 2). Washington, DC: GPO.

Grolin, Jesper (1988) 'Environmental Hegemony, Maritime Community, and the Problem of Oil Tanker Pollution', in Michael A. Morris (ed.) *North-South Perspectives on Marine Policy*, pp. 13–44. Boulder, CO: Westview Press.

Hawkes, Suzanne and R. Michael M'Gonigle (1992) 'A Black (and Rising?) Tide: Controlling Maritime Oil Pollution in Canada', *Osgoode Hall Law Journal* 30(1) (Jan.): 165–260.

Hirschman, Albert O. (1970) *Exit, Voice and Loyalty: Responses to Decline in Firms, Organizations and States*. Cambridge, MA: Harvard University Press.

IMCO (1962) *Resolutions Adopted by the International Conference on Prevention of Pollution of the Sea by Oil, 1962*. London: IMCO.

IMCO (1964) *Pollution of the Sea by Oil*. London: IMCO.

IMCO (1977) 'Resolution A.391(X) (14 November)'. London: IMCO.

IMO (1991) 'Resolution A.682(17) (10 November)'. London: IMO.

IMO (1993) '1994 Target for Port State Control Pact', *IMO News* (2): 24.

International Chamber of Shipping (1972) 'Consideration of Comments of Governments on the Draft 1973 Convention and Its Annexes: General Comments on the Draft Articles', MP XIII/2(c)/7 (2 June). London: IMCO.

International Chamber of Shipping (1973) 'Consideration of a Draft International Convention

for the Prevention of Pollution from Ships, 1973: Comments and Proposals on a Draft Text
of the Convention', IMP/CONF/8/4 (29 June). London: IMCO.

International Chamber of Shipping (1983) 'Questionnaire on the Adequacy of Facilities in Ports
for the Reception of Oil Residues from Ships: Summary of Replies' (MEPC 19/5/2). London: IMO.

International Chamber of Shipping (1985) 'Questionnaire on the Adequacy of Facilities in Ports
for the Reception of Oil Residues from Ships: Summary of Replies' (MEPC 22/8/2). London: IMO.

International Chamber of Shipping (1990) 'Questionnaire on the Adequacy of Facilities in Ports
for the Reception of Oil Residues from Ships: Summary of Replies' (MEPC 30/lnf.30). London: IMO.

International Chamber of Shipping, OCIMF and INTERTANKO (1991) 'Oil Tanker Design
and Pollution Prevention' (MEPC 31/8/5). London: IMO.

International Conference on Pollution of the Sea by Oil (1954a) 'General Committee: Minutes
of 3rd Meeting Held on 30 April 1954'. London: IMCO.

International Conference on Pollution of the Sea by Oil (1954b) 'General Committee: Minutes
of 5th Meeting Held on 5 May 1954'. London: IMCO.

INTERTANKO (1989) 'Provision of Reception Facilities: Reception Facilities and Recycling of
Oily Wastes in the Marine Industry' (MEPC 27/5/4). London: IMO.

INTERTANKO (1993) 'Provision of Reception Facilities: Lack of Reception Facilities in the
Mediterranean Sea – Commercial Implications' (MEPC 34/lnf. 26). London: IMO.

Kasoulides, George (1989) 'Paris Memorandum of Understanding: Six Years of Regional
Enforcement', *Marine Pollution Bulletin* 20(6) (June): 255-61.

Keohane, Robert O. and Joseph S. Nye, Jr, eds (1972) *Transnational Relations and World
Politics*. Cambridge, MA: Harvard University Press.

Kirby, J. H. (1965) 'Background to Progress', *The Shell Magazine* 45(697) (Jan.): 24-7.

Kirby, J. H. (1968) 'The Clean Seas Code: A Practical Cure of Operational Pollution', in *International Conference on Oil Pollution of the Sea*, pp. 201-212. Winchester, UK: Warren and
Son. Rome.

Levy, Marc (1993) 'European Acid Rain: The Power of Tote-board Diplomacy', in Peter Haas,
Robert O. Keohane and Marc Levy (eds) *Institutions for the Earth: Sources of Effective
International Environmental Protection*, pp. 75-132. Cambridge, MA: The MIT Press.

MARPOL 1973/78 (1978) *International Convention for the Prevention of Pollution from
Ships, 1973*, 2 November 1973, reprinted in 12 ILM 1319 (1973) and *Protocol of 1978
Relating to the International Convention for the Prevention of Pollution from Ships, 1973*,
17 February 1978, reprinted in 17 ILM 1546 (1978) London: IMO.

M'Gonigle, R. Michael and Mark W. Zacher (1979) *Pollution, Politics, and International Law:
Tankers at Sea*. Berkeley: University of California Press.

Ministry of Transport, United Kingdom (1953) *Report of the Committee on the Prevention of
Pollution of the Sea by Oil*. London: Her Majesty's Stationery Office.

Mitchell, Ronald B. (1992) 'Membership, Compliance and Non-compliance: The International
Whaling Commission, 1946 – present'. mimeo, Cambridge, MA. Paper presented at the 17th
Annual Whaling Symposium, Sharon, MA, October.

Mitchell, Ronald B. (1993) 'Intentional Oil Pollution of the Oceans', in Peter Haas, Robert O.
Keohane and Marc Levy (eds) *Institutions for the Earth: Sources of Effective International
Environmental Protection*, pp. 183-248. Cambridge, MA: The MIT Press.

Mitchell, Ronald B. (1994) *Intentional Oil Pollution at Sea: Environmental Policy and Treaty
Compliance*. Cambridge, MA: The MIT Press.

Moss, James E. (1963) 'Character and Control of Sea Pollution by Oil.' Washington, DC:
American Petroleum Institute.

National Academy of Sciences (1975) *Petroleum in the Marine Environment*. Washington, DC:
National Academy of Sciences.

National Academy of Sciences and National Research Council (1985) *Oil in the Sea: Inputs, Fates and Effects*. Washington, DC: National Academy Press.

OILPOL 1954 (1954) *International Convention for the Prevention of Pollution of the Sea by Oil*, 12 May 1954, TIAS No. 4900, 327 UNTS 3, reprinted in 1 IPE 332. London: IMCO.

OILPOL 1954/62 (1962) *International Convention for the Prevention of the Sea by Oil, 1954 as Amended in 1962*, 600 UNTS 332, reprinted in 1 IPE 346. London: IMCO.

Olson, Mancur (1965) *The Logic of Collective Action*. Cambridge, MA: Harvard University Press.

Peet, Gerard (1992) *Operational Discharges from Ships: An Evaluation of the Application of the Discharge Provisions of the MARPOL Convention by Its Contracting Parties*. Available as MEPC 32/lnf.8. Amsterdam, the Netherlands: AIDEnvironment.

Pritchard, Sonia Zaide (1987) *Oil Pollution Control*. London: Croom Helm.

Putnam, Robert D. (1998) 'Diplomacy and Domestic Politics: The Logic of Two-level Games', *International Organization* 42(3) (Summer): 427–60.

Reiss, Albert J., Jr (1984) 'Consequences of Compliance and Deterrence Models of Law Enforcement for the Exercise of Police Discretion', *Law and Contemporary Problems* 47(4) (Fall): 83–122.

Secretariat of the Memorandum of Understanding on Port State Control (1992) *Annual Report 1992*. The Hague: The Netherlands Government Printing Office.

Stein, Arthur A. (1983) 'Coordination and Collaboration: Regimes in an Anarchic World', in Stephen D. Krasner (ed.) *International Regimes*, pp. 115–40. Ithaca, NY: Cornell University Press.

Sutton, C. T. (1964) 'The Problem of Preventing Pollution of the Sea by Oil', *BP Magazine* 14(1) (Winter): 8–12.

United Nations Secretariat (1956) *Pollution of the Sea by Oil*. New York: United Nations.

United States Congress (1972) *Ports and Waterways Safety Act of 1972*, Public Law 92–340, 10 July 1972, Sec. 201(13).

Young, Oran (1983) 'Regime Dynamics: The Rise and Fall of International Regimes', in Stephen D. Krasner (ed.), *International Regimes*, pp. 92–113. Ithaca, NY: Cornell University Press.

INDEX

Abreu, Dilip, 77
Acheson, James M., 2, 28
acid rain, 3, 36
actors
  endogenous, 47-68
  heterogeneity, 4, 6-10, 22-3, 62-7
  non-state, *see* non-state actors
  numbers of, 4-6, 57-62
Adams, J., 114
Advisory Committee on Oil Pollution of the
    Sea (ACOPS), 225, 226
Agency Managed Irrigation Systems, 149,
    151
agreements, collective action, 18, 168-9
Agricultural Adjustment Administration
    (AAA), 181-6 *passim*
Agthe, Donald E., 216
air quality regulations, 12, 207-14
Akerlof, George, 9
Alanya fishery, 60-2
allocation
  distributional conflict, 93-5
  of endowments, 95-108
  rules, 17-18, 19, 164-7
Altshuler, Alan, 211
Ambler, John, 146, 151
American Institute of Mining and
    Metallurgical Engineers, 171
American Petroleum Institute, 170
analytic puzzles (human/environment
    relationships), 29-31
anarchy, 2, 51, 52, 60, 68, 77
Andren, L., 244
Antarctic Airborne Ozone Experiment
    (AAOE), 199
anti-trust laws, 11, 163, 176, 181
Aristotle, 8
Artesian valley, 193, 201-6
assets (capabilities), 7
asymmetrical information, 9, 18, 71, 82,
    94-5, 167-8, 170-4
asymmetry
  of interest, 73
  of power, 73, 80

auction prices, 104-5, 107
auction process, 95
  common price auction, 102-6
  discriminative price auction, 106-8
'auction winners', 106
audience costs, 12, 85
Aumann, Robert J., 130
authority, 2, 31, 68
  delegation, 7, 12, 72, 78, 89, 243
  enforcement, 60-2, 244-5
  exclusion, 60-2
  ratification rules, 83-5
autonomy, 83
Axelrod, Robert, 2, 29, 77

Bacon, Francis, 9
Baden, John, 30
Bain, Joe, 171
bargaining
  collective action, 133-4, 138-41, 143,
    147, 152-7
  conditions for success, 161-89
  conflict resolution, 114-15, 118
  institutional, 36-7, 80-1, 83
barter arrangements, 35
Bates, Robert H., 128
behavioural models, 38
beliefs (heterogeneity), 7, 9-10, 23
Bendor, Jonathan, 5
Benedick, Richard E., 3
benefits
  concentrated, 20, 192-206
  diffuse, 20, 207-18
  of regulation (cartels), 20, 191-209
  of regulation (oil pollution), 20-1,
    223-49
  rules to allocate, 134-6, 146
Berkes, Fikret, 2, 31
'BFP Dummy', 117-18
Biersteker, Thomas, 38
Binmore, Ken, 112-13
biological diversity, 3, 207
Blomquist, William, 19
Bolton, Gary, 115

boundary conditions, 50–1, 60, 62, 66–8
Bromley, Daniel, 2, 28
Buchanan, J.M., 81, 202
Bundesbank, 80
Bureau of Mines, 170
Burke, William T., 229
Bush, George, 212
Buyer Investment Cost Share, 117–18
buyer investments, 109–19

California Air Resources Board, 212
California Fruit Growers Exchange, 181–3,
    187
California Motor Vehicle Pollution Control
    Act (1960), 208
California orange growers, 181–4, 186–7
Calvert, Randall L., 128
Campbell, Bruce M.S., 31
Canadian fisheries, 216–17
capabilities (heterogeneous), 7–9, 23, 63
  collective action and, 18–19, 127, 165–7
  conflict resolution, 19, 93, 121
  issue linkage, 19, 71–89
  producing public goods, 237–8, 248
  social capital, 19–20, 138–45
capital investment, see investments
Caporaso, James A., 5
capture (common-law rule), 169
cartelization, 162, 181, 188–9
  by regulation, 20, 191–219
Carter administration, 195, 216
Carter Initiatives, 233, 243
Central Council on Environmental
    Pollution Control, 213
CFCs, 14, 15, 20, 193–201, 205, 218
Chayes, Abram, 39, 41, 243
Chayes, Antonia H., 39, 41, 243
Cheung, Steven N.S., 164
Clark, Colin W., 6
Clarkson Research Studies, 234
Clean Air Act (1970), 208–14
climate system (global), 27–8
codes of conduct, 30–5 passim
coerced compliance, 232, 243–4
coercion, 2, 68
Cold War (end of), 74
Coleman, James S., 126
collaboration problems, 76–80
collective action, 15
  agreements (sequence), 18, 168–9
  conditions for success, 161–89

costs, 4–5
  heterogeneities, 10, 165–7
  politics of scope, 47–68
  social capital and, 125–57
collective action problems, 3
  fisheries, 174–80
  issue linkage, 71–89
  oil field unitization, 169–74
  orange marketing orders, 180–7
  scale and, 11–13, 29–33, 35–6, 38–9, 41–2
collective belief systems, 54
collective-choice rule-making games, 152,
    153, 154–5
collective outcomes, 38, 39
common information (investments), 114,
    115, 116–20
common knowledge, 21, 22, 84, 130
common-pool problem
  fisheries, 174–80
  intentional oil pollution, 237–8
  oil field unitization, 169–74
  orange marketing orders, 180–7
  successful resolution, 161–5
common-pool resources (CPRs), 9
  heterogeneities and, 95–108
  human/environment relationships, 11, 28–42
  international relations, 1–8, 47–52,
      55, 59–63, 67–8
  issue linkage, 19, 71–89
  open access, 3, 4, 14, 162–9, 176
  politics of scope, 47–52, 55–68
  public goods and, 10, 13–15
  successful collective action, 161–89
common price auction, 102–6
commons problems (linkage), 71–89
commons property, 162–3
communication, 10, 21–2
  common price auction, 102–5
  discriminative price auction, 106–7
  face-to-face, 95, 98, 104, 106, 119
community, 10
community subgroups, 65–7
compensation, 167, 191
  Olsonian cases, 207–8, 214–19
  Stiglerian cases, 192, 201, 205, 218–19
Compensation Standards Governing Electric
    Power Development, 214–16
competitive advantage, 199, 201
compliance
  coerced, 232, 243–4
  non-compliance, 240, 243–5

configuration of power, 37
conflict resolution (sharing
  contracts), 93–121
*Congressional Quarterly Weekly
  Report,* 211
constitutional rule-making games, 152–6
contracting, incomplete, 108–19
contracts (sharing), 93–121
Convention on the Law of the Sea, 34
cooperation
  effects of heterogeneity, 7–10, 71–89
  politics of scope, 47, 51, 58, 61, 62–8
coordination problems, 71, 76–80
costs
  concentrated, 207–18
  diffuse, 192–206
  regulatory, 20, 192–218 *passim*
  rules to allocate, 136–8, 146
  transaction, 2–6, 16, 65
Council of the European Communities, 195
Coward, Walter, 126
Cowhey, Peter F., 85
Cox, Robert, 33
Crabb, Cecil V., 84
Craig, Paul, 218
Crosbie, John Carnell, 216
crude oil washing (COW), 233–4, 246

Dales, John H., 14
Dasgupta, Partha, 128
DDT ban, 205–6
decision-making, 78, 81, 82
  rules, 7, 83, 85–8
decision-setting, 96–8
defections (allocation schemes), 106, 107–8
delegation, 7, 12, 72, 78, 89, 243
democracies, 82
Dempsey, Paul Stephen, 240
Department of Agriculture, 183, 186–7, 204
Department of Commerce, 180
Department of the Environment, 194
Department of Justice, 163, 180, 181
desertification, 3
design
  institutional, 52–6, 67–8, 75–7
  principles, 2, 40–2, 51–2, 55 56, 57, 68
development, social capital and, 125
DiMaggio, Paul J., 33
discount rates, 6, 64, 114–15, 117
discriminative price auction, 106–8
distributional conflict, 93–5

dominium, 31
donor assistance, 146–51
Dotto, L., 194
Doyle, Michael W., 7, 82, 216
DuPont, 20, 193–201, 205
DuPont Corporate News, 200

ecosystems, 28, 34, 39
efficiency, 39, 40
Eggertsson, Thráinn, 2, 33
Eichengreen, Barry, 74
El Nino phenomenon, 28
Ellickson, Robert, 40
Elster, Jon, 29, 129, 131
endogeneity and institutional design, 52–6
endogenous actors, 47–68
endogenous parameters, 54–5, 67
endogenous variables, 15, 54–5
endowments
  allocation, 95, 96–108
  heterogeneity, 7–8, 175–80, 182–7
energy crisis (1973), 210–11, 213–15
enforcement, 244–5
  exclusion and, 60–2
environment, 14, 36, 81
  management, 191–219
  motor vehicle emissions, 208–14
  oil pollution, 12, 20–1, 64, 223–49
environment/human relationships (scale
  problems), 27–42
Environment Reporter, 210
Environmental Data Services Report, 197,
  200
Environmental Protection Agency, 195,
  197, 209–13, 216
equal absolute reductions, 101
equal allocation rule, 101
equal proportionate reductions, 101
equilibrium institutions, 75, 79–80
equity theory, 39, 40, 114–15
European Central Bank, 80
European Court of Justice, 78, 80
European monetary system, 80
European Union, 59, 72, 77, 80–1, 83, 86–7
Evans, Peter B., 32
exchange/exchange rate, 82
exclusion/enforcement, 60–2
exogeneity, 15–18
  institutional design and, 52–6
experimental evidence on sharing
  contracts, 93–121

explanation (issue linkage), 82
external assistance (results), 146–51
extortion (issue linkage), 82
Exxon, 228
Exxon Valdez accident, 235

face-to-face communication, 95, 98, 104,
    106, 119
fairness effect, 115, 117–18, 120
Faiz, Asif, 125
Farman, J.C., 196
Farmer Managed Irrigation Systems,
    149–51
Faulkner Committee, 225
Fearon, James, 38, 80
Federal Hazardous Substances Act, 216
Federal Insecticide, Fungicide and
    Rodenticide Act, 216
Federal Oil Conservation Board, 170–1
Feeny, David, 2, 29
Field, Barry C., 39
first proposer advantage, 116–17
fisheries, 3, 8, 11, 13, 15, 50, 60–2, 65,
    161–3, 174–80, 216–17
Florida Citrus Exchange, 182–3, 185, 187
Florida Control Committee, 183, 185–6
Florida Control Growers Clearing House
    Association, 182–3, 185–6
Florida orange growers, 181–7
'forced breakdown', 114
Fowler case study, 11–12, 193, 201–6, 218
Frank, Robert, 5
free rider problem, 108, 127, 143, 237
Friedman, James, 77
Frohlich, Norman, 5, 13
functional differentiation, 72, 76–8, 80, 88,
    89, 243
Furubotn, Erik G., 29, 33

Gaia hypothesis, 28
game theory, 9–10, 54, 58
    bargaining, 133–41, 143–4, 152–7
    coordination games, 77, 79, 80
    decision-setting, 96–8
Garden City Water District, 202–4
Gardner, Roy, 13, 145
Garrett, Geoffrey, 80
GATT, 21, 59, 77, 86
Gaubatz, Kurt Taylor, 82
general circulation models, 27–8
Germany (recycling policy), 206

GESAMP, 224
global
    level (comparisons), 12, 13, 15–17
    macro-level institutions, 11, 27–41
    see also international relations
global warming, 3, 200
Godoy, Ricardo A., 31
Goldstein, Judith, 79
Gordon, H. Scott, 6, 30, 164
Governing the Commons (Ostrom), 11
government
    head of (ratification rules), 84–5
    intervention, 163
Grad, Frank, 210
Granovetter, Mark, 9
Gray, William O., 247
Grieco, Joseph M., 37, 58
Grolin, Jesper, 230
Grossman, Sanford, 108–9
groundwater management, 14, 19, 50, 193,
    201–6
Gulf Coast shrimp fishery, 178–80
Güth, Werner, 114–15

Haas, E., 42
Haas, Peter M., 2, 3, 30, 37, 41, 75, 128
Hackett, Steven C₁, 73, 94, 95, 108, 128
Haggard, Stephan, 36
Hardin, G., 1, 28, 30, 76–7
Hardin, Russell, 5, 29, 94
Harral, Clell G., 125
Hart, Oliver, 108–9
Hawkes, Suzanne, 224
head-enders, 19–20, 140–51
head of government (ratification rules),
    84–5
hegemonic stability theory, 8, 63, 74–5
heterogeneity
    of actors, 4, 6–10, 22–3, 62–7
    beliefs, 7, 9–10, 23
    capabilities, *see main entry*
    collaboration problems, 71, 76–80
    collective action, 10, 165–7
    conflict resolution, 93–121
    CPRs and, 95–108
    decision-making rules, 85–8
    effects on cooperation, 7–10, 71–89
    information, 7, 9–10, 23
    institutions and, 47–68
    interests, 19, 63–4, 71–89
    issue linkage, 71–89

levels, 223–49
  power, 238, 240, 248
  preferences, *see main entry*
  provision of public goods, 235–47
  scope and, 15–21
hierarchy, 2, 52, 68, 72, 78
  enforcement, 244
Hirschman, Albert O., 240
Hobbes, Thomas, 8
Hoffman, Elizabeth, 187
Hokkaido Electric Company, 215
Holt, Pat M., 84
Homans, George, 114
homogeneous actors, 6, 65–6, 67
homogeneous situations (social capital),
  132–8
'horizontal orderings', 72, 78, 79
Hudec, Robert E., 78
Hughes, Barry B., 29
human capital, 126, 148
human/environment relationship (scale
  problem), 27–42
human rights, 78

ICI (product substitution), 193–201, 205
imperium, 31
implementation review, 41
incomplete contracting, 108–20
individual equality rule, 115
information
  common (investments), 114, 117–20
  conflict resolution and, 93–121
  exchange, 21–2
  heterogeneity, 7, 9–10, 23
  private (investments), 114, 117–18,
    119–20
information asymmetries, 18, 71, 82, 94–5
  sequence of agreements, 167–8, 170–4
institutional design, 75–6, 77
  endogeneity and, 52–6, 67, 68
institutional effects on issue linkage, 72–3,
  83–8
'institutional hegemony', 75
institutional scope, 47–68
institutions
  consequences of, 37–8
  design principles, 40–2
  formation of, 35–7
  heterogeneity and, 10, 47–68
  nature of, 33–5
  performance of, 39–40

intentional oil pollution, 20–1, 223–49
interests, 19, 63–4, 71–89
Intergovernmental Maritime Consultative
  Organization, 227, 229–30, 232, 233,
  240
internal authority, 7
International Chamber of Shipping, 231,
  242, 245
International Conference on Pollution of
  the Sea, 225
International Convention for the Prevention
  of Pollution of the Sea by Oil, 224–6,
  235
International Convention for the prevention
  of Pollution from Ships, 230–6, 239–41,
  243–8
international donors/aid, 146–7
international law, 31–2, 79
International Maritime Organization, 234,
  240, 245
international Oil Pollution Prevention
  Certificate, 232
International Oil Pollution Prevention
  Convention, 224–30, 232
international regimes, 2–3, 11–12
  macro-level institutions, 11, 27–41
international relations
  CPR and, 1–8, 47–52, 55, 59–64, 66–8
  macro-level institutions, 11, 27–41
  new institutionalism, 28–9, 33
  power distribution, 73–5, 79–80
INTERTANKO, 242, 244
investments
  buyer/seller, 109–19
  contract sharing, 93–4, 95, 127
  external assistance, 146–51
  incomplete contracting, 108–20
  predictions, 115–16
  in social capital, 146–51, 156–7
irrigation systems, 1, 9, 13
  Fowler case, 193, 201–6, 218
  huertas, 60, 62
  Nepal, 11, 12, 21, 127, 148–51, 179
Isaac R.M., 5
Israel, Arturo, 125
issue linkage, 19, 71–89

Jacobson, Harold K., 32
Japan, 12, 85, 207–14
Japanese air quality regulations, 12, 207–14
Japanese Environmental Agency, 213

Jodha, Norpat S., 40
Johnson, R.N., 6, 71, 94, 128, 178
joint surplus, 93–5, 115–21
Jones, Charles O., 208

Kamala Irrigation Project, 148
Kanbur, Ravi, 73, 94
Kansas (Fowler case), 11–12, 193, 201–5,
  206, 218
Kansas State Division of Water Resources,
  202–4
Kasoulides, George, 234
Katzenstein, Peter J., 7
Kennan, John, 115
Keohane, R.O., 2, 8, 36, 63, 71, 74, 78, 83,
  85–6, 128, 237, 241, 244
Kindleberger, Charles P., 4, 63, 74
Kirby, J.H., 226, 228–9, 241
Knight, Jack, 127, 129, 138
knowledge, 21, 22, 41, 84, 130
Krasner, S.D., 2, 30, 50, 55, 68, 74, 79
Kreps, David, 10
Krier, James, 209
Kutan, Timur, 9

laboratory (contract sharing experiments),
  99–119
Lachmann, Ludwig M., 125
Laitos, Robby, 148
Lasswell, Harold, 9
'Law Merchant', 77, 78
Law of the Sea process, 34, 50, 75
League of Nations Committee of Experts,
  225
learning, institutional, 245–7, 248
lease values, 171–3
Lesbirel, S. H., 214
Levinthal, Gerald, 114–15
Levy, M. A., 3, 38
Lewis, D. K., 128
Libecap, G. D., 6, 71–3, 94, 128, 169,
  171–3, 178, 187
Liu, D., 244
Load-on-Top (LOT), 228–30, 233,
  241–2
local
  CPRS, 22, 23
  level (comparison), 12, 13, 15–17
  micro-level institutions, 11, 27–41
Locke, John, 8
Logic of Collective Action, The (Olson), 8

Maastricht Treaty, 81, 86–7
McCay, Bonnie J., 2, 28, 41
McGinnus, Michael, 128
McKean, M. A., 2, 30, 39, 145
macro-level institutions, 11, 27–41
majority-rule process, 81
majority voting, 81, 86, 87–8
Mäler, Karl Göran, 128
Marine Environment Protection Committee,
  232, 235
Maritime Safety Committee, 227
market failure, 71, 76, 79
Martin, Lisa, 12, 35, 50, 58, 75, 81, 85–6
Mawelle fishery, 59, 60
Maxwell, James, 197
Mayer, Frederick W., 81
meso-scale phenomena, 27
M'Gonigle, R. M., 224–34 passim
micro-level institutions, 11, 27–41
Milankovich cycle, 28
Milgrom, Paul R., 77
military alliances, 108
Milner, Helen, 29
Ministry of Finance, 213
Ministry of Trade and Industry, 215
Ministry of Transport, 214, 225
Mitchell, R. B., 227, 234, 236, 240–1
Moe, Terry M., 2, 7
Molina, M., 194
monetary policy, 74, 80
monetary union, 83, 86–7
monitoring, 41, 75, 77–8, 240–1, 243
  costs, 4–5
Montreal Protocol, 64, 193–201, 205
Mookherjee, Dilip, 5
Moran, M., 7
Moravcsik, Andrew, 83
most-favored-nation status, 4
motor vehicle emissions, 208–14
Motor Vehicle Pollution Control Act
  (1965), 208
Mutual Orange Distributors, 187

NASA, 199
Nash equilibrium, 97–8, 100–1, 103–4
National Academy of Sciences, 194–5, 210,
  224
National Research Council, 224
NATO, 47–8, 59, 64
negative sanctions, 244–5
negotiation, 36–7, 82, 109

ratification rules, 83-5
Nepal Institutions and Irrigation Systems, 11, 12, 21, 127, 148-51, 179
nested enterprises, 57, 62, 66
Netting, Robert M., 2
new institutionalism, 28-9, 33
NIMBY syndrome, 215-16, 218
no communication
    common price auction, 102-5
    discriminative price auction, 106-7
non-cooperative game theory, 97-8, 100, 114
non-democracies, 82
non-governmental organizations, 12, 241-5
non-state actors, 12
    heterogeneities, 223-49
North, Douglass C., 2, 128
Norway (salmon farming), 206
Nowell, Gregory P., 212
Nye, Joseph S., Jr., 71, 241

OCIMF, 242
Ogallala Aquifer Formation, 193, 201-6
O'Hare, Michael, 218
oil companies, 241-5
oil crisis, 210-11, 213, 214-15
oil field unitization, 7, 11, 162, 169-74
oil pollution, 12, 20-1, 64, 223-49
Oil Weekly, 171
Olson, Mancur, 8, 13, 35, 57, 62, 166, 207
Olsonian cases, 192, 207-19
open access, 3, 4, 14, 162-9, 176
opportunism, 9
orange marketing orders, 8, 11, 162, 180-7
ordinary least squares (OLS) estimates, 117-18
Osherenki, Gail, 36, 37
Ostrom, E., 2, 5-6, 11, 19, 28, 33, 40, 50, 55, 57-8, 60, 62-3, 68, 71, 77, 94-5, 125, 127, 145, 149, 153, 179, 237, 244
Ostrom, V., 128
outcomes/policies (preferences), 7
'outturn' (oil delivered), 228
overappropriation (oil pollution), 237
ownership (and rights), 31
Oye, Kenneth A., 2, 5, 57, 66, 82
ozone layer, 3, 41
    CFCs, 14, 15, 20, 193-201, 205, 218
Ozone Trends Panel, 199

Pareto optimality, 76, 81, 86
Parson, Edward A., 3

Peet, Gerard, 240
perfect equilibrium theory, 114-15
performance, external assistance and, 146-51
physical capital, 125, 126, 127-51
physical resources, 14
policy implications, 21-2
political union, 80-1, 83, 86-7
politics of scope, 47-68
pollution, 14, 36
    motor vehicle emissions, 208-14
    oil, 12, 20-1, 64, 223-49
Porges, Amelia, 213-14
Port Lameron fishery, 60-1
Ports and Waterways Safety Act (1972), 230, 243
Powell, Walter W., 33
power, 7, 57-8
    asymmetry of, 73, 80
    configuration of, 37
    distribution, 73-7, 79-80, 88
    heterogeneity, 238, 240, 248
predictions, 114-16
preferences (heterogeneous), 4-5, 7-8, 23
    intensities, 9, 80-2, 88-9
    issue linkage, 19, 71-2, 80-2, 85, 87-9
    producing public goods, 237-8
price auctions
    common, 102-6
    discriminative, 106-8
principal-agent relationship, 2
prisoner's dilemma, 29, 58, 76
Pritchard, Sonia Zaide, 225-8
private costs, 164
private information (investments), 114, 117-18, 119-20
'privileged group', 13, 35, 62-3, 71
problem-solving, 36, 39
product innovation, 109
product liability, 216, 217
product substitution, 193-201, 205-6
property rights, 31, 37, 67, 126, 164-7, 169, 174-5, 203
prorationing, 181-6 *passim*
protectionism, 77-8
public goods, 11, 36, 50-1, 74, 88
    CPRs and, 3, 4, 10, 13-15, 20, 22, 60, 62-4
    provision of, 223, 224, 235-47
    regulation and, 20
punishment strategies, 77-9
Putnam, Robert D., 10, 32, 83, 243

qualified majority voting, 81, 86

Rabe, Barry G., 216
Rabin, Matthew, 115
Ramsayer, Mark, 7
ratification rules, 83-5, 88
rationality assumption, 3, 5
Reagan administration, 195, 211, 216
regime formation, 35-7
Regimes Summit (1991), 33
regulation, 191
    air quality, 12, 207-14
    cost, 20, 192-218 *passim*
    of fisheries, 176-8
    oil pollution, 12, 20-1, 223-49
    see also rules
Reinhardt, Forest, 198
Reiss, Albert J., Jr., 232, 244
rents, 104, 107, 165, 167, 171
    dissipation, 162-4, 166, 168-70, 175-7,
        188
    seeking, 193, 218
Repetto, Robert, 125, 151
reputational effects, 86
res communis/res nullius, 31
resistance, compensation and, 217-18
resources
    allocation, *see* allocation
    open access, 3, 4, 14, 162-9, 176
    rent dissipation, 162-4, 166, 168-70,
        175-7, 188
    see also common-pool resources (CPRs)
Richter, Rudolf, 29, 33
Rittberger, Volker, 30
Rivkin, Kenneth A., 195
Rosenbluth, Frances M., 7
Rowland, F. S., 194
Rubinstein, Ariel, 112
Ruckelshaus, William, 210, 211
rules, 2, 75-6
    allocational, 17-18, 19, 164-7
    boundary conditions, 50-1, 60, 62,
        66-8
    codes of conduct, 30, 31-2, 33
    decision-making, 7, 83, 85-8
    enforcement, 60-2, 77-9
    exclusion, 60-2
    international law, 31-2
    -making situations, 151-6
    punishment strategies, 77-9
    ratification, 83-5, 88

sharing, 93-5, 114-15
social capital, 127-38, 143-8, 152-6

Sanderson, Debra, 218
scale
    collective action, 11-13
    problem of, 27-42
Schachter, Oscar, 31
Schelling, T. C., 9, 131
Schiff, H., 194
scope, 5, 22-3
    heterogeneity and, 15-21
    politics of, 47-68
Scott, Anthony C., 30
Sebenius, James K., 41, 81
security issue, 48, 51, 74, 81
segregated ballast tanks (SBT), 230-1,
        233-4, 236, 239, 241-2, 244, 246-7
self-governing institutions, 93-121, 128
self-help, 1, 12, 52, 72, 77
self-interest, 5, 9, 28, 41, 52, 76, 79, 81
    environmental management, 191-219
self-monitoring CPRs, 1
seller investments, 109-19
Selten, Reinhard, 98, 114
shared beliefs, 32-3
sharing rules, 93-5, 114-15
Shell, 228, 241
Shepsle, Kenneth A., 75
Sherman Act, 163, 180
Shirk, Susan L., 84
Simmons, Beth A., 36
Singleton, Sara, 32
Small, Leslie, 149
Snidal, Duncan, 2, 8, 30, 35, 50, 58, 75, 76
social capital, 10
    collective action and, 125-57
    creation of, 127-51
social costs, 30, 164
social institutions, 33-42
social learning, 41-2
social settings (human/environment
        relationships), 31-3
socialization process, 33-4
sovereignty, 33-4, 71, 78, 81
Stahl, Ingomar, 112
states
    heterogeneities among, 238-40
    heterogeneities between non-state actors
        and, 243-5
Stein, Janice G., 36, 50, 76, 240

Stigler, George, 20, 192–3
Stiglerian cases, 192–206, 218–19
Strange, Susan, 37
strictly proportionate rule, 115
Subcommittee on Oil Pollution, 227–8
subgroups, 65–7
suboptimal outcomes, 76, 79
subtractability (CPR rivalry), 14–15
Sugden, Richard, 128
surplus-sharing, 93–5, 115–21
Sutton, C. T., 228

tail-enders, 19–20, 140–51
tanker operators, 12, 20–1, 223–49
Tanker Safety and Pollution Prevention
    Conference (1978), 233
Taylor, Michael, 5, 10, 32
technological externalities, 162
technology, 108
    access to, 200–1
    air quality and, 208–14
    politics of scope, 50, 52, 58–60, 62, 63,
        67
Telser, L. G., 128
Texas
    oil industry, 170–4
    shrimp fisheries, 178–80
Thatcher, Margaret, 200
Thomas, Lee, 197, 200
Three Electric Power Development Laws,
    215, 216
token allocations, 99–108
Tolba, Mustafa, 199
Tollison, Robert D., 81
Törbel (alpine pasture), 59
Torrey Canyon accident, 228, 233
'tragedy of the commons', 1, 28–31, 36,
    39–40, 76, 88, 95
transaction costs, 2–6, 16, 65
transaction-specific investment, 115, 118
transparency (role), 39, 41, 42
Treaty of Rome, 87
Tris ban, 216

Udéln, Lars, 5
unanimity (decision-making), 87–8
UNCED, 3

underinvestment, 108
unit shares (oil industry), 171–4
United Nations, 48, 76
    Conference on Environment and
        Development, 3
    Conference on Human Environment, 230
    Environment Programme, 199
    Secretariat, 225–6
    Security Council, 72, 78–9
United States, 85
    air quality regulation, 12, 207–14
    fisheries, 174–80
    oil industry, 169–74
    orange marketing, 180–7
Ursim, Edmund, 209

Vienna Convention for the Protection of
    the Ozone Layer, 195
violence, 51, 61
von Hayek, Friedrich, 35

Walker, James, 95
Wallace, Henry A., 183
Waltz, K. N., 2, 7–8, 51, 72, 78
Warr, K., 196
water availability difference, 150–1
Watson, R. T., 199
Waxman, Henry A., 211
wealth, 39, 98, 167
Weber, S., 86
Weingast, Barry, 7, 80
Weiss, Edith Brown, 32
Weissing, Franz, 153
Wiesmeth, H., 86
Wiggins, Steven, 94, 171, 173
Willett, Thomas D., 81
Williamson, Oliver, 2, 9
Wilson, Robert, 10, 115
World Bank, 125

Yarnell v. Hillsborough Packing Co., 186
Yoder, Robert D., 140
Young, Oran R., 2, 3, 29–30, 33, 36, 37,
    38, 41, 128, 238

Zacher, Mark W., 225–34 passim
Zurn, Michael, 32

Compiled by Jackie McDermott